Barry and Alice

Barry and Alice

Portrait of a Bisexual Marriage

Barry Kohn
and
Alice Matusow

Prentice-Hall, Inc., Englewood Cliffs, New Jersey

Barry and Alice by Barry Kohn and Alice Matusow
Copyright © 1980 by Barry Kohn and Alice Matusow

Printed in the United States of America

Prentice-Hall International, Inc., London
Prentice-Hall of Australia, Pty. Ltd., Sydney
Prentice-Hall of Canada, Ltd., Toronto
Prentice-Hall of India Private Ltd., New Delhi
Prentice-Hall of Japan, Inc., Tokyo
Prentice-Hall of Southeast Asia Pte. Ltd., Singapore
Whitehall Books Limited, Wellington, New Zealand

10 9 8 7 6 5 4 3 2

Library of Congress Cataloging in Publication Data
Kohn, Barry
  Barry and Alice.
  Bibliography: p.
  Includes index.
  1. Bisexuality in marriage—United States.
I. Matusow, Alice, joint author.
II. Title.
HQ734.K675   301.42   79-24551
ISBN 0-13-056150-9

To our families, our friends, and our son

Contents

Acknowledgments

This is a very personal book, and the fact that it has been written is a direct result of the very personal involvement of many people.

Before we began writing, we imagined that we would be holed up somewhere in a room with a typewriter, isolated and alone. Certainly, we had to do a lot of that, but we also gathered around us many people, as we do in our day-to-day lives, whose contributions have been emotional, intellectual, and literary.

We sincerely thank: Jeffrey Bell, Oliver Bjorksten, Steven Carson, Margarita Concha and colleagues, Gary Delfiner, Peter John Dorman, Robert Garfield, Karen Godett, Dorothy Johnson, Cheryl Keats, Maureen Keen, Cindy Kohn, Dorothy Kohn, Elaine Kohn, Mulford Kohn, Perry Kohn, Ronald Kohn, Arthur Matusow, Eli Matusow, Florence Matusow, Howard Matusow, Marty Matusow, Linda Noble, Jean Orr, Richard Petrino, Elaine Radiss, Rita Reneaux, Elayne Rhoads, Brenda Samara, Toby Schmidt, Tony Silvestre, Robert Toporek, Cathryn Ufema, Keith Wagner, Pierre Weigand, Tom Wilson, and Wayne Wright.

We appreciate the work of Roz Burak and Barbara Stokes who typed portions of the manuscript and were consistently available when we needed them. Thanks to Barbara Stokes for the support she provided in helping to care for our son this past year.

For significant contributions to the manuscript, we are grateful to Jeffry Galper for his clarity of thought, and Carolyn Washburne, David Kirk and Angus Davis for their assistance with revisions. Angus Davis provided encouragement and advice. Bill Stayton has been a valuable resource and teacher about human sexuality. Larry Teacher taught us a lot about the publishing business.

We want to acknowledge the hundreds of men and women in relationships similar to ours, across the country, who have been willing to tell us the truth about their lives.

Thanks also to: Virginia Barber, our literary agent, and Mary Evans, her assistant who believed in our idea for the book from the beginning.

Robert Stewart, our editor at Prentice-Hall, who had a major impact upon shaping this book.

Barbara Julius for her commitment and belief in us as individuals and as a couple, and for always knowing when to step in.

Paula Bell for her tireless efforts in helping us organize, reformulate and develop our ideas. Her caring and guidance came at a critical time.

Miriam Galper got us started, gave us direction when we were floundering, and managed our book and our days for three months. For many years she has been the friend whose wisdom we've consistently relied upon.

Helen Matusow, Alice's mother, was our principal emotional support throughout the process of writing this book, and she typed the major part of the manuscript. Always open to new ideas, she has been willing to examine conventionally accepted values.

Danny Kohn, our son, was a "good kid"; he was willing to be included in the process of writing and included himself. He's glad it's over and he's looking forward to spending more time with his mother and father.

Introduction

The debris of broken marriages is everywhere, yet last summer Barry and I celebrated our thirteenth wedding anniversary. Our marriage has lasted longer than the marriages of most of the people our age. From outward appearances, we look like any other family on the block, and in many ways, we are. We have a home in the center of the city, on a narrow treelined street, and a small red station wagon with wood paneling on the sides. We have a seven-year-old son, Danny, and, from the view around us, a relatively stable life. We care about our child's school and the community and have an extensive network of family and friends. Both of us have led active professional lives: Barry as an attorney and I as a psychiatric social worker.

What is different about us is that our marriage is no longer based on traditional notions of monogamy, fidelity, and heterosexuality. We are both bisexual, we are open about this with each other, but we continue to view our marriage as the primary relationship in our lives. Although we are more in love now than ever, we don't keep each other from taking part in separate activities and involvements, or from being free to have other intimate relationships in addition to our marriage.

Most people don't know that relationships like ours exist, let alone flourish. Our marriage would be an interesting, if somewhat idiosyncratic, phenomenon were it not for the fact that we think there are literally millions of people across the country dealing with similar issues. Though we constantly hear a lot about open relationships, freer sexuality, new-styled marriage contracts, very little has been written about the specific issue of bisexuality and its implications within a marriage. In fact, when Barry and I had to face our personal crisis seven years ago, there was no single book, or even person, that we could turn to.

Our marriage still continues against a backdrop in which more and more marriages are failing. Whether in Maine, where one in

1

four marriages ends in divorce, or California, where one in two disintegrates, there is no doubt that the divorce rate is soaring. Between 1968 and 1975, the number of divorces increased by 70 percent among married people between the ages of twenty-five and thirty. From our observation, three to five years seems to be the duration for most relationships these days.

It's not that Barry and I claim to have found the answer to marital strife. We have been through many rough moments, and certainly our marriage has not turned out the way we expected it to in the beginning. We are comfortable with the way we live, however, and we have the sense of continually reshaping our marriage. We also expect that our marriage will continue to change with time.

To be sure, our life-style would not be to everyone's liking. It's important to say that this is the way we've done it; it's one couple's experience, and we're not presenting our marriage as the right or the only way to live. There are many happy marriages around that look very different from ours. Yet there are also many people who feel trapped in their relationships and see no way out of the constrictions they feel. Our book aims to stretch people's imaginations, to expand their picture of what is possible in a long-term relationship.

Getting married is always an expression of hope: nobody ever gets married expecting to be disappointed. People want relationships that offer continuity over time, and they want relationships that are nurturing. Too often, however, marriages fail to live up to their promise. When this happens, many people are quick to end their relationships rather than to reshape their expectations.

We think that marriage has the potential to be an important and viable institution which should not be so readily abandoned. There's value in going through a crisis together, in discovering reservoirs of strength you didn't know were available, and in the process, finding tolerance and even wisdom. In marriages that can open up a little breathing room, issues between people—in our case, bisexuality—can be seen as challenges rather than as signals to retreat.

Some people have said to us, "It's okay if you want to live the way you do, but why do you have to write a book about it?" Many of them go on to say that they view their relationship and their sexuality as a private matter. They are put off and frankly distrustful about our willingness to be so public about our lives. The issue of why expose the details of our lives is a reasonable question. Certainly it's one that we have asked ourselves.

During the years when we were going through the experiences we are writing about here, we felt very much alone. We were naïve and uninformed at the time, but as far as Barry and I knew, we were the only married people in the world who had ever had to deal with bisexuality. Other couples we knew had experienced an occasional infidelity, but it seemed to us that no one else we knew had ever had to look at involvements with the same sex. We felt isolated, confused, and ashamed. There was no one to talk to and there seemed to be no models for what we were facing.

Years later, after we'd begun to develop our own solutions, we came in contact with many other married couples in the same situation. It really started when Barry placed an ad in a local paper to begin a support group for men who were married and either bisexual or gay. Eleven men came to that first meeting, and since that time, we have been in touch with hundreds of bisexual married men and women in Philadelphia alone, plus many others around the country.

Many people who have participated in these support groups have sought us out for individual or couple counseling with their partners, or have spoken to us by telephone about the issue of same-sex relationships within their marriages. As we have become more public about our own lives, the number of people who have contacted us has grown. In travels and contacts with people across the country, we have discovered individuals, groups, and organizations focusing on bisexuality from Miami to Seattle. It has become obvious to us that the issue of bisexuality within marriage is not an isolated issue by any means.

From this evidence, Barry and I have come to believe that by openly sharing our lives there will be a growing understanding and acceptance of bisexuality within marriage. We want to encourage more people to give up their secrecy and be freer to express the way they are living or the way they want to live. We've seen that it enables people to get on with their lives, to experience their own power, to deal constructively and creatively with problems that at one time seemed insurmountable, in short, to grow up. We know that feelings of isolation and fears of telling are common. People are sure that no one else could possibly understand. To realize that you are not just some aberration but that there are many people in identical situations can be a tremendous comfort. We are writing this book for others to know that there are couples, more people than they could even imagine, who have traveled the same route and have reached a satisfying resolution.

Many people who eventually come out as bisexual or gay were once married. Many of those we've spoken to have said that they were still in love with their partners at the time they separated. Often, they found it wrenching to leave a partner and children they loved, and yet they saw no other solution. Their need for same-sex relationships seemed just as pressing as their desire to keep the family together. We want people to take a fuller look at their options for maintaining bisexual marriages, and we want to share some insights that we have learned about relationships and about marriage.

We also think it is vital for the helping professions—therapists, counselors, attorneys, clergy—to understand and be open to other alternatives for relationships. When we speak at conferences and other meetings, professionals report that they are increasingly dealing with bisexuality and open relationships in their practices. Often, they are at a loss as to what to advise. Like us, they find little or no literature dealing specifically with the issue of bisexuality in marriage and are therefore forced to rely upon old stereotypes and misinformation.

It would be misleading, however, to say that the motivation for writing this book arises solely out of a desire to help others. In truth the book has served as a personal liberation for us. It is the final step in a long process of freeing ourselves from our stereotypes and fear, and acknowledging the validity of our own experience. Anyone who has guarded a secret, felt embarrassed or ashamed, been cautious and careful for many years, can imagine the sense of relief and new energy that emerges from knowing that there is no longer anything to hide.

A few words about how the book is organized. So that we can give a sense of who we are as people, the second chapter of the book presents sketches of our personal lives up to the time that Barry began to be aware of the significance of his bisexual feelings.

The rest of the chapters were written by either Barry or me according to which of us was more familiar with the issues covered. In the third chapter, Barry details the beginning struggle of his coming to terms with his bisexuality and recalls what it was like for him to reveal himself to me. In the following chapter, I relive the shock of my reaction to learning about Barry's bisexuality. I describe how I began to resolve a situation that for a while seemed unresolvable and, in doing so, moved toward greater personal strength and independence. Barry then talks about his experience in therapy and the effect of the gay rights movement on his ideas about himself and his life as a bisexual married man. I then discuss my continued development as an independent woman, which includes a description of my own sexual history, the kinds of relationships and experiences that have contributed to my own sexual awakening, and the process of becoming comfortable with myself as a sexual person. Barry then explores many of the issues around telling the truth to your partner and others.

The final two chapters describe our current life-style. In the chapter "A Family Portrait," Barry talks about the importance of our network of friends and family (our "extended family"), and of our relationship with our son, Danny. He discusses the issue of how to handle children in a bisexual marriage, using the experiences of others to present different points of view. He also explains our own arrangement of "coparenting" within marriage, which we have found to be a valuable way of arranging child care. In the last chapter, the two of us reflect on what we have learned about relationships, including a discussion of jealousy, monogamy, and open relationships in general.

Barry and I see this book as a beginning attempt to introduce the issues and to bring the subject into awareness. It is a book about our experience—about the two of us, about marriage, about sexuality—and it also includes the descriptions of other people who have dealt with similar issues. We have been moved by the willingness of those we have interviewed to talk freely with us. When we do draw upon the stories of others, some names and other identifying information have been changed where requested.

This has not been an easy book to write. To describe our deepest experiences, we have had to relive many of the most difficult moments and subject our lives to a relentless and ongoing scrutiny that has been quite painful at times. We could not have guessed, when we began, that the process of writing this book would also represent a kind of journey we would travel back into ourselves, enabling us in a very deep way to understand and make peace with our lives—our histories, our relationship, and our goals.

Moreover, we are confident that it will be helpful not only for those exploring bisexuality within marriage but also for couples in long-term relationships of all kinds. We have learned that people do have the power to shape their relationships according to their own unique and specific needs; and most important, we urge people—bisexual and otherwise—to explore a wider range of possibilities for making their relationships blossom and endure.

One

Alice and Barry

As we set out to write this book and tell about our lives, we wonder whether it would have been possible from our backgrounds and earlier experiences to predict the emergence of bisexuality as an issue in our marriage. Certainly we could not have imagined from our traditional wedding ceremony in 1966, at the ages of twenty-one and twenty-three, that our marriage and our sexuality would have moved along such a path.

Alice

The unspoken message in the close-knit, extended family I grew up in was that it wasn't necessary to venture very far outside. In my family two sisters married two brothers: Aunt Flossie, my mother's sister, and her husband, Eli, my father's brother, were virtually parents to me. Similarly, their children, Howie, three years older than I, and Artie, one year younger (my "double cousins" was what I called them), were as close to me as brothers.

The sense of family was intensified, I am sure, by the fact that as soon as school was out in June, we all trooped down to Ventnor, a suburb of Atlantic City, where we rented a summer house large enough to hold all of us, including my grandparents. During the week while the men returned to Philadelphia to work, the women and children remained at the shore, spending long, uncomplicated days on the beach. Once a week Aunt Flossie took us to the small public library on the Ventnor boardwalk to take out books. Between the library and whatever books were left behind in the houses we rented, I read three and four books a week. Every Friday night, Artie, Howie, and I had a boardwalk ritual—rides at Million Dollar Pier, miniature golf, Skee-Ball, fudge, and popcorn.

I grew up in a warm, insulated, primarily Jewish neighborhood in Philadelphia of 1920 stone row houses with small lawns and gardens. There were porches in front—some enclosed, some open. Our house sat on the corner of Sherwood Road, with big green canvas awnings on the porch and a small rock garden in front. My bedroom was in the back of the house. My favorite part of the room was a grand and wonderful, ornately carved French bed that my mother's father had bought at the auction of an old estate. The flowered silk fabric covering the headboard and footboard, the blue and white *Alice in Wonderland* wallpaper, and the framed prints of turn-of-the-century Frenchwomen made the room very feminine—an environment created especially for a little girl.

Like others of my generation, I was born at the end of the war, in March 1945, and grew up a child of the fifties, which meant that I was exposed to the cold war, a time of uneasy peace, intermittent conflicts, suspicion at home. While the setting of my day-to-day life was safe and tranquil, I also recall living with an ongoing sense of impending danger in the larger world outside. I am old enough, for example, to remember air-raid drills in the basement of my elementary school and Civil Defense tests on radio stations. The Korean War is a blur to me, but I have early memories of Adlai Stevenson. For what seemed to me an endless time in elementary school, I came home every day to see my mother glued to the Army-McCarthy hearings on television. I was nine on the summer day the Rosenbergs were executed, and I remember my grandmother campaigning on their behalf.

I wouldn't have dreamed of being apathetic or uninformed in the presence of either of my grandmothers. It was from them that the intellectual pressure I placed upon myself—to study, to know, to be educated, to understand history and politics—had its roots. They gave me their books—I still have them today—answered my endless questions, and explained their points of view, and I remember wondering if I would ever be able to know as much as they did.

My grandmothers also pushed me to recognize social inequities in the country, which I probably would have missed in my insulated childhood of the fifties; their heroes and heroines were the men and women who had led the political and labor struggles at the turn of the century, those who had risked their lives and bucked the criticism of others to fight for their beliefs. Neither of their husbands had the same social concern and passion for politics that they did (they were involved in making a living and building businesses), and I think I made an early decision that the man I eventually married would have to be willing to fight alongside me.

I always looked forward to sleeping at my grandmother Esther's house on Friday nights; it was always a trip back in time to my origins. My own home was not particularly religious—my parents, third-generation Americans, were concerned with assimilation and comfort—but religious orthodoxy, the rules and rituals of Judaism, were the anchor of my grandparents' relationship. I liked the old-fashioned quality of their home, the link with a European past that I could only wonder about, the sense of safety and sameness, the table set with my grandmother's good china for the traditional Friday night Sabbath meal.

Grandmom was a curious admixture of religious orthodoxy and political radicalism. We would lie in bed engaged in long political discussions. She was opinionated, dogmatic, and full of pronouncements. The "daren'ts" of her religion— "You daren't ride on Saturday," "You daren't mix meat dishes with milk dishes" —were expressed with the same absolute conviction as her political beliefs. "Madame Chiang Kai-shek is a terrible thing," she told me at seven. Most people, including my parents, did not take her politics seriously, but I listened carefully to what she said and appreciated her willingness to listen seriously to my ideas.

I think Anna, my other grandmother, also identified with and encouraged the thoughtful part of me. She was an intimate part of my childhood since I spent all my summers with her at the seashore. Irreverent and nonreligious, she was as deeply immersed in her Jewish heritage as my other grandmother. However, her concern was with Jewish identity—maintaining Jewish learning and carrying on the cultural experience.

She was a more worldly woman than my other grandmother and was an early model for me of what it was to maintain a measure of independence within the family. Every September she traveled alone to the White Mountains of New Hampshire and drove a car when few of her contemporaries did. It was from her that I began to appreciate the combination of intellectual and participator; hungry for learning and culture, she read avidly, attended concerts, went to endless political and literary discussion groups and meetings. She knew Emma Goldman, the famous anarchist, personally, and in the thirties, her house on Parkside Avenue became a kind of salon for anarchists of the day. She died not too long ago at the age of ninety-five, and I know that she lived as long as she did because she was curious and aware and threw herself into life.

When I was four years old, my brother Michael was born. The pleasant "Alice in Wonderland" years were suddenly darkened by the presence of not just an intruder, as I, like most firstborn, experienced the birth of my new brother, but of a child with whom it was clear almost from the beginning that there was something wrong. Mike is mentally retarded. I don't know when I became aware that he was not like other kids. It wasn't talked about directly until much later, but it seems like something I always knew without knowing. It was a tremendous shock to both my parents, and they could only face it a little at a time. A sensitive child, I observed the subtle changes in my parents; family life became heavier—less gaiety, more burden, more sighs.

It seemed to me after my brother was born that everyone had normal families but me. As I got older, it began to be uncomfortable for me to answer people's questions. It was as if I thought that the fact that I had a retarded brother said something about my own worth or my family's. I learned to dread the question, "Do you have any brothers or sisters?" I don't know the origins of my shame and discomfort. I only know that I felt embarrassed and then immediately selfish and guilty for feeling ashamed.

In my mind, having a retarded brother distinguished me too greatly from other people. One day I was in the schoolyard at Mann School and a girl in my class asked me whether I had any brothers or sisters. I lied. I said no and then felt terribly weak and disloyal. Later on, when people asked me whether I had any brothers or sisters, I compensated by supplying too much information. "Yes, but he's retarded and he's been retarded since birth and he lives in a home in Delaware and we visit him once a month."

In early May of 1956, my parents and I had driven to Delaware to take Mike to the home where he would be living. I was eleven. Mike was seven. I knew that we were putting him away even though it was a pleasant, small, private institution. In reality, there was a large part of me that was relieved to have him go so I could get on with my own life. At the same time, I was sad about losing him in ways I didn't have the words to express. For so long, Mike had been a part of my day-to-day life, and it was wrenching to let him go.

The morning we were to leave, my father and I had breakfast together, and gradually, we began to talk about Mike. The discussion became more and more somber, when suddenly my father broke down and began to cry. I had never seen him cry before. It was painful for me, deeply stirring, disorienting even. I hated it. I hated seeing him sad. He had always wanted a son, but to have one that was deformed was a blow to his self-confidence that he never really snapped back from. It seemed a validation of a certain point of view he had always held about things never quite working out, that life held cruel jokes. I said to him, "Daddy, everything will be all right." I vowed that it would. Try as I might, I was never really able to make up for his loss.

My father was a very special, vulnerable, and loving man who felt he had to hide that part of himself. He got up every morning and squeezed fresh orange juice for my mother and me. He taught me my multiplication tables and took me with him to his office when he went there sometimes on Saturday mornings. He was also needling, rough, and abrasive, and sometimes I was embarrassed by him. When I got older, I longed for a soft-spoken, patrician-looking father like Robert Young on the TV show *Father Knows Best*.

Many times when I was young, my father said to me, "Enjoy these years. They are the best of your life." It always seemed sad to me that he lived with as much regret as he did, sadness over missed opportunities, disappointment for some sense that life was not as full now as it had once been for him. His statement also scared me. As a very little girl, I decided that I never wanted to look back at my life and regret that I hadn't done something I wanted to do.

As much as I wanted to be seen as normal by others (after Mike's birth, being accepted, acceptable, appropriate became a preoccupation), early on, I also knew that I didn't want to be like everyone else. I wanted there to be something distinguished and distinguishable about my life. Maybe everyone feels this way. But it's amazing to me

now when I look at my own seven-year-old son that when I was not
very much older than he, I fantasized being written up in the "M"
book of the encyclopedia.

I don't know why this desire to excel, to achieve, was so
strong in me. I just know that it came from very deep inside. Perhaps
I assumed the burden of making up to my parents for their disappointment; it's possible that I thought I could be the son my father
had lost. Whatever the reasons, I worked hard at it; competition was a
way of life and I hated to fail. Maybe that was why later in my life, I
was unwilling to choose the option of labeling my marriage a failure
or acknowledging that I had made the wrong choice in marrying
Barry. It may also explain why when I first learned about the
homosexual side of Barry, it hit me so hard, tapping into all the shame
and pain associated in my mind with having a "freak" in the family.

The competition that was so much a part of my character
extended—or perhaps began—in my relationship with my mother. I
loved my mother, but we fought a lot too. I saw her as beautiful and
powerful, and wasn't sure that I could measure up to her. She was an
attractive, vital woman in her thirties, and her natural sexuality was
intimidating to me. I knew I was smarter and more intellectual than
she, so I developed that side of myself.

The relationship was frequently stormy, with periodic out-
bursts and fights, but she was the one in particular who instilled pride
in me. Unlike many of the mothers of my friends, who regularly
disparaged and criticized their daughters, the greatest tribute I can
pay my mother is to say that she never broke my spirit. She insisted
always that I was special and promised that when I grew up, I would
be able to have anything I wanted. Somehow I believed her when she
told me, a young awkward teenager, that I was a late bloomer and
someday I would feel better about myself.

Although these were not times when many mothers pursued
work or professions, my mother was never particularly happy in the
role of housewife. She went back to work when I was thirteen and was
a very competent administrative secretary in the Department of
Psychiatry of a major medical school in Philadelphia. When she did
return to work, her entire outlook changed. She felt more vital,
productive, appreciated, and she liked earning money. The fact that
she worked no doubt served as a good model for me.

Throughout my childhood, I played with boys and girls; it
seemed unnecessary to choose between them. It depended on my

mood and interests at any particular time, not to mention who was available. As a little girl, I loved to play with boys—more than that, to be accepted as "one of the boys," or at the very least, to have them notice me. I remember sitting on my porch in the spring and summer watching the older boys in the neighborhood playing boxball on the corner or stickball in the street, hoping that they would pay some attention to me. I formed crushes and concocted fantasies about one or another of them suddenly noticing me and wanting to take me out, or fighting among themselves about which one would get to have me as a girl friend. Sexually, my fantasies never went beyond being kissed. Frankly, at the time I don't think I had even given any thought to what else sex might include.

Most of all, I treasured the time I spent with my cousins, Howie and Artie, and their boyfriends. When we were younger, we did a lot of playacting and pretending. When we got older, we played highly competitive board games like Monopoly and Sorry and endless card games. We knew fifteen different ways to play solitaire. In a household where baseball and the Phillies were an obsession, there was constant ball playing. We also collected stamps together and watched M-G-M musicals and Esther Williams films at the movies.

Then there were the girls on my street. They were no less important to me and my relationships no less intense. I remember Joanie. When we fought, there was no torture more horrible than when she wouldn't talk to me and even worse, when she enlisted the other little girls to take her side in a fight. For me there was nothing more painful than fighting with a girlfriend. I could always handle it if Artie or Howie were angry. But there was something about having another girl angry with me that was much more basic and scary.

Whatever the hazards, and there did seem to be more storminess in relationships with girls than with boys, I loved my girl friends. There was nothing more wonderful than playing in my room on a Saturday afternoon with Joyce, dressing up in costumes from an old trunk that my grandfather had found at an auction. Joanie and I sat on the railing that enclosed my porch and pretended that we were cowgirls and the railing our horses.

With my girl friends, and with my cousins, overt sex play was not a part of our repertoire. We talked about boys and chose movie stars as pretend boyfriends, but I remember very little talk about sex or about our own bodies. I don't even have memories of masturbating as a child. If indeed I was aware of my own sexual fantasies or impulses, I kept them deeply buried. It just wasn't something I felt comfortable talking about.

When I entered junior high school at eleven, I was still a little girl, playing with dolls and jacks, jumping rope, fantasizing pretend games with Joanie. Suddenly, there was a lot to deal with. The school bus that delivered me to my door every day was gone, and I had to ride public transportation, two buses. More than that, other kids were growing up or had already grown up faster than I had. There was a popular crowd and I wasn't in it. I had few friends, boys or girls, and I felt very much alone, unwanted and out of it. I was miserable and spent all my time ruminating about how to gain acceptance. At the same time, preadolescent sexuality was surfacing. In the morning before the school bell rang, the girls stood around in clusters telling dirty jokes I didn't understand, talking about boys and parties I wasn't invited to, singing suggestive songs.

I was very naïve. Even though my family always told me I was pretty, among my peers I felt skinny, awkward, and unsure. Other girls were developing physically faster than I was. I was fascinated suddenly to see breasts and then bras on some of the girls in my class and I wondered—worried really—whether I would ever have my own. I awaited the coming of my menstrual period with eager anticipation—it seemed to me some type of badge of honor as a woman—but I was too proud and embarrassed to talk with anyone, my mother, friends, relatives, about my anxieties about myself. It wasn't as if I had not felt the faint stirrings of my own emerging sexuality. In fifth grade Jerry Golden had kissing games at his parties, and I even had a boyfriend or two.

Most of my sexual thoughts as a child involved fantasies of some male lover carrying me off à la Cinderella and Prince Charming. I spent a lot of time wondering what it was like to kiss a man and practiced kissing the pillow. I remember feeling uncomfortable watching other people kiss and be affectionate. I always turned away from scenes in movies that portrayed a man and woman kissing or making love. I was fascinated, but it also made me uneasy. Perhaps watching other people be demonstrative threatened too directly the lid I had placed upon my own sexual impulses.

For me, love was the M-G-M musicals I adored as a child. People fell in love simply and directly; they kissed and then they sang a song about it. Passion was never portrayed, and I had no idea what sexual intercourse was about. Falling in love—that was the key. In my own fantasies, the lover who carried me off was Howard Keel or Gordon MacRae, with choruses of radiant men and women singing in the background. Now that I think about it, though, it was probably Ava Gardner in the movie *Showboat* who interested me more than Howard Keel. I thought she was beautiful—mysterious and lusty in a way I had never seen before. No wonder I saw *Showboat* five times.

Still, this was the 1950s, the era of "good girls" and "bad girls," and one's reputation—dignity, self-respect, other people's judgments—was crucial to success and well-being. In the fifties a "good girl" was still someone who engaged in little or no sexual activity, or else kept it very quiet.

I remained fairly tight and controlled and directed most of my energies, which I can now look back and see as sexual, into more acceptable channels like school and reading. During this time I spent a lot of time in my room by myself, thinking about "life with a capital L," and the room became a kind of haven away from the pressures and rapid changes going on around me. It was a terrible time in which I had the recurring feeling that I was always going to be left behind.

I was delighted and enormously relieved when I finally got my period at age thirteen and a half. I had been waiting eagerly, especially since many of the girls I knew had already begun to menstruate. I perceived the event as a validation that I was normal, that I was like every other girl, that, indeed, I was on my way to growing up. My interest in sexual matters intensified as my body began to change. Sexual thoughts, questions, and fantasies began to occupy much more of the time I spent alone.

My body began to change and develop later than some of the other girls. I had hoped it would happen overnight, with the onset of menstruation, but it was a much more gradual process. For a girl, breasts were the important thing. The size of your breasts determined how grown-up and sexy you were. Suddenly, along with Westmore's pink lipstick, everyone was wearing bras. My mother bought me a 30AA, which I scarcely filled, but at least I had a bra. I felt a little better when I happened to glance at the sleeveless white middy blouse of the girl in front of me in seventh-grade math class and noticed blue toilet paper sticking our of her bra. It wasn't until I was fifteen or sixteen that my body began to fill out.

I avoided discussion about sex with my mother or even with my girl friends. In junior high school, I picked up what I could, but my information was very sketchy. My mother gave me a few booklets about menstruation like "What Every Girl Should Know," but I felt frustrated that they didn't reveal more about sexual intercourse. I was embarrassed to admit to anyone that I knew as little as I did. It was a question of pride.

When I was thirteen years old, I sneaked into the Woolworth's at the Bala Cynwyd Shopping Center near my home and picked up a copy of the best seller of the day, *Peyton Place*. Surreptitiously, I tucked it under my arm and avoided the eyes of the clerk as I went through the checkout counter. I took it home, kept it under my pillow, and read it every night. *Peyton Place* was my first sex manual, only I didn't understand it very well.

Even if I didn't know exactly what was happening, *Peyton Place* did give me a sense of the hotness and passion of sex. There was an element of violence to the description of sexuality that was scary and a bit overwhelming. I didn't know what all the words meant. Years later, when I learned the meanings of different slang words relating to sex, I would find myself remembering *Peyton Place* and thinking, "Oh, so that's what the word meant."

I finally found the book I needed in the synagogue library. It was called *Facts of Love and Life for Teenagers*. When I was fourteen or fifteen, I attended religious school at Har Zion Synagogue. I never had the nerve to take the book out on my library card; people might guess how much I didn't know. But every chance I got, I took the book off the shelf, tucked it inside an *Encyclopaedia Britannica*, carried it to the table farthest from the librarian's desk, and pored over its contents. It was a tremendous relief finally to have the answers I needed.

I recall wishing to be freer, but I didn't know what to do about it, and I readily accepted the "good girl/bad girl" division. Years later, I found out that girls I knew had many more sexual experiences than I had, but they had kept it quiet. In my case, concern about being careful, holding on to my reputation, began very early and was part of my upbringing. The freer sexuality and openness of today carries with it its own problems, to be sure, but how unfortunate it was for girls of my time—growing up during the last phase of a previous morality—to have to struggle against feelings and impulses that in reality are natural and appropriate for their age.

By the end of junior high school and the beginning of high school, I had matured sufficiently and was beginning to feel more comfortable with myself. But I was still frustrated socially. I wanted girlfriends. I set out on a personal campaign to win the friendship and respect of the other girls and to be included in the "in group." Everything I did was focused toward the goal of recognition including getting myself appointed chairman of a new tutoring project that was being started in the school.

By being chairman of this project, I was able to spend much more time with the girl I most admired, Betsy. She was vice-president of the school and was pretty, intelligent, refined, confident, and, above all, popular. She had all the qualities I desperately wanted for myself. More than anything I wanted to be her friend, and spending time with her became the highlight of my day.

The truth is that the excitement, the admiration, the thrill of being with her had all the components of falling in love with a boy. It is only as I review this experience, years later, that I am aware that I was falling in love with Betsy. No physical contact, no knowledge of what was happening, but love nonetheless. In retrospect, I understand that I have experienced a kind of falling in love with all the girls or women I have become close to in my life. The intimate confidences, the feeling that when we are together no one else matters, the attraction and the admiration, are as intense as any love affair with a man.

The girls I had longed to be friendly with had always been good students. With college looming ahead, they began to place more value upon intelligence and academic prowess. Fortunately in high school that side of me began to be noticed and respected, and, to my joy and relief, I found myself accepted as an integral part of a clique of girls, Betsy and others; in typical high school fashion, the "big six" was what we called ourselves.

I dated too. The custom among academically oriented, attractive girls at Overbrook High School in the early sixties was to date University of Pennsylvania freshmen; we went to mixers and fixed each other up. My sexual contact with boys increased from good-night kisses to "making out"; it was the era when discussions about sex involved the debate of whether to advance sexual intimacy beyond "first base." I was always careful not to go "too far," and I don't think I ever felt strongly enough about anyone to be very much tempted. At the time, it wouldn't have occurred to the kind of boys I dated to push me to change my mind.

The old pull between staying close to home and branching out on my own reoccurred when it came time to enter college. After my brother, Mike "went away" (the euphemism we used in our house to describe his institutionalization), my parents must have felt the need to keep me close to them. I was confused, torn between the responsibility I had always felt to please them and my own sense that it was important to me to experience living away from home.

The issue was finally decided on the basis of money. My father said that he did not have enough money to pay for my living away at school. I know now, and I must have guessed on a certain level then, that this wasn't true, and it created a rift between my father and me, an atmosphere of vague distrust, that lasted almost until he died a couple years ago. I blamed my parents for holding on to me so tightly, but I was too unclear about my own goals to put up very much of a fight for greater independence. Later in my life, I would reexperience my dependency anew when Barry proposed that we open up our marital relationship and all the old resistance I had to flying on my own came to the surface.

When I entered Temple University in 1963, my father was very determined that I become a teacher, because, as he said many times, he didn't want me to graduate from four years of college without the ability to get a job. Throughout my life, my father had always placed enormous emphasis upon financial security, the importance of my having the ability to make money on my own. Clearly, in the manner of the day, the message was that it did not have to be a huge amount of money, since eventually it would be my husband's obligation to provide most of the income. But I was encouraged to make something of myself.

I never wanted to be a teacher, I was sure of that. My father and I fought a lot until I put my foot down as a sophomore and categorically insisted that I was not going to take any more teaching credits. That was a big move for me—my first thrust at following my own direction rather than being under the influence of my family. I didn't know at the time what I was going to do instead. I just knew that I didn't want to be a teacher.

I still had that drive to make something of myself, the desire to be "somebody," but there was a big part of me that didn't believe it was really possible for a girl, for me. Women's liberation had not yet come to the foreground in 1963 or 1964. At the same time I was thinking about "what I wanted to be when I grew up," I was also giving a lot of thought to what kind of man I would marry. In those days, if you married well, you could hook on to your husband's star. I remember a recurrent fantasy of marrying a senator. In the conventional thinking of the time, it's not that I was at the point of seeing myself as a politician, but I could imagine entering that world by marrying one.

The field that interested me the most in college was publishing, and it became clear that I had ability in this area. I liked to write, and I enjoyed the subtleties of copy and layout. The entire process of producing a publication fascinated me, and I was also interested in the business end of it. I worked on the university yearbook from the time I was a freshman and eventually became managing editor and editor in chief, paid positions that were demanding jobs.

When I thought about pursuing publishing, however, I pictured New York and I got scared. I imagined myself as one of thousands of hopefuls. The summer before, I had applied for a job at the United Nations where my older cousin worked as a guide. When I got turned down, I was not only disappointed, but I think it must have also undermined my confidence in myself.

As a woman it seemed even harder to me to think about being completely on my own. Most of the other girls I knew well were either getting married, had plans to, were going on to graduate school, or were planning to work in the city. Without even realizing it, I made subtle little compromises. I looked around at job possibilities that seemed more manageable.

I was an English major, my courses were demanding, and I had a strong drive to be a good student. School, plus extracurricular activities and friends, kept me busy. I had begun to date frequently in college, but I never "went steady" or was "pinned" (the custom of the day), or had the kind of intense, ongoing relationship, emotionally or sexually, that some of my friends had. Although I did my share of "making out," it's rather amazing to me as I think back on it that the extent of my sexual experience probably involved some heavy petting, little or no genital contact, and that before meeting Barry, I had never even been naked with a boy. Some of the morality of the fifties had carried into the early sixties. If you did make the decision to lose your virginity, and it was a crucial decision indeed, you generally did it with someone you planned to marry.

During this time I ran into Barry once or twice very briefly. Always, there would be a physical reaction when I saw him, a shortness of breath, a knot in my stomach. And I had a sense that he was attracted to me. One summer he even went so far as to ask me out. At the time I viewed him as cocky and self-satisfied, and that impression was confirmed when he asked me out on a Friday for a date the next night. My automatic response was to say no, even though there was no one I wanted to go out with more than him. In those days, you measured how desirable you were to a boy by how much in advance he asked you out. After that, it took a year before I got to go out with him again, and by that time, gradual changes in morality, the beginnings of more permissive attitudes toward sexuality, had begun to have an effect upon even me.

As stereotypical a reaction as it probably is, it is unabashedly true that I was drawn to Barry from the first moment I met him. There was a brightness about him, a magnetism, an alive kind of energy. I liked his tall, lean body, close-cropped hair, deep-set brown eyes, cleft chin, and the easy way he carried himself. He was well dressed, 1964 style: an expensive-looking red crew-neck sweater, an oxford blue button-down shirt underneath the sweater, herringbone sport jacket, white sweat socks, and loafers. On his hand was a college ring with a red stone and diagonally across the stone were imprinted the Greek symbols of his fraternity, Pi Lambda Phi.

Even though he had more money than most of the people I knew—his family owned a large local beverage company—he carried it easily. And there's no doubt that I was attracted to the financial security Barry offered after growing up all those years with my father's preoccupation with that issue. Barry was also gregarious and outgoing, and I liked his social ease. Yet he seemed kind and sensitive too. Since I masked my insecurity and social discomfort under a guise of aloofness, I was fascinated by someone who made it look so easy.

We fell in love in Bethel, Maine, a tiny little gem of a New England town. It was late June of 1965 and the Maine summer was just coming into her own. The university had sent a group of ten students to attend a two-week group dynamics training, run by the National Training Laboratories. I hadn't seen Barry for some time, but when he smiled at me in the gymnasium of Gould Academy in Bethel, I knew without doubt that he was the one I wanted.

In the late 1970s, sensitivity groups are as much a part of the culture as compact cars, but in 1965, they were still a relatively new phenomenon. Fortunately for me, there had been an early interest in the field of group dynamics by some faculty and staff at Temple University and the university had become a center for research and study in the field. My participation in groups made me see that some of my motivation for doing the things I had always done was to win the approval of my parents and other people. For once, I began to explore what my own values were rather than fitting myself into the expectations of others. I saw that I could get angry at people and they would not fall apart and I could handle their criticism of me as well.

I also saw that other people were exactly like me, with similar fears and similar strengths. The intensity of my relationships expanded, and I felt surer relying upon myself as my own anchor. At twenty I had the kind of training in listening to myself—to my inner sense of right and wrong—that some people experience after thirty from psychotherapy or a comparable experience. I also learned to hear what other people were saying in a deeper, less judgmental way than I had known before. It was so satisfying that I knew then that any relationship that mattered would eventually have to be based upon these principles.

In the mid-sixties, when Barry and I began to date, no one we knew smoked pot. We went to fraternity parties and football games. We made out to Johnny Mathis and the Lettermen. There were fewer divorces, people stayed married a long time, and they got married with different expectations than they do now. The people I knew didn't live together, they got married. Ours was the prototypical college love, the fifties TV version of romance. When we got engaged, I thought Barry would answer all my needs, that marriage would be forever, that neither of us would require anyone else.

Barry gave me my engagement ring on my twenty-first birthday. He took me to dinner at the Wedgewood Room of the Warwick Hotel in Philadelphia and slipped it on my finger under the table. The band played "Make Someone Happy" and we stood up to dance. Five months later, on a late summer evening, I walked down the aisle in my white lace wedding gown, and we danced to that same song at our wedding.

A month after we married, we moved to Carlisle, a small college town in central Pennsylvania, so that Barry could complete his last year in law school. Carlisle was a nice place to begin a marriage. We lived in the center of town in a large, old apartment, above an optical company, the second floor of a Victorian house. Except for the periodic pressure of law school, our life was easy. We opened our wedding presents, bought furniture, and set about creating a home.

When I began my relationship with Barry, my sexuality had expanded incredibly. There was an attraction between us that I hadn't experienced with anyone before. Something about him—an essential decency, perhaps—I trusted in a very basic way. And he also was attracted to me. My body was never too thin for Barry; he liked my face, the way I dressed, my hair.

I was a senior in college and he was in his first year of law school when we had sex for the first time. I had grown up a lot—there had been more sexual experiences with men, my own sexuality was blooming, and I was ready for a more serious involvement. The first time, in Barry's Carlisle apartment, was anticlimactic and mildly uncomfortable; actually, I didn't feel very much of anything at all. It took me some time to learn how to reach orgasm. I had to discover what felt good to me and how to communicate that to Barry. In those days, there was not a whole lot of information available about sex or sexual response. Most people were reluctant to talk about it, and we all suffered under the weight of sexual myths and misconceptions. Obviously, what I considered good sex then I might find limited today, but generally, my memories of our sexual relationship in the early years of our marriage are pleasant. We grew looser and more open with each other, we experimented, and we learned in expanding ways how to satisfy each other.

Fresh out of college, beginning a new marriage, I also got my first job—as an administrative assistant in the Office of Mental Health in Harrisburg, the state capitol about thirty miles from Carlisle. My job was not particularly stimulating; basically, I wrote letters authorizing the transfer of mental patients from one state mental hospital to another. But I felt very grown-up commuting to work an hour and a half every day and making money of my own.

I knew nothing about running a home. Barry taught me everything. The most I had ever prepared before getting married was eggs or tuna fish. I read cookbooks and collected recipes, but cooking came more naturally to Barry, and he'd had much more experience. Sometimes when people came to dinner, Barry ended up preparing most of the meal. When our guests complimented me on a dish, neither of us would reveal that I hadn't actually done the cooking. Standard roles for husbands and wives were still narrowly defined in the mid-sixties. It was terribly important to my self-esteem as a woman to know how to cook and to be seen as skilled in this area by other people; and as unbelievable as it seems now, Barry was the only man I knew who was comfortable in the kitchen. More and more women were working, but it was still a time when womanliness was tied to competency in handling household chores.

From the time we started dating, Barry and I had talked about joining the Peace Corps after he finished law school. It was something that Barry was certain he wanted to do, and I also looked at it as a way of not settling down too fast, of staying young and open, of moving out from the insulation and expectations of home.

Barry's determination to join the Peace Corps represents the quality I've always valued most about him—his willingness to reach out beyond the conventional and try something new—and his ability to push me past my own fears and reluctance. He has ideas about the way things should be, and he sets about making them that way. Where I get stuck in day-to-day details, Barry forges ahead.

It's been over ten years since we were Peace Corps volunteers in the farming and cattle town of San Andrés, Panama. It seems like another lifetime. Sometimes people who meet me now are surprised that I was actually in the Peace Corps. To me, it's consistent with my history. The Peace Corps was merely a different expression of the political concern that has always been a part of me, the involvement with other people that my grandmothers encouraged.

Nor is it surprising that the major part of my efforts was with women, dealing with projects that were intended to mobilize them to recognize their own power. Working with local women's home economics clubs, I presented programs on birth control, nutrition, and sewing, and also organized women in San Andrés to pressure the government to provide a nurse and medical equipment for a health center that had been constructed but never used.

The Peace Corps taught me that I didn't have to be so careful with myself. I could learn Spanish because I had to; I could learn to sew a dress on a treadle machine even though I hated sewing. I could reach out beyond my limits and make contact with people very different from those I knew at home, not just Panamanian, but the other volunteers in my group. Until this time, I hadn't yet done very much traveling. During Peace Corps training, I met people from rural areas of my own country who had never visited a major city. Before this experience, I myself had never seen a pig up close.

Still, it was a strange time to be away from the States, 1967, '68, '69—a time of internal violence, civil disruption. One morning, Lalo, our neighbor across the road, rushed over to our house to tell us that he had just heard on the radio that Martin Luther King had been shot. Some months later we got the news that Robert Kennedy had been assassinated. There was the violence too at the Democratic National Convention in Mayor Daley's Chicago. In my house on a dirt road in a mountain town in Panama, I felt both involved with and disconnected from what was going on at home.

There is no doubt that the bonds of my relationship with Barry were deepening during the time we spent together in the Peace Corps. All our new experiences were shared experiences. There were so many hard times—long periods of boredom, frustration with the unstructured work, loneliness, the difficulty of learning the ways of a new culture. But we were growing too. We were pushing ourselves, and we pushed each other. We spent enormous periods of time together, visiting and working with the people, riding on horseback to neighboring towns, taking baths in a nearby stream. During the rainy season, when rains were so torrential that no one went outside, we spent hours alone together in our small cement block house.

When we returned to Philadelphia, I felt a tremendous need to settle down for a while. It had become very clear to me in Panama that I wanted a profession of my own, an area of expertise that was mine, work that was specified and directed, and work that involved people. Barry was about to embark on his law career, and I had no interest in being a mere appendage. The years in Panama had shown me that I had my own abilities, and I wanted to make my own contribution. Besides, by this time, it was considered quite acceptable for married women to lead independent professional lives as well.

For a year I worked in a day treatment program of a community mental health center, and then in 1970 I entered the Graduate School of Social Work and Social Research of Bryn Mawr College, a two-year master's degree program. In addition to my classes, I worked in field placements, first in a rehabilitation unit of a city hospital and then in a child psychiatry clinic.

The people I was drawn to at school were the political people, the ones who had gone South in the early sixties to take part in civil rights demonstrations, or those who were involved in the antiwar movement. The Vietnam War had marked my own coming of age politically. Back in 1966, when peace activists were still seen as traitors and dissidents, I had overcome my reluctance and fear about what people would say and joined a demonstration on the steps of the State

Capitol in Harrisburg. Over the years, I continued my involvement in antiwar activities.

Social change was in the air during the early seventies, the years I was a graduate student, and it influenced my personal development. Now in my mid-twenties, I felt suddenly bombarded by a whole rash of new ideas and issues that were being talked about, besides dealing daily with a curriculum within the social work program that already focused upon personal and societal change. It wasn't just the peace movement, which, of course, was at its height, nor was it merely concern for socially oppressed minorities—although a career in social work necessarily demanded attention to these problems. What was changing was the way I looked at myself as a woman: my consciousness and life-style began to be deeply affected by the women's movement, which was capturing more and more public attention.

It was time to examine the assumptions I had always held— the ones I had never thought to question until now—about what I had a right to expect of myself. In the consciousness-raising group I was in for two years, I began to talk openly with other women about our independence and our sexuality for the first time in my life. I had had no idea of the wide range of sexual activity and response among women. Masturbation was not something I had ever given much thought to. Nor had I realized that some women achieve orgasm through other means than intercourse with a man—oral sex, a vibrator—and others had never reached orgasm at all. And, certainly, it was the first time I heard open discussion of homosexuality between women, that I was even aware that it existed.

Barry and I were still very close, and many parts of our relationship were working. Our marriage had gone through many changes, as had we as individuals, and both of us felt an intimate connection with the social changes going on around us. Some marriages we knew were breaking up. It was clear that we loved each other, and there was no question that we remained committed to our marriage. The only problem was that after more than five years of living together, I was beginning to be mildly bored. Small wonder that the title of my master's thesis at the end of graduate school was "An Exploration of Some of the Dimensions of Marriage."

Perhaps it was something in our past, or the unrealistic expectations with which we had gone into marriage, or factors in our own personalities—whatever it was—something in our relationship had gone stale. I had married young, transferred my dependency on my family onto my husband, and I knew that in order to grow up, I needed to branch out on my own, discover my own separateness. But how to do that while I was still married? Like many other couples we knew at the time, we had always placed a lot of emphasis upon togetherness. Although we each pursued our individual interests in terms of work, socially we tended to see ourselves as extensions of each other.

Suddenly and with increasing frequency, I found myself drawn to other people. It seemed to me that something must be going wrong with my relationship with Barry for me to spend so much time fantasizing about other men, and I felt too guilty to talk to anyone about it. It's odd how after a number of years of marriage, some of the very qualities that had drawn me to Barry in the first place began to be objectionable in my eyes. "I am not your arm, Alice," he said sometimes to me when I criticized him, but the relationship was so much a part of me and the way I viewed myself that I saw anything he did as reflecting upon me.

Somehow our marriage has become ingrown, and it was obvious that sooner or later something was going to give. Barry seemed preoccupied, weighted down, involved with his work, less accessible. A few times during the early years of our marriage, I had been attracted to other men, but I never pursued any of the relationships. I was too frightened. I didn't want to do anything to risk hurting the intimacy and trust Barry and I had developed together. Now, however, I was restless and going through a period of self-examination and reaching out. I became involved in an affair with an older man, an intellectual, and as confused and conflicted as I felt, the relationship added a dimension of excitement to my life.

All of it seemed to be moving too fast, and to top it off, I became pregnant. For some time, Barry and I had planned to have a child when I finished graduate school, an expression of the positive feelings we felt toward each other, our marriage, the future. No doubt, it also was a way—or so we thought—of holding things together. At the same time I wanted to be a mother, I also knew that I would have to postpone beginning my career, at least for a while. The women I had gone to school with were all beginning exciting new jobs, but I looked ahead to being at home with a baby. For the moment at least, the separate options that I had worked so hard to develop for myself began to narrow.

Barry

My maternal grandparents, Mary and Manuel Frank, were the hub of my family when I was growing up and they played a key role in keeping everyone together. Their oldest son, Perry, had died when he was thirty-three—it was the tragedy of my grandmother's life—but my mother, her two brothers, and their families were very close. Almost every Sunday, my parents, aunts, uncles, and their children would visit my grandparents in their Wynnefield home. My cousins, brother, and I, dressed in our Sunday best, played together around the house while the grown-ups congregated in the living room to talk. Later in the day, my grandmother often served a huge meal that she had been preparing for several days. The rituals were established, and the relationship between my grandparents was devoted and solid. There was never any question about the deep love that existed between them or the love they had for their family.

Even when I grew older, I liked to visit them regularly. Their home was inviting to me, warm and welcoming, and I could always depend upon consistency in the way they lived their lives.

Mary, my grandmother, was born in England on Christmas Day, but as a young girl, her family moved to Elmira, New York, and she grew up there. She was a gracious lady, a woman of bearing, and she wore her prosperity and her propriety well. It was more than her generous contributions to charities; one had the sense in her presence that somehow everything would be taken care of. Her home was filled with handsome antiques, but her favorite room was her comfortable den where rows and rows of framed photographs of her family filled an entire wall.

My grandmother and I had a special bond; in some way, I think I reminded her of Perry, and she admired my sensitivity and concern for people's feelings that she said had been so much a part of her oldest son's nature. She was always delighted when I came by, greeting me with some sweets or a glass of soda, after which we would sit and talk.

On some visits, she would sit down at the piano and play two songs she loved —"The Girl That I Marry" and "Too Young"—and which she had taught me to sing. I can recall singing these two songs, at her urging, when I was five years old, in front of the guests at the elegant Shelburne Hotel in Atlantic City.

My grandfather was a proud man. He had a kind of earthy nobility to him. Sitting erect in his favorite chair, he'd talk to me about business. He loved to tell me the story of how, at nine years old, he would save five cents given to him by a teacher to do an errand, by walking across town rather than using the money for the trolley.

Manuel, my grandfather, was a Russian immigrant. Along with his father and brother, he started a business selling soda in their South Philadelphia garage in 1895. It was hard work, requiring long hours—in his early years he worked six and a half days a week—but my grandfather had enormous determination and drive and a very shrewd business sense. Besides having a unique taste for natural fruit flavors, he believed in using the finest ingredients, and insisted upon a high standard of quality. Under his and his brother's guidance, Frank's Beverages mushroomed and became the largest independent bottling company on the East Coast.

Mary was the power behind Manuel and his chief confidante. She provided a stable, comfortable home and looked after his every need. Their marriage was an early model to me of a successful relationship, especially after my own parents' marriage began to deteriorate.

As it did to many couples in the early forties, the war contributed irrevocable disruption to my parents' relationship. My mother and father were very young when they married—she was eighteen and he was twenty-one—and I was born ten months later. A year after that, my father was drafted. He was stationed at a series of bases throughout the South, and my mother with me in tow, traveled too, in order to be close to him. When it came time for him to go overseas, my mother moved back to her parents' house. She was pregnant again, and my brother, Ronald, two years younger than I, was born while my father was away.

Deeply protective of their only daughter, my grandparents watched over her with great caring. But in their single-minded devotion, they could be domineering as well. The force of both of them united on a position was formidable. For as long as I could remember, and certainly throughout the years I was growing up, my mother was caught between the struggle to please them and to break free from their domination. No doubt her own desire to be independent had an impact on the way she raised me. The contribution she made to me was her continual admonition to do what I wanted to do in life, that I need not follow anyone's direction except my own.

My mother's life was marked by tragedy from the time she was small. At two years old, her dress caught fire while she and her brother were playing with matches. She was rolled up in a rug, rushed to the hospital, and barely survived. One third of her body was severely burned, and for the next seventeen years, she spent every summer in the hospital enduring countless operations, skin grafts, and other medical procedures.

My mother's burns had a major effect upon the way I viewed life. Her scars never bothered me; to me my mother was always beautiful, but the effects of her being burned at such an early age was carried into my life. Her descriptions of the way she had been teased and ridiculed by other children for being different moved me deeply. I identified with the hurt and pain she had gone through. My empathy for people whom others don't find socially acceptable may have its roots in the compassion I felt for my mother. Certainly, she emphasized kindness and understanding as the most important attributes a person can have.

When my father returned from the war, he came home to two small children he hardly knew. My parents moved away from my mother's parents' house, to a newly built apartment complex across the city. The six years that we lived at the Lakeside Apartments were in many ways my happiest years. My family was reunited, and my parents' relationship was relatively tranquil. I felt comfortable in the self-enclosed, insulated setting with its trees and pleasant lawns and the two rosebushes I watched my father plant behind our apartment building. Both my parents loved plants and flowers, and throughout my childhood, gardening, planting, and nurturing living things was one of our more pleasant family activities.

As the youngest of four boys, my father, like so many men his age, was strongly affected by the Depression and World War II. When his older brother was drafted into the Army, my father left college and helped his father run their real estate business until he too was drafted. Although he had completed two years at the University of Pennsylvania, when my father returned from the war, he gave up his dream of being a doctor and decided to work for my grandfather at Frank's Beverages. It was a decision my mother never approved of. Still my father seemed to derive a lot of satisfaction from working in the business. His easygoing manner could soothe the most agitated customer, and within a short period of time, he became an excellent salesman and manager.

My relationship with him was more distant than with my mother, since he was away working much of the time. Where my mother has always tended to be high-strung and emotional, my father is steady and easygoing, more careful and cautious in his approach toward life, less adventurous than my mother. He is a man whose feelings run deep, but he has difficulty expressing them directly; it's through his sense of responsibility that he shows his caring and commitment.

Some of my problems as a child probably date back to when I was eight years old, and my family moved. I didn't want to leave my friends and the life I was used to, and I was angry at my parents for making me go. At eight years old, however, there didn't seem to be much I could do about it. Everything felt strange and bewildering to me when my family moved from our apartment to our new home in Merion, a suburb of Philadelphia. Our house had been built as part of a large development of single-family three- and four-bedroom homes, part of the postwar suburban sprawl into Philadelphia's Main Line. The homes on my new street seemed far apart and remote from each other, and the entire neighborhood appeared to be a large barren expanse, devoid of trees and people. Soon after we moved in, I remember standing alone on the corner next to my house feeling completely lost, as if I had been dropped down into a city on an alien planet.

I had trouble adjusting to the new ways; as soon as I entered my new school, I was sure I was more backward than the other kids in my class. They had already learned script, but in my old school we had been accustomed to printing only. From the very beginning, there was enormous pressure upon me to catch up. My parents hired a tutor to teach me script, but from that time on, I was always behind, and this tutor was to be the first of many I would have throughout school. That sense of being lost, the feeling of confusion and bewilderment, was with me for the rest of elementary school and through high school until my senior year.

My bedroom was used as a retreat from the world, and I spent many hours working with my expanding tropical fish collection. It was a large room with a desk and built-in drawers and shelves along one wall and a cherrywood bureau and twin beds. Years later, when I was in psychoanalysis, my psychiatrist accurately stated that I tried to study relationships and life by watching the interactions of tropical fish. For many years I thought that I could gleen hints about how to live from animals, birds, fish, and nature in general.

Another of my hobbies was building plastic models of boats, planes, and cars. Very agile with my hands, I loved the intricate models with their many small pieces. Many afternoons and evenings, my homework was left untouched while I concentrated on building and painting my models. When I completed a model, I felt a sense of accomplishment and pride in my work that I didn't experience in any other area of my life.

Most important, there was privacy. Indeed, sometimes it seemed to me that I was happiest when I could be alone in my room away from the pressures of peers, school, and family. I am a social person—the truth was that I loved to be with people even then—but I just didn't feel good about myself. It seemed after I moved that I couldn't do the things that were expected of boys my age. And my family life was far from happy.

My parents fought a great deal whenever my father was home. It was rare when he wasn't working—usually only Saturday afternoons and Sundays. Wintertime, Dad was away from seven-thirty in the morning until six-thirty every evening, and he worked as late as ten or eleven at night in the summer when the soda business becomes very heavy. Usually, he arrived home exhausted. After eating the dinner that my mother prepared for him, he would collapse into a chair in the den and doze. When they did fight, my mother would scream and cry while my father sat in another room, seemingly impassive, not saying a word. Perhaps fighting was the only way my parents knew to make contact.

There were very few times that I recall when my mother and father truly seemed to give each other pleasure. Instead of hearing each other out, their arguments became repetitive battles in which my father discouraged my mother's initiatives—new ideas for the house, plans for the children—while my mother, in turn, constantly pressured my father to be different from the way he was. I think my mother and father cared for each other, and probably still do today, but it seems that somewhere in the early part of their marriage, they stopped talking to each other and encouraging the other's goals and desires in life. I decided very early that when I got married, it was going to be different.

It's odd, given how much I enjoy physical activity now, that as a child I hated sports with such venom. I never seemed to do as well as the other kids, whether it was in school, camp, or on my block.

They made fun of the way I ran or threw a ball, and I was always the last one to be chosen for a team. Physical play seemed awkward, and my body never seemed to perform the way I wanted it to. I don't know what got in my way. Maybe it was fear, or embarrassment about doing it the wrong way, or the fact that no one ever took enough interest to work with me on developing the fundamentals.

The problem was that it seemed that most of the kids wanted to play some type of sport almost all the time; if it wasn't basketball season, then it was touch football. There must be something wrong about me, I thought, something basic that I was lacking, and there didn't seem to be anything I could do about it. Often, I spent an entire game worrying when the inevitable moment would come that I would mess up—drop a fly ball, strike out, miss a basket—and then have to face being attacked fiercely by one boy or another.

I longed to be included, to be accepted in the popular group. There were several crowds in my school, cliques of kids who spent time together, but I wasn't even in the unpopular crowd. Other kids who were not particularly good at athletics achieved recognition by being smart and performing well in school. I couldn't do that either. I know that people generally thought of me as a "nice person," but what did that matter if you were nice but dumb?

When things got bad, I went to my mother in tears and complained to her about being beaten up by one of the other boys. I know that it was hard for her to see my pain. She listened sympathetically and made suggestions, but they didn't seem at all helpful. Sometimes her response was that someday I would be better than all the other boys and eventually they would look up to me.

Some of my happiest times when I was young were the evenings when my parents went out and my younger brother Ronny and I were left with Doris, our housekeeper. Doris had worked for my mother from the time she was seventeen, and she was very attached to my brother and me. There's no doubt that she provided some of the basic nurturing in the household. While Ronny and I usually fought when we were alone, when we were with Doris, we got along with each other much better. Doris was very much a part of my family: she was caring, she liked to laugh, and her steady disposition was a continual comfort to me. She was there when I came home from school, to make dinner, and to celebrate my birthdays.

My parents almost separated after twelve years of marriage but then decided to stay together and try to make it work once more.

They had two more children, Perry, who is thirteen years younger than I, and Cindy, two years younger than Perry. From the time they were born, I adored Perry and Cindy and because of the large age difference, I felt a kind of parental responsibility toward them. As my parents' relationship deteriorated further, I assumed more responsibility in the home. My mother was frequently upset and depressed, and many evenings I took Perry and Cindy out to a restaurant for dinner.

I had difficulty understanding why with so much unhappiness my parents stayed together for twenty-one years. I know from living with them that they probably should have separated about ten years sooner. During the 1950s, however, there was a greater stigma attached to divorce, and more social pressure to stay married and make a go of it, whatever the circumstances. To be sure, my grandparents were very much against separation and did not conceive of divorce as a possibility worth considering. They were very fond of my father, and I don't think they ever understood why my parents didn't get along. Divorce meant social embarrassment, and they were also concerned about emotional damage to the children.

Even though it was a blow to me when my parents finally did separate, I realized that it was best for all of us. Much of my sadness came from an unrealistic feeling of responsibility, wondering how I had failed in my goal of turning the Kohns into a model "Ozzie and Harriet" type of family.

Sex was hardly ever mentioned directly in my home. On a trip to California when I was thirteen, my father took me aside to have a "talk." He began by telling me that since I was growing up, there were certain things I needed to know and then described in a somewhat mechanical manner how sexual intercourse produces a baby. The discussion was grimly serious. From the stiff vocabulary he used, and the distant manner of his lecture, he could have been telling me how to change a tire. The subtle message was that a man had to take responsibility and that sexual intercourse was a serious matter. He never added that there was any pleasure involved in sex. I was left with the impression that the sole reason for intercourse was to have babies.

As I look back, I think I have always been a highly sexualized person with intense sexual curiosity. The first sexual experience that I recall occurred when I was about five or six years old at my cousin's house. While my parents were occupied talking inside, two neighbor-

hood girls and I quickly undressed and began to touch one another's
bodies, laughing at the new and different unknown areas.

Like most boys, when I was growing up, I spent most of my
time with other boys rather than girls. Whether it was in school, at
overnight camp, or playing hide-and-seek after dark on Friday nights,
boys played with boys. Girls were people that you saw at school,
talked to in the halls, or danced with at "Younger Set" parties
sponsored by the junior high school. Physical contact was generally
off limits.

When I was twelve or thirteen, one of the boys at camp, a
neighbor from home, showed me how to masturbate. After camp
ended and we returned home, we continued to meet privately once
every two or three weeks for a period of more than four years. At first
our sex was limited to mutual masturbation. Gradually we expanded
our repertoire to include lying together, oral/genital sex, and, unsuccessfully, anal intercourse. The feelings of touching or being touched
by my friend were always different and unpredictable. Sometimes it
was thrilling, sometimes loving, sometimes playful.

Despite our pleasure, we knew, somehow, that what we were
doing was wrong. After we reached orgasm, we'd put our clothes on
and leave one another as quickly as possible. I always experienced a
tremendous letdown as all the good feelings from minutes before
disappeared. I was filled with guilt and shame for having given in to
my physical need, and I was confused about the sexual excitement I
felt with the other boy. After sex with him, the desire would leave and
I was sure that we'd never do it again.

After our sexual relationship began, our friendship became
strained. We kept our distance from one another and went out of our
way not to show our affection in front of other friends. We had a secret
that we intended to keep. We never talked about not telling our
friends; we just knew that neither of us would reveal what we had
done.

Even though there was tension between us, when the desire
returned, we found ourselves getting together again. Each time, we'd
talk about our latest fantasies and then experiment with them.
Neither of us labeled our activities as homosexual—we didn't even
know what the word meant. We just saw what we did as homework,
so to speak, for the day when we would transfer our skills to girls.

In my early teens I began dating girls and having limited
sexual experience with them, kissing, hugging, petting. Each encoun-

ter whetted my appetite for more. What I wanted was to experience the "real thing" with a girl. Although I had many concerns about the consequences, I was excited about the possibility of exploring sex with a girl. Except for several experiences about the age of sixteen of being masturbated by a girl, sex with girls from ages thirteen to eighteen was fairly limited. This was the morality of the day and I bought it, although it didn't stop me from having continual fantasies about girls.

In the eleventh grade I began dating Sandy, a girl in my high school class, and we continued to go out together off and on for the next six years. As we grew to trust each other, I began to open up and Sandy and I had long talks. I don't think that either of us had ever talked as honestly with another person. Our relationship gave me a sense of security during a time I was not feeling very confident about myself. Unlike me, Sandy came from a very stable family. It's interesting that throughout my life, I have always been attracted to friends whose familes seemed more "normal" than mine.

Sandy had very strong views about how involved she wanted to get sexually, and she always stopped my advances at heavy petting. She wanted more of a commitment than "I like you," which was all I was willing to say until years later.

Other boys seemed more willing than I was to say the magic words "I love you" in order to have sex. In fact, some boys would boast openly about lying. I took the question of love very seriously, and was not willing to say I loved Sandy when I wasn't sure that I did. Love for me was closely tied to marriage and that was something I wanted to be completely sure about before making a commitment. Also, since I believed totally in the "good girl/bad girl" philosophy, I went along with Sandy's reluctance to have intercourse.

My high school years were not happy ones for me. Most of the time at school I was in a daze, just going from class to class but not connecting at all with the material covered. Although I astonished everyone one semester by getting a B in Chemistry, the only subject I consistently got A's in was choir, which was my favorite subject and the only class in which I was recognized as being special and competent. Several times I was chosen to sing solo selections for our choir performances. However, because my high school was very academically oriented and choir seemed a subject of little importance to one's post high school needs, I devalued the experience.

During my senior year, I was asked to be advertising manager for our school yearbook. I was delighted to be given the opportunity and wanted to prove that I could do a good job. I worked hard, and by the end of the year was highly complimented by many of the students and teachers for doing a competent and responsible job. My yearbook achievement and the recognition I received were important to my self-image. I felt lighter and less depressed about my life than I had in many years. I had been starved for that kind of acknowledgment. It was also during that year that several girls pursued me in addition to Sandy. That was new for me. They told me that I was very sensitive, that I was fun to be with, and that I had a lot to offer as a person.

The summer before entering college I made a conscious decision never to have sex with boys again. To renounce this kind of behavior seemed a necessary step toward becoming an adult and beginning a new grown-up life in college. I knew that sex with boys was wrong and unacceptable, that if anyone ever found out about it, I would be very embarrassed. Besides, sexual experiences with girls were becoming more accessible. I still hadn't had sexual intercourse but I assumed that it was just a matter of time. I looked at entering college as an opportunity to begin a new life, with new people and eventually new friends. It seemed an appropriate time to give up what I saw as one of my old "bad habits."

It wasn't until college that I really began coming out of my shell and radically changed my behavior both academically and socially. Although I felt dejected about going to Temple University because most of the kids in my high school were going to Ivy League or other prestigious colleges, it turned out that Temple offered me a lot.

One woman I met at Freshman Camp, a three-day orientation program for new students, had a special impact on my life at Temple. She was advertising manager of the college newspaper and took me under her wing as her possible successor when she heard that I had been involved in high school yearbook advertising. Ellen encouraged me to work hard during the first semester so that I could achieve an academic average high enough to become involved in campus activities.

Ellen's continuing interest in me was a major factor in why I was able to change so much during Freshman Camp and my first semester. I never before had any person show such concern about me and my well-being. Besides, she was beautiful as well as smart.

Almost every day we would see each other in the student activities office or go to lunch together. Ellen introduced me to her friends, who were also very involved in student activities and equally intelligent. Within weeks of beginning college, my entire attitude about myself began to shift.

From the beginning, I did well academically. I was astounded. Here was Barry Kohn, who had always thought of himself as a mediocre student, with a B average. I was a member of the men's honorary society, president of my fraternity, and—perhaps coincidentally, although I doubt it—co-director of Freshman Camp. I received many awards as a senior, including the coveted Sword Award for outstanding service to Temple. During my four years at Temple, my whole life seemed to flip over. Everything I had hated about myself in high school had changed. I could no longer describe myself as lonely, withdrawn or dumb. I was astonished by the change, and I loved it. I wondered to myself, "How did all this happen?"

Among the most powerful of the college experiences that contributed to my new self-image was my life as a member of a fraternity. Replacing the many unhappy experiences with boys in my childhood were new ones based on the values of brotherhood rather than competition. I had never before been as intimate with a group of other young men, spending time together, talking seriously at meetings, or just horsing around. I developed close friendships with two or three fraternity brothers and we shared a variety of experiences—double-dating, participating in student activities, and vacationing together. At weekly fraternity meetings I was challenged to improve my ability to speak comfortably in front of a group and I grew increasingly confident about my skills in working with people.

During this time, homosexuality was mentioned only in a ridiculing manner, and I participated in the negative comments as much as anyone else. I had put my earlier sexual experimentation with boys behind me, and my sexual awareness—thoughts, fantasies, involvements—was focused entirely upon girls. Words like "fag," "queer," and "homo" were loosely thrown around as put-downs. No one really believed that any brother in our fraternity was a homosexual. I know now that there were brothers in the fraternity who were gay and were actively having sex with men at the time. But, of course, they were extremely secretive about such activities and were not about to take up any banners defending their rights.

I was nineteen when I first had sexual intercourse with a girl; finally I was experiencing "the real thing." The college semester had ended and most of the brothers who lived in the fraternity house had returned home for the summer. I knew that a certain girl had a crush on me and also had a reputation for being sexually loose. One late summer evening, I drove her to my fraternity house, both of us aware of the purpose of the evening. I was so excited that I had an orgasm before I even entered her. The second time, I was able to hold out a little longer. I loved it. It was everything I had fantasized and more. I felt proud of myself and had a sense of finally coming of age.

My first few sexual experiences with girls seemed to increase my desire for more. At the same time, though, I was still hung up on the idea that only promiscuous girls would consent to have sex. Every time I had sex I chose a girl that I didn't respect. While we were together, I loved it, but as strong as the desire had been to have sex, so too was the urge to get away from the girl the moment after I had reached a climax. I felt a lot of guilt about using girls merely for sexual satisfaction, yet at the time, I saw no other alternative.

My feelings toward men were still tightly repressed, but faint stirrings occurred periodically. During one summer while I was in college I worked as a camp counselor in the Pocono Mountains and developed a very close friendship with another male counselor named Arty. Arty was very handsome: lean, tight-skinned, wiry, and very athletic. Almost every night after dropping off our dates, Arty and I talked until late in the night about sex, love, and relationships. The talks we had were very important to me. There was an intense feeling of energy, a kind of electricity that passed between us as we talked and shared our deepest thoughts with each other. I didn't even think about how to characterize my feelings for Arty except to think of him as my best friend.

During the summer of 1964, having graduated from college, we traveled around Europe for two months. I have vivid memories of a warm night in Paris, sharing a hotel room as we always did, when I became aware of a strong sexual desire for Arty. I remember debating with myself whether or not I should touch him. I knew that to be physical was to risk our entire friendship, and I was too frightened to explore my attraction for him.

After my summer in Europe with Arty, I began a new stage of my life as a freshman at Dickinson School of Law in the small central Pennsylvania town of Carlisle. My decision to enter law school came more from not knowing what else to do with my life than out of any certainty that I wanted to practice law. I had liked my college courses in constitutional and business law, and my family was enthusiastic about the prospect of my attending law school. Besides, at the time, continuing my education was far preferable to the draft.

That autumn of 1964, when I entered law school, Sandy, my girl friend of five and a half years, began asking serious questions about our future. There was another man in her life now, and she did not want to close out her options if I had no intention of marrying her. Actually, I had never really given serious consideration to marrying Sandy. Marriage was a subject that I just was not ready to think about.

Looking back, I realize that I was very much affected by the failure of my parents' marriage, and I didn't want to be married to someone whom I had any doubts about. I knew Sandy was my closest friend and I thought to myself, "Maybe this is what love is." Perhaps I might never meet another woman with whom I would feel as close. After all, we had grown up together and shared many experiences during a significant part of our lives. But marriage was forever, and I just didn't hear bells ringing; deep down I knew that Sandy was not the one.

After a lot of indecision, and a halfhearted marriage proposal on my part, Sandy decided to marry the other man she was dating. When she told me of her decision, I was shocked and relieved. I was sad about ending our relationship, but I was excited about the prospect of not being tied down and maintaining my freedom.

I've always been happier putting ideas into practice than studying about them in school. Although later on I liked being a lawyer and grew increasingly confident about my own competency, I found law school to be boring, draining, and detached from the real world. Consequently, I had to work very hard at my law courses, plugging away in the library. Still, I loved living the life of a student in Carlisle. In college, even though I spent most of my waking hours at the fraternity house, I had lived away from home for only one semester. Now, however, I had an apartment in a beautiful, clean, small college town where people greeted one another when they walked down the street. There was time for squash, fishing, and parties with the Dickinson College students.

I was happy to see my first year of law school come to an end. It had been a period of constant academic pressure and I was looking forward to the summer. I took a summer job at Temple University, counseling incoming freshmen, and as part of my training for the position, I was invited to participate in a two-week sensitivity group experience in Bethel, Maine. In many ways, my time in Maine represented my first real contact with myself. Being part of a group for eight hours a day, I discovered the joys of introspection as well as the personal growth that resulted from sharing my deepest thoughts and feelings with other people.

I was shocked though, one afternoon after one of the group sessions, when the leader of my group called me aside and asked me if there was something I was hiding from the group. Was he talking about my past, adolescent homosexual experiences? How could he know? Of course, deep down I knew he was right because several times during the group I had thought about sharing that part of me and then immediately held back. Instead of telling him the truth, I lied. I was too frightened to take a chance and let him know. I thought that if he knew the truth he would tell me to leave the group and seek counseling.

It was also at Bethel that I began dating Alice. I had met her two years earlier at Temple and remember thinking she was special from the first time I saw her. I found her beautiful and was especially attracted to her blond hair, brown almond eyes, and delicate body. I loved seeing the shape of her breasts in a tight sweater.

She was very bright, and her directness in confronting me was fascinating. I had never before met someone who would not allow me to shut down when I was depressed. She would keep urging me to talk about my feelings, and for the first time, I was able to share a lot of the sadness that I carried around with me. Within a few weeks of dating I knew that I was falling in love with Alice.

I remember the first time I arrived at Alice's family's house at the shore. I had known her only a short time. When I arrived, Alice, her mother and aunt were out shopping. The only people around were her grandparents, whom I hadn't met previously. I was warmly welcomed, not as a stranger, but as a friend of Alice's, and the warmth I felt from her grandparents was repeated by each of Alice's relatives the whole weekend. I was deeply drawn to this family, realizing quickly that they shared a lot of love.

Within a few months after we started dating, Alice and I began discussing the possibility of marriage. While I still felt uneasy about making a commitment, I also knew that Alice had become very important to me. I loved the times we spent together and I always looked forward to seeing her. I was able to talk more openly with her than I did with any other person in my life. Even our fights, which many times were intense, seemed to end with us moving closer together. Unlike my parents' marriage, I began to realize that fighting could have a positive effect on a relationship. It grew harder to imagine life without Alice, and I saw that my own marriage could indeed be different from my parents' experience. After seven months of dating Alice and I became engaged. We were married the following summer on August 20, 1966.

I shared everything I knew about myself with Alice except one thing—my past adolescent, sexual experiences with boys. I didn't tell her because I feared that she would reject me and I didn't want to risk that. Now I felt even worse than I had before about my earlier sexual experiences because they forced me to lie to Alice. In some ways I knew I was cheating myself from the very closeness that I desired to have with her. I always felt that Alice's ease and freedom in expressing her thoughts was because she had nothing to hide, no secret that she felt she had to keep from me. During the next five years, I remember wishing many times that I had not withheld any part of me.

After my graduation from law school, we entered the Peace Corps. The training was demanding on us both physically and mentally. For me, learning a foreign language had always been difficult, while for Alice the deprivation of living without modern conveniences and the rugged life-style were a constant challenge. During our training in Puerto Rico, Alice spent hours tutoring me in Spanish in addition to eight hours of instruction we received daily. In a similar way, I helped Alice in doing many of the physical tasks that were a part of living in very poor countries. Alice's and my relationship deepened as we talked, cried, and joked about the problems that confronted us in being in a strange culture, far away from the support of family and friends.

When we moved back to Philadelphia, after returning from the Peace Corps, I began to work at Community Legal Services in a Puerto Rican area of North Philadelphia. It was just the kind of job I wanted. The work was challenging and required all of my energy. I was able to use my legal skills and the Spanish I had learned in Panama, and I could continue to be involved in working with the problems of the poor.

Before college, living in Lower Merion, an affluent, upper-middle-class suburban community, I had been insulated from poor people. During my college years, I became aware of the hardship and suffering of the poor. Each day I took public transportation or drove through the worst slums in the city to reach Temple University's North Philadelphia campus. The daily sight of poverty made a lasting impression, and was still with me when I made my decision to join the staff of a legal services agency.

For the next year, Alice and I went through a difficult time adjusting to our life in Philadelphia, what the Peace Corps calls "culture shock," a frequent occurrence for returning volunteers. Our interests and concerns had changed from our experience of living in a small Latin American town, and we didn't seem to be able to relate as easily to the friends we had had before entering the Peace Corps. We had become politicized and were now concerned with the social problems of poverty and discrimination. It took some time for us to find other people who held similar views to ours. We felt isolated, and we experienced a longing for the intimate friends we had made in the Peace Corps.

Slowly, we began meeting people whose political views were similar to ours. Alice and I became heavily involved in the People's Fund, a local organization devoted to raising money for the support of community-based groups working for social change.

While I was committed to seeing greater changes in the living conditions of the poor in this country, it seemed that the majority of the people wanted a rest from the turmoil of the sixties. People were frightened by the rising crime rate, the assassinations, and the growing unrest on the part of black people and women. At the same time that my work continued to focus upon social problems, and Alice and I attended peace marches and other demonstrations, the press talked about a backlash developing from Nixon's "silent majority."

Even between Alice and me, things were calmer in our relationship than they had ever been in our five years of marriage. We had moved into a modern, appliance-equipped apartment complex where many other young professionals lived. For the first time we purchased new furniture and took our wedding gifts out of storage. We were really settling down. Many of our nights were spent taking bridge lessons, relaxing by our apartment pool, or trying to make friends with people with whom we had very little in common.

The one area where I felt constantly challenged was at work. From the day I began the job when I interviewed my very first client, and had to turn to the office secretary for advice on how to proceed, I realized that this job would require all my energy. With the situation relatively dormant at home, I was excited to go to work. There I was dealing with real people's problems, like tenants being left without heat or welfare personnel who were insensitive to the needs of poor families. Some nights I was required to attend meetings and be an advocate for the community in dealing with problems of housing or police abuse. Within six months of taking the job, I was promoted to managing an office of three attorneys, which meant additional responsibilities.

It was a welcomed escape from the dinner parties, bridge games, or worried discussions with Alice about why we didn't have more intimate friends. Whatever problems existed between us were vague and unformed, and there was no doubt that we continued to love each other. But, for the time being, my major area of growth and movement was my work.

Two

The Beginnings

Many Panamanians think of Chiriquí province as the "pioneer province" of Panama. Farthest from Panama City, the capitol, until the Inter-American Highway was completed in the early sixties, Chiriquí was not easily accessible except by air. It is the richest province in Panama. Unlike other areas where peasants barely eke out one harvest a year, the rich, lush land of Chiriquí has two growing seasons and is well suited for a variety of crops—rice, tobacco, beans, and corn. Some of United Fruit's vast banana holdings are located in the province. Like our own early settlers in the West, the people in Chiriquí are accustomed to being left alone, and generally they like it that way. But when the Peace Corps sent volunteers to San Andrés, the largest town in a cluster of mountain villages, the people were friendly, if also a bit wary until they got to know us.

As we were getting acquainted with the people and the rural surroundings, we also became close friends with another American couple, John and Mary, volunteers who were stationed in the same remote province as we were, in a town about six hours away from ours. We had liked them from the time we met them during the three-month Peace Corps training in Puerto Rico in 1967. Once in Panama, they became the most important people in the world to us. Living in a strange, new culture, far away from home, struggling to develop meaningful projects for ourselves in a highly unstructured setting, we began to rely upon each other and eagerly anticipated the times we could get together. After weeks of speaking nothing but Spanish except to each other, it was a pleasure to hang out with people our own age away from the pressures of the work we were doing, to be able to share what we were going through with other people who were encountering similar experiences.

44

Every three or four weeks, the four of us arranged two or three days off in the centrally located city of David—a small town, by our standards—but it looked good to all of us after weeks in our more primitive sites. We were off duty, so to speak. For weeks before, we would look forward to the prospect of relaxing at a restaurant or bar or getting rooms at the Hotel Iris facing the plaza (where for seven dollars a night we could take showers, even if there was no hot water). The limitations of David didn't matter to us. We spent hours talking together about home, our families, what we were learning, our frustrations and problems, our hopes.

Occasionally, Alice and I traveled to the small village where John and Mary lived in an unpainted wooden one-room house. They also visited us in our town, San Andrés. Sometimes Alice and Mary went off together to a women's conference in Panama City, and John and I attended a co-op conference or other regional meetings. When we couldn't arrange to see each other for an extended period, we wrote letters.

In many ways, much of Alice's and my exposure to new ideas came from our friendship with John and Mary. They were a couple of years younger than we were and had graduated from college at a later time. They were political people, sincere in their social activism, and like other college students of the late sixties, in many ways looser and less career-oriented than we were, less willing to settle down as fast as most of the people we had gone to school with had been. They were more a part of the generation that had come of age in the late sixties— restless, searching, rebelling from the passivity of the late fifties and early sixties, and deeply affected by the questioning and change going on in the society. They were both from the Southwest, from large all-American families, and they had grown up in very different settings from ours. The difference in their backgrounds only enhanced their appeal. Nobody would have thought in these terms then, but there's little doubt that as couples and as individuals, we had become infatuated with each other.

When John and I got together, we talked about our Peace Corps projects and the problems we were having with them. We'd brainstorm ideas and solutions. After a while, though, our talks would turn to personal matters. It was one thing to share things with Alice, but I also needed a man I could talk to. One evening John and I were having a drink in a small bar in Panama City, killing an hour before Alice and Mary joined us to see an American movie, always a treat when we visited Panama City. Over a beer, we began to discuss our relationships with our wives, and the talk turned to sexual experiences we were having. It had been a long time since I felt comfortable talking freely to another man about such matters. Before I got married, I had often talked to men friends about girls I was dating, but after I got married, I somehow held back. I bought the unspoken but widespread mystique of the time, which still goes on today, about keeping matters of the conjugal bed confined to the bedroom.

It was an incredible relief when John and I broached the subject of sex. All the things we had wondered about, or questioned, or felt good about, or worried if anyone else in the world ever experienced, turned out to be not so unusual or terrible. It's almost laughable now to think back to the subjects we hesitated to talk about, but we had a lot of reluctance then. For example, we found that the way both of us knew that our wives were sexually excited was when their vaginas felt moist. We discovered we reached orgasm in different ways, and that sometimes we or our wives didn't have an orgasm during sex. How would we have known these things? Like other men our age, we had grown up with such pressure on performance that we had placed an undue emphasis on climax, a kind of tyranny of the orgasm. Just talking about it lessened the pressure we had imposed on ourselves.

Neither of us ever entertained the thought that our relationship had anything to do with homosexuality, with any kind of attraction to each other, but it was interesting that many times as our discussions grew more open and intense, both of us would find ourselves sexually aroused; suddenly, we would become aware that we had erections and we let each other know that obviously our talks were stimulating. Naturally, though, we attributed the fact that we were aroused to the subject matter or to the fact that we were turned on to our wives.

About eight months after we returned from Panama, John and Mary returned to the States. They moved to New York City, about a two-hour drive from us and we visited them a number of times during 1970. Whether shopping in the Village, sight-seeing, attending peace marches, or eating rice and beans in a Cuban restaurant, we continued to be very close and to enjoy spending time together. It's often difficult when you're part of a couple to find another couple that both of you like, where the four of you get along and can be intimate in different combinations. We had that kind of relationship with John and Mary.

About a year after our friends returned from the Peace Corps, we arranged to spend Memorial Day weekend with them in my grandmother's apartment in Atlantic City. They were planning to move to Maine from New York the following week, and we all knew that we would be seeing each other less. This particular Memorial Day weekend, which traditionally marks the opening of the summer shore season, was rainy and dreary, so we ended up spending most of our time indoors.

John and Mary had brought some marijuana with them, which Alice and I had only smoked a few times before. The grass seemed to allow us to relax and talk openly for once about our closeness and caring for each other, but it also opened up a more permissive atmosphere to acknowledge the sexual attraction that had existed among us for a long time, but had never been discussed openly. Immediately, the atmosphere in the room became heightened. People who we knew just didn't talk openly about sex back then, yet here we were, having the most explicit sexual discussion that any one of us had ever experienced.

All of us were lounging on the living room floor with our eyes closed. It took me a few minutes to realize that Mary's hand was touching my arm and shoulders. I was aroused immediately. I hadn't been with another woman or felt anyone else touch me since I was married. The high-rise apartment overlooking the boardwalk and ocean was warm and enclosed. With the rain beating down steadily outside, we felt as if we were in a tiny, isolated corner of the world, detached from any outside reality.

Before we knew it, all of us had begun touching and massaging each other, and someone raised the possibility of our actually having sex.

Alice was the most reluctant of the four of us. It wasn't that she wasn't feeling the same stirrings of sexual tension that all of us were, but she said she was worried about the effect it would have on our relationship. It's important to realize that at the time, "open marriage" wasn't even a concept spoken about freely in the culture. We had all been completely faithful to our partners for a number of years. To talk about having sex with each other with all of us present was embarking upon the unknown and forbidden. None of us had even heard about such a thing as group sex. Nevertheless, the three of us—regardless of prohibitions—were more willing to experiment and jump in—and Alice eventually agreed.

As time passed, we decided to go into the bedroom. Mary and I began hugging and kissing each other while Alice was doing the same with John. But there was something uncomfortable about all of us being together. Alice and John left the room, leaving Mary and me alone. Mary and I spent the night together and had sexual intercourse a number of times.

I had felt warmly toward Mary for years, and she had grown to be one of my closest friends. But to be physical with her was surprisingly passionate and intense. Despite my previous training and ideas about the way things should be, the truth was that I loved being with her. She was very responsive and obviously enjoyed having sex with me. We were very free. She and I both reached orgasm each time we had sex. I knew that John and she had been having sexual problems since the Peace Corps, that John would lose his erection in the middle of intercourse. It made me feel good to perform well and please her. She was obviously very much in need of reaching orgasm.

As soon as we awakened the next morning, I needed to make contact with Alice to talk about what had happened, perhaps to reassure myself, to know that everything was all right. The two of us also ended up making love. We needed to get back in touch. Alice told me that John and she had spent the night together but didn't have intercourse. John had problems getting an erection and keeping it. Alice and he talked about it and decided just to cuddle and touch.

I felt fine about Alice and John having been together. I didn't feel jealous. Alice felt a bit uneasy about her experience with John but told me she liked sharing the intimacy of a private time with him. She was not particularly upset about my having had sex with Mary, and rather, seemed almost proud that I had been able to give Mary pleasure. During breakfast, we alluded to the experience but none of us seemed very comfortable talking directly about it. We laughed about it, but it was the kind of uncomfortable laughter that you often hear when no one knows exactly what to say.

Later in the day, the four of us were again lounging in the living room. It was still raining. John was subtly trying to seduce Mary, but she was ignoring his efforts. Mary seemed more interested in the talk she was having with Alice; they were both intense women and they loved the kind of heady, involved talk that was very much a part of their friendship. John and I exchanged glances from time to time, and it occurred to me that he was trying to indicate that he was having sexual thoughts about me. No, I thought, I'm imagining it. Not John. But as the minutes passed, I became aware that I was having the same feelings. I was becoming aroused, thinking about being physical with my friend John, touching him, being close, hugging, expressing the depth of the feelings I had toward him. But I was scared. And I wanted to. And I was reluctant. It was something very old that I was feeling—a pull toward John, but also into myself—back through the years to a part of myself I thought I had forgotten.

I remember the rain. It was beating down incessantly upon the apartment patio outside as if it would never stop. I watched it form puddles and for a while didn't say a word. Then I took a chance and said, "John, do you want to go into the other room with me?"

"Sure," he said.

Alice recalls that she and Mary noticed us go into the other room and had a good idea of what was going to happen. But we were all caught up in a kind of "let it be" atmosphere; neither woman moved to stop us, but when Alice turned to Mary with a questioning look, she remembers Mary saying, "It's all right."

As soon as John and I were in the other room and the door was closed, we began hugging and holding each other. It was incredibly passionate and fiery. We quickly stripped off all our clothes. Like being fourteen again, it brought back all the memories of having sex as a teenager.

Whatever prohibitions we had seemed to disappear, for that moment at least, and for me, pent-up feelings that I had had toward John without even realizing it were suddenly released.

We tried everything. There was lots of touching, hugging, and kissing. It was very hot. We sucked each other's penises and even tried unsuccessfully to have anal intercourse. We were obviously doing something wrong because even though we used lubricant, the pain was unbearable. Totally worn out, each reached orgasm through mutual masturbation.

Later in the day, John and I got together again. This time we were much less spontaneous. John lost his erection in the middle of the experience, and we began to talk about whether we were doing something wrong. Both of us felt somewhat guilty, a little embarrassed, and uncertain about what it all meant.

John was convinced that the episode had been an aberration on his part and that he would not want to do it again. I, on the other hand, felt resentful when John negated the time we had together. The sexual experience with him was a profound one for me, the first time I had had sex with a man in more than ten years. This time, however, it was an entirely different experience for me because it was with a person I had grown to love. No matter what the taboos, I couldn't ignore the tremendous release that occurred within me, the sense of wholeness and satisfaction that was very deep.

Sometime toward the end of the weekend, the four of us talked about our experiences together, but again, we became very uncomfortable with the discussion. We knew there were many things left unsaid but we weren't sure what they were.. The discussion was awkward and not totally truthful. I learned that while John and I were together, Alice and Mary had spent time talking and had also touched one another tentatively. Neither one had ever experienced touching another woman's body before.

All of us felt uncertain about what it all meant and somewhat leery about the repercussions of what we had done. In some ways we wanted to forget what had happened, and in other ways the experience had been deeply stirring. It was striking that our excursion into homosexuality took place in a setting that had a definite heterosexual component. Perhaps none of us would have felt the freedom we did to act on our same-sex impulses if we hadn't been in a couple environment. We did not yet know that there was such a thing as bisexuality.

Some months passed after our experience with John and Mary, during which we spent a quiet summer at the shore with Alice's family. But I couldn't put my experience with John out of my mind. A part of me had been reawakened, a terribly personal and intimate part of myself that I thought I had been done with long ago.

John and Mary had moved to Maine, which seemed a very long way from Philadelphia. I fantasized having sex with John, just being close again, even being able to talk to him, and I felt depressed that he was so far away. I agonized about my desire to have John next to me again and felt guilty about my thoughts. "You're married, Barry Kohn," I told myself. "You can't have sex with a man. It's not done. It's sick. It's unacceptable." Sometimes, I missed him and my thoughts had nothing to do with sex. I missed the ease and comfort of our friendship and surprised myself at the intensity of my longing.

Our communication with John and Mary was very stiff and disjointed during this time. We were used to spending time together, not just talking to each other on the telephone, and while Alice and I wrote letters, they were rarely answered. For me, this period was one of the loneliest times in my life. I couldn't understand why John and Mary didn't want to talk with us as much as Alice and I wanted to make contact with them. Even if they felt uncomfortable about the time we had spent together, I didn't see why we couldn't talk it over—after all, they had been our closest friends. For a while after we left the Peace Corps and moved back to Philadelphia, we didn't have very many other good friends and we were having difficulty acclimating ourselves to life back home.

Many nights after returning home from work I felt depressed and it seemed to me that I was in a kind of mourning over the loss of the relationship that had become so important to me. A year and a half later John and Mary finally told us that they had distanced themselves from us because of preoccupation with their own marital problems, which eventually ended in their separation and divorce.

By 1971, however, Alice and I had settled in fairly comfortably to our life in Philadelphia. She had just completed the first year of her graduate program in social work at Bryn Mawr, and I had recently changed positions at Community Legal Services. For two years I had been the managing attorney at a neighborhood law center in North Philadelphia, handling various types of individual poverty law cases—landlord-tenant problems, welfare disputes, consumer fraud, and domestic relations. As the number of clients continued to grow steadily, I was becoming increasingly frustrated dealing over and over with the same problems on a case-to-case level.

When the opportunity was presented to head a law reform unit dealing with landlord and tenant problems, I jumped at the chance. My interest in working with social problems on a broader level was becoming stronger. It seemed to me that by concentrating my efforts on a particular problem area, in this case landlord-tenant relations and, more specifically, the lack of adequate low-cost housing in the city, I could have a more direct impact.

I put a tremendous amount of energy into mastering the new position. By pouring myself into work, I didn't have to look at all the feelings that were emerging, especially that I was thinking a lot about having another sexual experience with John. I began to realize that the strong sexual desires I had had for boys as a teenager were returning, and I felt uneasy and confused.

How could I talk to Alice about these thoughts? Now that she knew I had had a sexual experience with John, it seemed even less safe to talk to her about my desires than before. She was convinced that my having sex with John had been a fluke, brought on by the intensity of our friendship and the help of drugs.

Even in my own mind, there seemed to be an ongoing tug-of-war between the part of me that longed for John and the part that was totally repulsed by the idea of homosexuality. Thinking about homosexuality in the abstract horrified me and I wanted to see myself as 100 percent heterosexual. Yet fantasies about men began creeping into my thoughts.

What about my marriage? I still loved Alice, we had wonderfully close times together and continued to have satisfying sex. Still I felt more distant from her than I had at any time since we were married. She was very involved in graduate school—working hard in her classes, learning to work with people in a field placement three days a week, and in whatever time was left, researching and writing her master's paper. It seemed that she was developing her own life apart from me, and when I had free time, she was not always available.

I spent some of my evenings and weekends going to movies or other events with Elaine, one of our few friends left from college days. Elaine lived in an apartment two blocks away from us. She was an attractive, vital kind of person in her late twenties whom I had always enjoyed spending time with. It was a difficult time for her too since she had a small baby and was having her own marital problems. Although we were also very close, I was unwilling to tell her about the internal struggle I was waging. I worried that she would react negatively and also feared that she would probably tell Alice, since they were also very close friends.

Some nights when I was walking to Elaine's apartment I would purposely walk down Spruce Street, "the homosexual street" in Philadelphia. I would see people who, according to the usual stereotypes at the time, I assumed were homosexuals. They were the thin, soft, effeminate men with tight blue jeans, carefully groomed and particularly self-conscious about their appearance. Their speech was affected, as if they were trying to imitate women. But I had never heard women quite like them: a conversation would begin with an effusive "Hello, darling," continue with a few "Isn't she lovely," or "She's just too much!" and end cheerfully with a "Good-bye, sweetie!" I couldn't understand why a man would want to talk like that.

What I didn't know then was that I was seeing only a small, particularly visible group of homosexual men. There were plenty of other homosexuals on Spruce Street, but they walked, talked, and dressed just like any other person on any street in the city. They were businessmen, truck drivers, waiters, professionals, students.

As I was walking I'd think to myself, "How can I be married to a woman and continue to think about having sex with John?" "Do my sexual desires mean that I shouldn't be a lawyer?" "Am I some sort of pervert?" I was fascinated and also put off by these men, wondering who they were, what they did, and where they lived. At the time I thought that all homosexuals were either hairdressers, decorators, or waiters. Certainly, there couldn't possibly be any lawyers who were homosexual. It seems strange now that I was so naïve about homosexuality, but in 1971 the gay rights movement was not particularly visible nor had I even heard the word "gay." In fact, I had never heard anyone speak even mildly positively about homosexuality.

Increasingly that fall, I became more withdrawn from Alice when I was with her. Many times I'd be deep in thought about missing John. Alice seemed to be able to put the experience with John and Mary behind her, although from time to time she expressed sadness about missing them.

From the time we moved back to Philadelphia from Panama, we had formed a weekly ritual of eating dinner out on Friday nights, just the two of us. It was a chance to unbend from our work week and it always signalled the beginning of the weekend for us. Often, we drove to the outdoor Italian Market in South Philadelphia, bought fresh fruits and vegetables, and then stopped at a favorite restaurant of ours on Ninth Street for mussels in marinara sause and manicotti. As we sat across the table from each other in the noisy restaurant with its red flocked wallpaper and menu posted on the far wall, I would often become quiet. Frequently, Alice asked, "What are you thinking about?" I evaded her questions and said that I was preoccupied with work or thinking about a case. If we talked together about missing John and Mary, I lied and said that I was thinking about both of them, careful not to reveal that my major thoughts were centered on John.

On a number of brisk Philadelphia November nights, I found myself roaming the streets of Philadelphia not knowing exactly what I was looking for. At the same time I began to fantasize about having sex with men other than John. One evening I walked into an adult book store near Twelfth and Arch streets, its bright fluorescent lights revealing racks of magazines and books, a front counter filled with dildos and other sex objects, and booths for quarter movies lining one of the walls. I began by looked at the heterosexual pornographic books and magazines in the front of the store and then slowly made my way toward the all-male section, trying to be inconspicuous. I was embarrassed that the clerk, perched on a high stool behind the front counter, might see me looking at pictures of men and assume that I was homosexual. I didn't want anyone to know—not even a store clerk—that I was even having such thoughts, let alone looking at that kind of material. Yet when I felt the drive inside me, it was so intense that no fear, not even the possibility of being observed, could stop me. It seemed that the desire to have contact with men came over me in waves and whatever negative repercussions I feared became secondary until my desires were in some way satisfied.

My recurring fantasy was to see men having anal intercourse, which at the time I saw as purely homosexual activity. From several of my teenage experiences, as well as the one with John, I had become both titillated by the idea and, at the same time, questioned whether such an act was physically possible. After looking around for a while, I found pictures and films of men having anal intercourse. The pictures only seemed to intensify my desire to experience it myself.

This was a very somber period in my life. I felt out of control and more closed off from the rest of the world than I had ever felt at any time. The thoughts and fantasies that I was having seemed like a time bomb that would eventually would go off and destroy my marriage and me in the process. What's more I didn't see any way that it was going to get any better.

Instead of openly confronting the issue, I absorbed myself further in my work and tried not to think about what the future would bring. I wanted so much to believe that I could keep the fantasies under control. But I wasn't sure. No sooner had I controlled my feelings for one day, or not even thought about them, than I would find myself back walking the streets or stopping in an adult bookstore several days later.

In December 1971 Alice and my mother went on a spur-of-the-moment vacation to Jamaica. Alice was on her Christmas break from classes but I couldn't get away from my job. We hadn't been separated for any period of time since our stint in the Peace Corps, but now she would be gone for a week. Once she left, I was not able to keep my fantasies under control. I thought continually about going to a homosexual bar and seeing whether I could meet a man to have sex with. Yet I had so many fears. Were the bars as dark and seedy as the one I remembered from the movie *Advise and Consent*? Would I be physically abused? It took me several days to overcome my apprehension, but finally I decided I had to see for myself.

I had often walked past the Victorian, four-story, stone building, located on Spruce Street in the heart of the homosexual district, which I was certain was a gay bar. About 8:30 on an unusually clear and mild Wednesday evening in December, I left my house and headed for Spruce Street. As I entered the Mystique, an appropriate name for the bar given the circumstances, I was convinced that I was committing the lowest, most degrading act of my life. I thought to myself, what if someone sees me go in—it will be the end of my legal career—I was sure I would be disbarred. Why, look at what happened to an important aide in the White House when he was arrested in a men's bathroom—total disgrace and the loss of a high administrative job under Lyndon Johnson.

Yet, when I walked into the room, the people didn't look at all the way I had imagined. There were about ten men scattered around the bar and all were wearing ties and jackets. They were older than I expected, middle-aged. Self-consciously, I sat down on a stool and gradually began to study the men more closely. The bar was dimly lit and looked like any of a hundred other bars I had been to in my life. None of the men "looked like" homosexuals; I didn't see any who were particularly effeminate.

After a few minutes I noticed that one man, a few stools away, was looking at me. I looked away and then a few minutes later, glanced back at him. He was still staring at me. Then he walked over and sat down on the stool next to mine. I remember thinking, "He can't be a homosexual." He didn't look like one; or at least like the image I had of homosexuals at the time. He was tall, a little heavier than average, and he was dressed in a dark suit and tie.

He said hello, introduced himself, and told me that he was a doctor, a specialist in rehabilitative medicine, visiting from California. I was struck by his specialty because Alice's field placement at school that semester was in the Rehabilitative Medicine Department at Jefferson Hospital. I thought, "Well, he's not a homosexual, he doesn't dress like one or talk with a lisp and, besides, he's a doctor." When he asked me questions I was very evasive in talking about myself because I didn't want him to find out why I was in the bar. I reasoned to myself that being from out of town he had probably wandered into that bar unknowingly. But after a few minutes of conversation, he invited me to go with him to his sister's house in Germantown, in the northwest part of the city where he was staying.

He was a homosexual after all. My mind was going a hundred miles an hour. "He's bigger than I am," I thought. "Maybe he'll beat me up. What if Alice finds out?" I was terrified, but it was exactly what I had come to the bar to find. I agreed to go with him provided he would drive me back into the city later in the evening.

Driving out of center city, on the Schuylkill Expressway, I again had second thoughts about being with him and having accepted his offer. Here I was, a happily married man, who had a close relationship with his wife, enjoyed having sex with her, who loved her and wanted to stay married, and I was on my way to have sex with a man that I had met ten minutes ago at a gay bar.

We arrived at the house and were stripped naked five minutes later. I was tense and didn't enjoy it. I wanted to leave as soon as I could. We began to have oral sex, and I reached orgasm quickly. It reminded me of times years earlier when I first started having sex with girls who were supposedly "loose." As soon as I reached orgasm, I always wanted to get as far away from them as I could. I felt guilty for cheating on Alice and was worried about adding one more lie to the already formidable pile between us. Why was I there? The whole idea of sex with another man seemed deviant and self-destructive. It's hard to describe the feeling I was left with; it was more a non-feeling, a numbness, an emptiness, regret for having been so impulsive.

He said he wanted to make several phone calls to friends, so I fidgeted while waiting for him to take me home. As I listened to him joke with his friends on the phone, his speech now seemed more effeminate than my first impression. I was developing a growing disgust for him. On the drive home, I listened to him talk about the various other doctors he knew at Jefferson and Pennsylvania hospitals. He even knew a homosexual attorney. I was amazed.

While I now knew that there were other gay professionals, I was reinforced with the impression that they were all neurotic and sick. In fact, this doctor had confirmed those thoughts. While he said that he accepted his life-style, he also told me that he regretted his "lot" and would have chosen to be straight if that were possible. "If a pill were available to make me a heterosexual, I would take it," he said.

When Alice returned from vacation, I didn't tell her what had happened, although I mulled over my evening with the doctor many times. Over the next few months, I became more moody and depressed as I thought about my predicament. I tried to absorb myself in the law, but even when I was at work, my mind would wander frequently, and I would start having homosexual thoughts about John or the doctor. When I became preoccupied with these thoughts—obsessed would be a more appropriate word—I would usually masturbate and feel temporarily relieved.

I was twenty-nine, and for ten years I had successfully repressed the need to have sex with a man, except for my two recent experiences with John and now the doctor. I had never talked to another soul about my homosexual feelings, and yet it seemed that, day by day, these feelings were growing like a strange new disease. To make matters worse, at the same time that I was coming to grips with my own sexuality, Alice admitted to me that she had become involved with another man. When she told me, I don't remember being jealous or angry. Rather I felt numb, almost as if her affair had left me with no reaction whatsoever. I certainly didn't want to lose her. But once it was clear that that wasn't going to happen, I remember feeling almost relieved, somehow less guilty about having had sex with the doctor and then withholding the fact from Alice.

As if there wasn't enough happening in our life, Alice began to talk about wanting a baby. We'd made a decision early in our marriage—actually it was made quite consciously—to put off having a child for five or six years, so that we could have the time to get to know each other and build our marital relationship without pressuring ourselves with the added responsibility of a child. We had been married five and a half years now, Alice was going to be finishing her master's degree in the spring, and it seemed that it was a good time for her to take some time off to have a child.

When I look back at that period of our marriage, it seems that it was probably the worst time to deal with such a basic decision. My life seemed to be growing more complicated by the day. I have since learned that it is not unusual for a couple to make major decisions like having a child or buying a home when their relationship is in turmoil. It may seem like a strange time to have decided to have a child when we were facing problems as major as the ones we were dealing with, but it was as if there was another part of us, separate from these problems that was trying hard to bolster the positives we had built together. Having a child came from a desire to renew the bonds we still felt for each other.

About six months after Alice's vacation and my encounter with the doctor, I met a man who openly raised the issue of telling Alice about my sexual attraction for men. It was a warm, bright Easter Sunday, 1972. In the early afternoon, while Alice was studying, I walked the two blocks from my house to Rittenhouse Square to find the annual Easter fashion show already underway. I took a seat in the grandstands next to a young man and as we watched the parade of people, we began to chat with each other. About my height, he was slim and muscular; his shoulder-length, curly hair, pulled back in a ponytail, made him look like a hippie. He was twenty-five and taught at an alternative school in the suburbs.

We went to a nearby restaurant for coffee and I poured out the details of my bisexual activities and my marriage. Why was I suddenly ready to talk about my sexuality with Timmy when I had held back from telling anyone else for so long? I'm not sure. I think I suspected that he might be homosexual. It's interesting how one begins to have a sixth sense about that. At the very least, I sensed that he was understanding and easy to talk to. And it's quite possible that I was willing to be open with Timmy precisely because he was a total stranger. He listened sympathetically and talked to me about his own confusion about his bisexuality. He told me that he had a girl friend but also was attracted to men and had had a number of experiences with men. It was a relief finally to talk with someone who was in a similar situation.

Timmy invited me to visit him at his home and the following week I accepted the invitation. He lived in a commune in Gladwynne, a suburb of Philadelphia, with seven other people. The late sixties and early seventies was the era of communes. Many people had begun to experiment with some variation of a group living situation in which a number of people shared a large home and household responsibilities, often going so far as to pool incomes. The life-style in Timmy's house was very different from what I was used to: folk and rock music, marijuana, health foods, family-style dinners with lots of people, fresh vegetables and homemade breads. I was warmly welcomed by Timmy's friends when I arrived, and they seemed genuinely interested in hearing about my job and about my life generally. After dinner everyone would sit around, get high, talk, and listen to music. Their "live and let live" approach to life was a refreshing change from many of the people Alice and I knew at the time.

I visited Timmy and his friends often. After my visits, I'd tell Alice about Timmy and his friends. She listened but did not appear especially eager to meet these new people. I probably didn't encourage her to come out to the house because I was enjoying having a life apart from her where I could be myself in any way I wanted to be.

It was either the third or fourth time I visited Timmy that he seduced me. I hadn't thought we were going to have sex because it seemed that Timmy's attraction to men was less insistent than mine; in fact, we hadn't talked about bisexuality since our first meeting. One night after dinner he asked me up to his room and turned on a Neil Young record. He rolled a joint, and as we were sitting together talking, Timmy touched my arm. Within a few minutes, we were embracing each other. It was exciting to have sex with Timmy, reminiscent of the time John and I had been together a year before. Afterward I didn't have the need I had had with the doctor to get away. We'd found it easy to talk to each other from the beginning, and had begun to build a friendship, an easy intimacy during the month before, and sex was just one more dimension of our relationship.

I continued seeing Timmy every week or so, and on several visits we had sex. One day as we were taking a walk in the woods near Timmy's house, he asked me whether I had told Alice about him and the fact that we had had sex together. "No," I responded abruptly, "I haven't told her and I don't see any reason to do that." Timmy paused for a few seconds, obviously wanting to say something, but then held himself back. He never told me directly to tell Alice, but he did say that at some point he thought I would have to let her know.

The thought that I would ever have to confront Alice openly about this issue irritated and upset me. The truth was that I had been having thoughts about talking to her, but the idea was troubling to me. Why couldn't I just let things continue the way they were? Sure I was living two lives, but I seemed to be handling it okay so far.

My mind raced ahead to visions of what it would be like if I did tell Alice the extent to which homosexuality was dominating my thoughts and my life. I was terrified, certain that my telling would lead to the end of our marriage. I just saw no way that Alice would tolerate Timmy's and my relationship continuing in this way and, frankly, I didn't see how bisexuality and marriage could be compatible.

The conversation with Timmy stayed with me long after that afternoon. It was as if his question about telling Alice forced me to recognize that my attraction for men *was* a central issue in my life. I could no longer lie to myself about having to confront it eventually. But I certainly wasn't ready yet.

Sometimes I made excuses to myself, wondering whether the fact that I hadn't told Alice really did matter. I rationalized that this was only a small part of me that I didn't share, and yet I wasn't sure how to judge the significance of my unwillingness to tell her. The fact that thoughts about my secret appeared and reappeared every time I was with Alice made me suspect that the secret was too important for me to withhold. It was becoming enormous in my own mind. Sometimes I'd be washing the dishes after dinner and think to myself, "You're lying." At work, I'd fantasize about having sex with Timmy, or think about telling Alice, or worse yet, imagine someone else finding out and telling her. Mostly my thoughts focused on my overwhelming confusion and my sense of being trapped.

I missed the free and easy quality of the talks I had always had with Alice. Every time Alice and I had a close and intimate conversation, I felt a strong urge to tell her about my bisexuality. Preoccupied with my internal struggle, I withdrew more and more. Alice often probed, asking me, "What's wrong? Why are you so quiet?" "Nothing," I would answer, "I'm just tired and want to be left alone."

I spent long stretches of time thinking about the relationship that I was developing with Timmy. Suddenly there was another person in my life. I'd had sex with him three times, I really liked him, and I wasn't telling Alice about it. It wasn't as if I wanted to leave Alice for him but I didn't like lying. It certainly didn't make me feel very positive about myself. Sometimes, I thought that perhaps I would find a way to cure myself, that it was just a passing phase, and that if that was the case, I didn't want to tell her and risk everything.

Everytime my thoughts turned to telling Alice, all I could think of were the negative consequences that were sure to result. Separation certainly, followed probably by an angry and complicated divorce. Lots of embarrassment in facing family and friends. And what about the baby that was due in five months? "No," I decided, "I'd have to be crazy to tell her and risk all that." It seemed to me that I had one of the most confusing and complicated situations that anyone ever had to handle. I had no idea of what to do, and I felt very alone. Although I had friends, I didn't feel I could talk to them.

Sometimes there would be moments when I could forget about my bisexuality as we shared our excitement over Alice's pregnancy. I didn't even realize then that I was ambivalent about her having the baby. She used to say to me, "Why aren't you more involved in my pregnancy? Why aren't you as excited as I am?" The truth was that I was thrilled about having a child, but I was also very frightened. Here I was, bringing a child into the world at the same time that I was leading a secret life.

One day I was in one of my funks, withdrawn, preoccupied, distant. This time Alice confronted me directly and asked, "Once and for all, tell me what is going on with you. You are not yourself and you haven't been for a while." Spontaneously, just like that, I told her. I couldn't hold on to the secret anymore. Why I picked that moment finally to tell, I don't know. The words just came out.

Interestingly enough, I can remember few specifics of the conversation and neither can Alice. I have some memories of where we were, and I am not sure if they are accurate. Alice says we were on the way to a concert. She remembers crying several times during the performance and coming home in a fury. I remember her looking over at me during the performance, just glaring at me with hate and contempt in her eyes. I recall having a series of conversations over a two-day period in which I revealed that I was involved in a sexual relationship with Timmy and also let her know something that I had never shared with her, that I had had sexual relationships with boys as a teenager. "I don't know why I have this need, Alice," I told her. "I feel very guilty but I don't know what to do."

It was actually a relief to reveal all this to her, and it took far less time than I had anticipated. Before I knew it, the secret I had carried around since the time we began to date was out. In some ways, an enormous weight was lifted. But I was also filled with apprehension, knowing immediately the ramifications of sharing this information would be far-reaching. The relationship that had been so secure and constant was moving very quickly into uncharted territory.

Alice responded with anger, confusion, fear, and lots of tears. Sometimes she seemed almost out of control. She couldn't handle this problem in the insightful, nonjudgmental way she had dealt with so many other situations. She had very little knowledge about bisexuality or homosexuality and had the same stereotypes as most people. In the next few days she called me "faggot," "fairy," and every other hate word she could think of to express her absolute disgust.

Both of us were in a tailspin from the assaults on our marriage. The values we had held when we married no longer seemed operable, but we had no idea what to replace them with. The trust in each other that we had devoted so much time to building now seemed shattered irrevocably. I began to wonder whether I had made a serious mistake. The knowledge was only going to bring us pain and grief. Couldn't I have kept this one secret from her? Why wasn't I big enough to handle it by myself? I felt selfish for burdening her with the problem, and I now had to deal with her anger. Many times I was sorry that I had told her. I also knew there was no way to take these words back.

I didn't know what was going to happen to my life. It was as if my anchor to reality had been lifted, and I was just floating out there somewhere. Anything that would happen to me could only be bad. Alice was continually crying hysterically, yelling, or completely withdrawn. It seemed that I had caused her great unhappiness just for my own sake, for my own neurotic needs. The situation seemed to be my fault yet I wasn't sure that I could do anything about it. How could I stay married now? I loved Alice. It was incredibly painful for me to see her so unhappy.

Three

Dealing with the Crisis

I was furious. The thing I remember most clearly about the night Barry told me about his bisexuality is my anger.

It was a Thursday evening in early May 1972. We had our usual subscription tickets to a concert series at the Philadelphia Academy of Music. We both got home about 5:30, Barry from his job as an attorney at Community Legal Services, I from classes at the Bryn Mawr School of Social Work. The concert was at 7:30, so we had to make dinner and eat quickly.

Barry seemed preoccupied and distant—for a while I had been noticing him this way when he was with me, as if he were in a world of his own—and I didn't like it when he was so passive. I kept pushing him to tell me what was going on. Throughout our relationship, there had always been periods where he would withdraw into himself. I often went to great lengths just to get some definite response from him, cried, provoked a fight, whatever.

Finally, in the kitchen, after dinner, as I was doing the dishes, he told me. "Alice, I had sex with Timmy," he said. I was stunned. I didn't know what to say. I had heard Barry mention Timmy as a man he had recently met, but I had no idea. . . . We dressed and went to the concert.

The Philadelphia Orchestra was playing the Symphony in D Minor by César Franck—I still remember.

I had been calm and reserved at the concert, but once inside our car, I began to scream, and then cry, surprising even myself with the intensity of my fury. How could Barry, the most decent person I knew, deliberately hurt me so. I couldn't understand it.

As we parked the car and crossed Eighteenth Street, I

screamed, "You faggot!" at the top of my lungs. I wanted to beat him up with my fists.

For days my anger was of an intensity I didn't even know was in me. Barry had been having sex with a man and he hadn't told me. With a man!

How could he risk losing me, the relationship we'd built together, the life-style we'd come to value? What kind of strange and unknown need did he have within him? And what would people say? How could I even tell anyone? My head was splitting, and I felt bombarded by a confusion of thoughts.

Then Barry told me that this wasn't even the first time. I had thought I knew everything there was to know about him, and now he was telling me he'd also had homosexual experiences as a teenager. Why did he wait until now to reveal it all? All the repressed anger I'd ever had toward homosexuals came exploding to the surface. I was angry that I had to deal with the question at all. Why me?

Strangely enough, mixed in with the shock and repugnance, there was also a sense of relief. Perhaps it seems odd, given my feelings at the time, that I should have experienced any relief at learning that my husband had actually had sex with a man. But finally, we had a distinct issue that could be pinpointed, something real, rather than vague suggestions of boredom and discontent. It was as if we needed something big—a crisis—in order to mobilize ourselves to deal directly with the subtle differences that had emerged in our marriage over five and a half years.

And maybe it was easier for me to look at the situation as "his problem," regardless of the fact that I had already gotten involved with someone else and was uncertain about the direction in which I was going. I suppose it was comforting to view Barry as the one with more serious problems.

Nevertheless, it's important to realize—as I would many times in the next few years—that I was not an innocent victim of Barry's transgressions. Almost precisely to the month of Barry's first homosexual liaison, I, too, became infatuated with another person.

I didn't get involved with another man easily. The focus of my life in graduate school was no longer my marriage but rather my own intellectual awakening. It was an intellectual attraction at first. He was one of the smartest men I had ever met, and he became a mentor, a kind of father-confessor to me. The sexual part of the relationship was short-lived, but we had deep, soul-searching talks, long after we stopped being physical with each other.

Suddenly there were things in both Barry's and my life, individual preoccupations and separate intimacies, that we didn't feel quite so free to share. The fact that I had strayed may well have given Barry some added permission to explore his own impulses, but I suspect that our experience with John and Mary the previous spring had moved both of us along our individual sexual journeys.

Once the impact of Barry's involvements with men hit me, I tended somewhat unfairly to underestimate and make light of my outside relationship, focusing all my energies on dealing with my reaction to what Barry was doing. It was as if Barry and I were now in battle. Suddenly, our lives had become too complicated, more emotionally charged than either of us had known before, and I was fighting to return to a past time when life had been more quiescent. We had never been enemies; neither of us wanted to see each other that way. It was difficult to view Barry as the villain, painful, disquieting, but there were times I felt I was defending my very life against him.

Thinking of Barry being involved with someone also stirred a very basic fear in me. "Does he love me?" I wondered. "Does he really want me?" It didn't matter that I too had been attracted to others; I couldn't understand how he could actually choose to be with someone else over me. I was angry, but underneath the anger was a tremendous sadness and sense of loss. Things would never be the same. It was as though someone I once knew very well, someone close to me, had died. I was mourning the loss of a way of life, the loss of a person I thought I knew better than anyone else.

More than anything else, I felt abandoned. It was as if I could no longer count on Barry, the person in my life I had always counted on the most. Why wasn't I enough for him? As the crisis crystallized, he became the only one who mattered. It seemed as if my future, my well-being, my happiness, were dependent upon holding on to him, holding on to the way things had been, holding on to the way things were supposed to be.

I couldn't think rationally. I tried. I tried to plot out the situation, examine it point by point. But I was gripped by basic, primitive emotions. It seemed to me that my very survival was at stake, that if something like this could happen, then I could no longer count on being safe.

My own strength and sense of self seemed to be slipping away, and I suddenly felt a desperate need for reassurance. Needing to know Barry still loved me, I asked for proof in hundreds of ways, directly and indirectly. At times, I could be so angry that I was without mercy—scornful, vitriolic, cruel; at other moments I became a little girl—clinging, frightened, begging for comfort.

It was an endless dialogue. "You wish we had never married, right?" "I suppose you'd be happier if I were a man." "I guess you never were attracted to me." On and on went my barrage or my pleadings. "That's not true, Alice," he'd answer. "I do love you, and I'm still attracted to you." "Wanting to be with men really doesn't have anything to do with you," he said. I wanted to believe that more than anything but I could never be sure. Each time we'd go out together, I'd watch him for signs of disinterest, disloyalty, and boredom.

I was plagued by the question "If he is attracted to men, how can he be attracted to women?" I wondered whether Barry was actually homosexual, not bisexual, and had just been hiding that fact from himself and from me. Surfacing was the gnawing, undermining feeling that there must be something wrong with me as a woman for him to have sought out relationships with men. That was the hardest thought to deal with. Whatever doubts I had ever had about my own appeal, the questions about my worth, my desirability, my womanliness, which dipped back into my earliest childhood, emerged with an intensity that was frightening.

Barry tried to comfort me; in many ways, as I look back, he was stoic in his patience. But sometimes after interminable questions, he would become exasperated, get angry himself, give up; other times, he said he just didn't know. He didn't always give me what I was looking for, and I didn't even know what I was looking for. I had always assumed that if you loved someone, you didn't need anyone else, so it was hard for me to understand how he could still love me, and at the same time want to have relationships with others.

Before Barry told me, homosexuality could not have seemed further removed from my life. I didn't know any homosexuals, nor did I particularly want to, and I wasn't aware of any homosexual feelings on my part. Homosexuality seemed foreign and bizarre to me, something that made me vaguely uncomfortable and, in some faint but insistent way, scared. I tried to picture, to graphically imagine, Barry having a sexual experience with a man. Then I stopped myself, and I later would wonder about it again. I must be the only person in the world who ever had to deal with a problem like this one. It was a problem without a solution, a kind of secret ailment.

All those questions, thoughts, fears, became my private little torment, an interior dialogue that never stopped. I told no one. The day after Barry told me, I went to work as usual. As part of my social work training, I was working three days a week in a child psychiatry clinic. The day was filled with client after client, and I remember sitting at my desk listening to their problems and thinking to myself that I no longer knew anything about anything. How could I help them when my life was a shambles? All the things I was used to doing with ease in the course of a day became a struggle. Distracted, preoccupied, I could hardly be with other people.

Almost deeper than my anger and confusion about homosexuality itself was the even stronger concern about people finding out. What if our families or friends knew? My pride was at stake. I didn't want people to talk about me or, worse, pity me. Nobody would ever understand. And as angry as I was at Barry, I felt strangely protective of him. I didn't want anyone to think less of him. I really liked the view most people held of us as a happy, successful couple. We had never had any serious problems in our marriage, and it was hard for me to admit to anyone that we were facing one that appeared to be unsurmountable.

The secrecy, though, was driving me crazy. Barry seemed like a stranger, and I felt isolated and alone. Finally, I couldn't keep it in any longer. I blurted it out to an old friend of mine, a woman I had been close to since high school, and who had also known Barry for years. When I told her the story (including my own extramarital involvement), she couldn't believe it. As far as she was concerned, she said, the two of us were very mixed up. "I can't understand what's happened to the two of you. You better seek some help," she responded.

Her shock and repugnance so mirrored my own feelings that I made a vow that that was it, I was never going to tell anyone else. All the shame and embarrassment left over from my youth—the feelings of not wanting anyone to know about my brother—came barreling to the surface when I thought about Barry's sexuality.

I had a strong urge to flee, to walk out. It seemed that if I could leave him then and there, I'd be freed from further hurt. It was an appealing prospect, but I also had a clear sense even then that it would not be him or my marriage that I would be walking away from. Rather, I knew that if I ended the relationship at this point, I would be avoiding something in myself, that I would be giving up the chance to come to a deeper understanding of what I wanted out of life. I could live the rest of my life as a victim of this drama, or I could use it as an impetus to embark upon my own growing-up process—to see how such a thing could have happened in my life and why.

It may seem strange that I would have had the clarity of thought, that kind of vision into the future at such a tumultuous time. But it was one of those occasions that I think happen in a lot of people's lives, when you have a moment of knowing the simple, inalterable truth of it all. It doesn't matter whether you feel good or bad. You just know it's the way it is.

The differences between us had been just under the surface. When Barry shared his bisexuality with me, they all came out. Otherwise, it might have been years before we dealt with them directly. A number of my friends had separated or divorced by this time, so I knew that pulling out was a clear alternative, but that was a decision I just wasn't ready to make.

I've thought a lot about why I didn't leave him. Was it just dependency, was I too scared to be on my own—I can't be sure. My decision probably had those elements mixed up in it. But the deepest truth went beyond the rational. I simply couldn't imagine life without Barry. He meant too much to me; sometimes I felt I knew him better than I knew myself. Nobody had ever loved me the way he had, unabashedly, directly, almost ingenuously. As young as we were, we had become devoted to each other. Maybe it was the old-fashioned way we had gotten married. Surrounded by our parents, our grand-parents, our families and our friends, we had pledged our vows for a lifetime. We had no thought of five years together or ten, if we were lucky; we knew when we married that we were linking two lives, and we planned to grow up and grow old together.

I think I would have done anything to save our relationship at that point—so would Barry—it was clear to me that we had both gotten involved over our heads. I had already decided to give up my other relationship, the sexual part at least, and go back to a monogamous life, if only we could find peace together again. When I asked Barry whether he was willing to forgo relationships with men, he said that he wanted to, he really did, but he wasn't sure it was possible. I had an ominous sense, but I was also reassured by his desire to try.

We had finally come to a problem that was too big for us to handle alone. I knew we needed professional help. My hope was that through therapy, Barry would be able to remove the problem, and Barry agreed he would do anything he could to resolve the situation. Within six weeks after Barry brought up the issue of bisexuality, both of us were in therapy. We saw the same person, a psychoanalyst recommended by my supervisor at the child psychiatry clinic. I had confided to her that I had marital problems, but never revealed exactly what they were. Barry saw Dr. Green four times a week for psychoanalysis, and I saw him twice a week for intensive psychotherapy. Early on, I remember Dr. Green asking me, "Are you willing to live with a husband who is homosexual?" My answer was an emphatic No!

Yet it's important, as I look back, to recognize that my own decision to enter therapy was not made to deal with Barry's problem alone. In my late twenties, having just completed an intensely psychological graduate program, I had also begun to recognize areas in my own life that were uncertain—discontentments, fears. I was in an affair and I felt guilty. My own behavior didn't match the standards I had had when I married. As naïve as it seems now, I really did get married expecting to live happily ever after and I didn't know whether my expectations were wrong or my marriage was. I knew also that the therapy I was doing with people could only be improved by my going through the same process myself.

I never hit it off with Dr. Green, never found it comfortable or reassuring or pleasant to talk to him. For four years, I used to have a recurring fantasy as I sat across from him in his office; I was a vaudeville performer, the old "one-man act." There I was on stage, all by myself, singing, dancing, juggling, playing a harmonica, putting out everything I had, and despite everything, the audience was still throwing tomatoes.

The beginning of therapy marked a new stage in our marriage. From the time we had gotten together in the group dynamics environment in Maine until now, we had always based our relationship on being as open as we could with each other. But by the terms of our therapy, we could not discuss with each other what we discussed with Dr. Green. His concept of honesty in a relationship was different from what ours had always been. He said we had been too close; that we each needed privacy from each other. It was clear that our assumptions weren't working. I was willing to do whatever he told me, so for the next three years, I followed his directions, mentioning homosexuality to Barry only at periodic intervals and keeping a whole range of private emotions to myself.

Our sexual relationship had changed soon after Barry told me about his encounter with Timmy and his interest in men. Strangely enough, the intensity of our contact heightened. Even though in many ways I looked down on Barry for his behavior, and felt embarrassed and ashamed, I also needed to prove to myself that I could still please him sexually. We hadn't talked directly about sex for a long time—what we liked, what pleased us, fantasies—but now we were talking again, even, at times, sharing what we had done with others.

It was angrier sex than we had ever experienced, but somehow, the expression of some of that anger physically made us both more passionate. As angry as we were at each other, we were also starved for each other's touch. Sometimes the only way we could connect with each other, break through all the hurt and pain, was to be physical. As with many women, my pregnancy had freed me up physically: I was more conscious of my body and I didn't have any attention on birth control. I was less passive, more sexual.

On the surface everything appeared to return to normal. During the summer of 1972 we rented a house at the shore for the summer with a friend. Barry and I were not very close that summer since there were many things we couldn't talk about because of our mutual agreement with Dr. Green. I had finished my thesis on marriage, and my love affair had evolved into a friendship. I became focused on the pregnancy, and enjoyed planning for the new baby. With autumn, Barry began to get more excited about the pregnancy, more involved with me, as we attended Lamaze natural childbirth classes. Preparing for the birth of our child became an important bond between us.

Danny was born in late November, a few days before Thanksgiving, after nineteen and a half hours of intense labor. Barry was with me throughout, and our eight-pound, eleven-and-a-half ounce boy was delivered without anesthesia. All the problems and struggles of the last few months—leveling with each other about our outside involvements, our emotional distance, the decision to enter psychotherapy—were forgotten for the moment in the rush of excitement about being new parents. For me, it was hard to believe that the man who had not left my side even once, who had coached and counseled and cheered me through a hard labor and delivery, had made love to a man just a few months earlier.

Suddenly, I was a mother, and my life changed radically. A friend of mine, Carolyn Washburne, included in her book, *For Better, for Worse: A Feminist Guide to Marriage*, a short piece about motherhood that I wrote describing my feelings at the time:

> You exist in a kind of distinct subculture when all you are doing is taking care of a baby. Generally, you are either alone or relating to other mothers. As I look back, it was not the actual responsibilities of mothering a small baby that were hard, it was my total immersion in this subculture and the way of life it represented.*

Like many mothers I've talked to, I put aside my sexuality when my baby was born. Caring for a small baby was like taking on a new lover. Child development literature and "nursing your baby" books that I read pointed to the deeply sexual nature of the nursing relationship. It's only in retrospect that I can recognize the intimacy and bonding that went on between my new son and me.

For the first five months, Danny received nothing but breast milk, so I was nursing at least six times a day. There's hardly room for anything else when you're nursing that seriously. But giving birth and caring for a baby during the early months of his life was also a profound experience for me. Being a mother was a tremendous validation; it was the beginning step in recognizing myself as a mature woman.

When Danny was about six months old, I began to grow restless. While I had been used to being active and involved in school and work, I now felt alone and isolated in the house. It seemed as if life had ground to a standstill; the highlight of my day was watching

*Jennifer Baker Fleming and Carolyn Kott Washburne, *For Better, for Worse: A Feminist Handbook on Marriage and Other Options* (New York: Charles Scribner's Sons, 1977) p. 188.

the soap opera *Another World* on TV while Danny napped in his room upstairs.

I can remember pushing my baby carriage along the city streets, feeling heavy and burdened. I wasn't telling anybody about Barry's bisexuality and the fact that I had had an affair. Other mothers would sit in the park chatting freely with each other and sharing all kinds of intimacies. I couldn't. My secret kept me feeling isolated and alone, different from everyone else.

At home with a baby, without a job, it seemed as if I had no separate life of my own. Barry, on the contrary, going off every day to work, seemed to have all sorts of freedom. Usually, I tried not to think about it, but sometimes I let myself wonder what Barry was up to. Was he involved with anyone? Did he want to be? Every gay person I saw on the street reminded me of my own situation.

In the fall of 1973 I started looking for a part-time job, but finding one was very difficult. Finally, in January 1974, when Danny was a little more than a year, I took a position as a family therapist in a mental health clinic in Camden, New Jersey, across the river from Philadelphia. It felt good finally to be putting my training into practice, to feel like a useful, competent person again, and to get back in touch with the natural talent I had always had in working with people.

More important, work was vital to me because it enabled me to experience myself once again as a person separate from Barry. I saw that I was competent, that I could earn money on my own, that I could be independent, that I could survive.

As I look back to that time—I'm talking about the two or three years after Barry first told me about his homosexual involvements and our subsequent decision to enter therapy—I realize that my total energies were divided between mothering and my work. My marriage, my problems with Barry, other interests, social life, were all secondary to proving myself as a working woman, and it was my work that enabled me to survive all the emotional ambivalence and confusion I was feeling.

The growing realization that I had to develop my own separateness was triggered by the increasing influence of the women's movement. Today, with so many mothers working, it may be difficult for people to remember (it's even difficult for me, and I went through it) that as late as the early seventies, young mothers who didn't stay at home with their babies and chose instead to return to work were resoundingly criticized and accused of not being good mothers. I recall my psychiatrist, for example, disapproving of my decision to work.

I participated in a consciousness-raising group, and was also involved with Women in Transition, a feminist-oriented program that worked out of the Women's Center in Philadelphia, providing counseling and legal advice for separated and divorced women. I took part in workshops and training programs and also led a group. To be involved with women in this way was new for me. These were women who recognized their own abilities and were concerned with developing them but in a women's context, without the pressure of pleasing or competing with men. It was also the first time I heard women discussing the need for sexual independence from men.

Probably my willingness to explore my attraction for women can be partly attributed to my involvement in the women's movement in the early seventies. My interest in feminism provided an impetus to examine my feelings for women, as I was growing more aware of an emotional and experiential kinship. The "sisterhood" I felt for other women before this time had always been masked by competition. There was more talk about women's sexuality, and a more permissive attitude toward women loving women. Female homosexuality was entering my consciousness. Before this time lesbianism had been absolutely foreign to me. I had pretty much buried from consciousness the brief experience I had had of touching Mary two years before and I had absorbed a lot of the negative cultural stereotypes. Now I was meeting gay women who felt good about their sexuality. Some feminists were openly advocating lesbianism as a valid sexual alternative for women. At the least, I became curious, but I maintained my distance.

In October of 1974, when Danny was almost two, I began working full-time as chief social worker and therapist in a new Inpatient Psychiatric Unit at Crozer-Chester Medical Center, about thirty-five minutes from home. It was exactly the kind of job I wanted, a challenging environment, a chance to counsel patients and their families, and the opportunity to help develop the treatment program.

Barry and I both arranged to work one night a week so we could each spend an afternoon with Danny. The rest of the time he was cared for by Dorothy, the housekeeper who worked for us three days a week, or he was in a day-care program. The combination of full-time work, mothering a two-year-old, and therapy twice a week left little time for myself, but also less time to think about my problems.

Of course, underneath it all was the off-and-on anxiety about what was happening with Barry's homosexuality. Occasionally, I asked him about it and generally he said he didn't want to talk about it. I could only hope that he was "getting better." Our nights at home were somewhat strained. I would spend hours talking to my girl friends on the phone while Barry sat in the living room reading or watching TV.

Barry was doing very well in his job. He moved from Community Legal Services to an appointment as Deputy Attorney General for a state civil rights and civil tensions unit. He was very successful in a number of well-publicized public-interest cases. Given my ongoing concern about "what people think," Barry's success as a lawyer was one of the bright spots in my life. To me it was some compensation for his bisexuality, which I still saw as a deformity.

After I gave birth to Danny, it was several months before I really felt like having sex again. Once we resumed sexual relations, it was not with the passion that had characterized our sex prior to Danny's birth. Absorbed in our own thoughts, we weren't talking directly to each other. More important, I wasn't turned on to myself. It was a period of sexual dormancy in which I was holding in my sexuality. I continued to have sex with Barry as I always had, but I certainly gave no thought to another involvement during this time. I stayed away from bright colors, from tight-fitting clothes, from anything that would draw attention to myself. Along with Barry's secret, I covered up my sexuality, my playfulness, my warmth.

It wasn't until late spring of 1975 that some significant changes began to occur. I took part in a two-day workshop about counseling preorgasmic women (women who have not yet achieved orgasm) given by Lonnie Barbach, author of *For Yourself, The Fulfillment of Female Sexuality.* For the eight women who took part, all therapists and sex educators, the workshop also turned out to be an intense training about female sexuality, about our own sexuality. It was the first time many of us, for all our degrees and training, had talked directly with other women about our feelings, about our own bodies, our patterns of sexual response, our sexual likes and dislikes. Lonnie Barbach's point of view was that every woman has the potential to reach orgasm. Once myths and misinformation are stripped away, women can become more conscious of their own sexuality, specifically from learning how to masturbate.

During the training we went through many of the discussions, exercises, and homework that we were being trained to teach the women we'd eventually be working with in small groups. The first night she encouraged us to go home, make sure we had privacy, and then put aside an hour to create a sensual scene for ourselves, in whatever way we chose. Our assignment included standing in front of a full-length mirror, looking at and touching our bodies, even the parts we thought we hated, and then discovering what turned us on.

In Lonnie's workshop, I discovered the importance of exploring my sexuality and making peace with my own body as a means of gaining a fuller sense of myself as a person. I saw that the capacity to appreciate my body and give myself pleasure made me feel like a whole and complete person, separate from men, separate from needing anyone. That was important to me, given my relationship with Barry at the time and my fears of flying on my own. As I shared my growing-up stories, my development, my sexual experiences, I saw that I had not been alone in being a stranger to my own body. None of us knew our vaginas very well, and very few of us felt positively about our bodies, no matter how much sexual experience we had had.

I had, like many girls, developed the feeling very early that my vagina was something that required special attention. When I was a very little girl, I can remember my mother bathing me and explaining to me that it was especially important to cleanse that part of my body. It became a forbidden area to me; I felt cut off from it. It had a smell that was strange and different from any other part of my body. I know from speaking with other women that I was not alone in having these feelings; the popularity of feminine hygiene sprays attests to women's preoccupation with vaginal odors. We all have been socialized to view our natural smells as offensive.

It's amazing and sad too that I waited until high school to explore my own genitals. Even now, I know grown women who have no idea what their vagina looks like. And many women are not aware of the fact that vaginas come in as many colors and shapes as penises.

It wasn't until my late twenties that I was given Betty Dodson's book *Liberating Masturbation*, in which she presents drawings of a variety of women's vaginas. I had had no idea there was so much variation from woman to woman. I remember one evening, when I was in high school, getting out a mirror, stretching out on my bed, and looking at my genitals. I had never seen my clitoris before. I was fascinated. "So that's what's down there," I thought.

I had no memory of masturbating as a child, but the more I talked with other women, the more I saw that I was in the minority. Those who did masturbate felt guilty and secretive about masturbating, but they did it anyway. I realized that reaching orgasm with a partner was only one way to achieve satisfying sex and that I had neglected the part of sex that had to do with self-pleasure. I began to read books on masturbation and I talked more openly with several women friends about sex.

My friend Mimi gave me a vibrator for my thirtieth birthday. It was a plug-in model from Sears with several attachments. I had been wanting one for a while. I had heard about them, and I wanted to see what they were like. Women who used vibrators talked about them as being reliable. "You can count on your vibrator," they said. The feelings of anticipation about masturbation were similar to those I had when, as a virgin, I knew I was ready for intercourse. Once I got comfortable with the vibrator, it was good to know that I could get individual pleasure without having to count on anyone else.

By the end of 1974, Danny was growing older and more independent, and Barry and I were both feeling more secure and recognized in our professions. The Vietnam War had ended, our social involvement in the People's Fund lessened, and it was a time generally when people wanted to relax a little, to play, to lighten up. We felt the same way. We had more room for fun in our life than before. We began to smoke grass when we were together with our friends, started to go out more, and worked with less intensity.

By this time we had formed a group of friends whom we enjoyed and could talk to, although I insisted on not revealing the issue of Barry's bisexuality to them. We began to enjoy dancing again. Our friends Cheryl and Oliver, who were therapists with special training in sex education and sex therapy, were starting out in their relationship and were swept up with all the passion of a fresh involvement. They were actively engaged in exploring their sexuality and talking about it. Given how much I had been holding in for a long time, I was uncomfortable being around them, but I was also intrigued.

During the spring of 1975 the issue of homosexuality seemed to creep into my life in more and more ways. TV programs on homosexuality and gay rights activities appeared more regularly. In the course of his work, Barry had taken on several cases involving gay rights. It made me uncomfortable. I remember reading an article in *The Philadelphia Inquirer* about his testimony before a City Council committee examining gay rights. I wondered if this would give people cause to wonder about him.

Barry began to take me out to dinner at the Astral Plane, a restaurant in our neighborhood with a funky, bisexual flavor. He had grown accustomed to going there alone, but now he took me and often our friends went along too. Barry had an easy familiarity with the waiters and waitresses there, some of whom were obviously gay. He called them by their first names and they did the same with him.

I watched Barry in that environment and I couldn't figure out why he seemed so happy there. What did he see in these people? They seemed so superficial. We had so many friends who were intelligent, accomplished people, and yet he seemed happier, more relaxed with the people who worked in this restaurant. I tried not to think about it, but I wondered whether he was involved with any of them sexually. If I asked him, he said no, and I wanted to believe him.

Although it seems quite innocent to me today, at that time the restaurant had a somewhat bizarre, slightly macabre feeling to it; decadent and inviting, it evoked scenes from the movie *Cabaret*. Most of the people who worked there were artists or actors, and if their role at this moment in time was to wait on tables, they played it to the hilt. They would strut around, listing the specials of the day as if they were delivering a highly dramatic scene in a play. The food was good, but that was not my reason for going there. It was like watching a show, entering a different world, far away from Crozer-Chester Medical Center, a world suggestive of drugs and sex, a world pushing the limits of conventionality.

The restaurant had been put together on a shoestring budget by a couple of former art students who took two row houses (I can still remember when one of the buildings was a Black Muslim dry cleaner's) and furnished them with kitsch from the thirties, gathered at flea markets. In one room an old parachute was draped on the ceiling. Antique beaded bags decorated one wall. Nothing matched—dishes, silverware, glasses—and yet great care was taken to achieve a certain effect. You might find a sugar bowl or a vase on your table that was outrageously tacky. Or perhaps you could be struck by a delicate and sweet old-fashioned picture hanging on the wall. All of it was very sensual and very permissive, not serious and significant as we and many of our former lawyer and social worker friends had been.

Without realizing it, our life was opening up and things were coming to a head.

On a Thursday evening in May 1975—three years from the time he'd first told me about his homosexuality—Barry announced to me that he had something to talk about. He led me to the living room sofa and we sat down. Then he told me gently but clearly that he was bisexual, that he'd accepted that about himself, that he wasn't going to change, and he didn't want to change. His goal was no longer to cure himself in therapy. He said that he loved me, he wanted to stay married to me, but he intended to pursue outside relationships with men.

Every feeling that I had the first time he told me came back to me. I was angry and very disappointed. I felt steamrollered, as if my life were being ruined and I had nothing to say about it. I saw Barry as "driven." He was giving me up for something I couldn't understand. Something abhorrent and unnatural. No more could I hold on to my hopes that homosexuality would disappear as an issue in our lives.

Surprisingly, I also realized more than ever that the truth was I loved Barry, I had always loved him, and that hadn't changed. I felt very sad. Bittersweet emotions. My marriage was over. I saw no way of integrating our marriage with his pursuit of outside relationships, especially with men. This was not what I had bargained for. No one else I knew lived in a way that even approached the kind of life-style he was suggesting. As much as I knew I loved him and valued our life together, I saw no other choice than to separate. Yet it seemed so unfair to have to give up all the good things we had in our life together.

The most intolerable thought was picturing other people as they found out about Barry's bisexuality. Anytime I was with people and a subject came up that even remotely touched on the areas of homosexuality, sexuality in general, or marriage, I became tense and cautious. I made Barry promise not to tell anyone and was always worried that he would slip and reveal the information to someone. I felt as if I were in hiding. It reminded me of the old David Jannsen TV program *The Fugitive*. If all this seems overly dramatic, then you haven't ever had a secret that you thought was so horrible that your life would fall apart if people knew about it. Every time I heard a disparaging joke about a homosexual or read an article critical of gay rights, I felt reinforced in my belief that no one would ever understand or sympathize.

But I no longer could keep it to myself. The next day I had a drink with my friend Mimi and told her everything. Even though she was a very close and intimate friend, I was embarrassed to tell her. I was afraid of rejection, disapproval, laughter. I had kept the secret to myself for so long that I couldn't be at all realistic regarding other people's reaction to the truth.

Instead of rejecting me, Mimi was very understanding. She wasn't shocked or horrified; she didn't even give me advice. She was sympathetic and warm, urging me not to do anything rash. The news didn't seem as upsetting to her as I had anticipated and she didn't condemn Barry or me.

The next person I told was the man I had been involved with at Bryn Mawr a few years before. I called him the next day from my office at Crozer-Chester and told him everything. It was he who gave me the most helpful advice of anyone, or at least for some reason, he was the one who was able to get through to me. He encouraged me not to feel compelled to come to a decision right away, to give myself time. Released from the self-imposed pressure to make an immediate choice, I talked to him and felt relieved, almost buoyant.

Within two weeks I revealed the truth to my parents and all my closest friends. I needed to know I could count on their support because I felt very alone. Telling people close to me meant that I was finally ready to deal in earnest with our marriage as it was, openly, without all the avoidance and uncertainty. Once they got over their initial shock, everyone was kind and concerned although no one knew what advice to give me.

At times I wanted it all to be over yesterday, and at times I felt certain I could never live without Barry. In the process of looking at whether I could actually live with this situation, I had to reexamine completely all my expectations of marriage, sexuality, fidelity, and jealousy. But as I went up and down, I realized that the real question was no longer about Barry or my marriage. The real question was about my own life and how I wanted to live. "What about me?"

To redefine my marriage in new terms meant that I would have to come to a new understanding of myself as a woman and as a wife. I didn't know whether I could do that or not. I didn't even know whether I wanted to.

Although I knew that I loved Barry, I also knew that my views on homosexuality and monogamy were fixed and rigid in my mind. I was unable to envision when it would be all right with me for my husband to have feelings for other men. I could be tolerant of homosexuality as long as it did not touch my life too directly.

This new proposal of Barry's demanded that I give up all my images of a "normal" married life. The phrase that kept coming back to me was "I wasn't raised to be in the vanguard." Propriety was important. I felt alone, distrustful, and fearful of other people's judgments.

When I see photographs of me then, I look older than I do now. There is a held-back, proper air to my demeanor. Everything is in studied good taste. Nothing outrageous. I don't even think that I knew there was a flamboyant part of me. I don't look very sexy in these pictures, and I know that's not how I felt. The important thing was to be attractive and successful, not sexy.

Now a whole new set of options was before me. Could I be part of an open marriage? I saw myself as a possessive person. I wanted to be number one. How could I live with constant jealousy? And why should I have to compete for my own husband? While these questions plagued me, I also knew that I would never be content to play the role of dutiful wife sitting at home waiting for her husband to return. I had tried that one already—all those Friday nights when Danny was small and I fell asleep on the sofa while Barry went out for a "walk"—and I didn't like it. I wanted more for myself. I did not want a life where I would be constantly rebounding off Barry's actions.

For a while, I didn't want to know anything about homosexuality. As time went on, however, I began to ask a lot of questions, direct and indirect. It just wasn't helpful to keep all these questions inside myself. I wanted to know what being with a man was like for him, what kind of sex he had, how it was different from being with a woman, from being with me. Sometimes it seemed as if we talked of nothing else.

I wondered whether I could ever make peace with homosexuality. I had spent hours talking to Barry, but I didn't seem to feel any better about it. Sometimes I believed what he told me and sometimes I didn't. The sexual feelings he expressed for men seemed detached from anything I had ever felt toward women. I began to be curious about myself. What was sex like between women? Could I be turned on to a woman?

About a month after Barry told me he was bisexual and wasn't going to change, my close friend Cheryl, whom I had known since graduate school and now lived in Charleston, came to visit. I was always comfortable with her; she was easy, understanding, accepting. Some years earlier she had told me about a homosexual experience she had had in college. Perhaps that made me feel freer to tell her about my problems with Barry.

Cheryl was wonderfully accepting and matter-of-fact with me. Barry's involvements with men were not the end of the world to her as they had seemed to me. She knew him well, she understood him, she had a good sense of the strengths in our relationship, and she was the first person able to offer me some perspective. She also loved me dearly and was willing just to be there to comfort me. I had never been a particularly demonstrative person, especially with women friends. But Cheryl was warm and physical. It was her way. Other friends would be there with words, but Cheryl would push through my reserve and hug or touch me in some way. She had always done that.

One night, we talked about my dilemma. I cried for a very long time and she held me. I had never allowed another woman to hold me and comfort me in that way. Another day we went shopping and she encouraged me to be frivolous and buy an expensive gold chain I had been admiring. She asked nothing of me and was willing to take care of me. That was what I needed, someone to focus all her attention on me.

One evening, toward the end of her stay, we stayed up one night and talked for hours. After years of friendship, for the first time, we actually touched each other, faces, hair, arms, and then we held each other. We explored each other's bodies. It was the first time I had ever kissed another woman or touched her breasts. Contrary to everything I would have thought, it was a very warm, safe, and tender time. I began to see the uniqueness of being with a woman. It was like making love to myself. I could begin to understand all the things that Barry had described about being physical with a man. No longer could I accuse Barry of being weird and deviant.

Even after my experience with Cheryl, I alternated between periods of retreat and times of opening up to my feelings for women.

Sometimes it felt as if the experience had never happened, and other times I knew it had had a profound effect.

Gradually, I allowed myself to meet Barry's new friends. This wasn't always easy. Sometimes I had to force myself to go to parties or events where I knew his bisexual or gay friends would be. It was as if I were testing myself, seeing whether there was a way I could be comfortable in this kind of setting. At times, I was very uncomfortable. I felt different from these people because I was married. I wondered whether they were laughing at me. It didn't seem as if I had anything in common with them. And some of them looked so stereotypically gay.

Yet, as I began to warm up and talk with them, I discovered that the parties I went to with Barry's friends were a whole lot more lively than the old lawyer-social work parties I had been used to. I rediscovered music and dancing. I had always loved music, but in the last couple of years of taking care of a baby, working hard, struggling in my marriage, I had lost track of my appreciation of it. The people I was meeting cared about music; it was part of their life. They were creative and sensual and liked to have fun.

Barry now began to level with me more, to tell the truth when I asked for it. We had more fights, more confrontations, more emotion than we had ever had in our relationship. One time I threw a jewelry box at him, and was so enraged that I forgot to close the catch. But, at the same time, we were also dealing more directly and spontaneously, more forthrightly, with each other. We began to see a depth and range in each other's behavior that we hadn't recognized before—the irrational, the petty, as well as the ennobling, compassionate parts.

At the same time that I was beginning to feel better about my own sexuality—or perhaps because of it—Barry and I began to open up to more experimentation and pleasure within our relationship than we had in the past. His experiences with other people had made him freer and more confident sexually. He had things to teach me, fantasies to talk about, and although I usually resisted at first, when I went along with him, I enjoyed myself. It was a strange irony—and countless numbers of people have told us of similar experiences—that the sex in our marriage got better as we were able to be more open with each other.

In the spring of 1976 Barry started a support group for

bisexual and gay married men. He told me about the men who came to the weekly meetings, and hearing about them, they seemed no different from straight men I knew. I began to meet some of them—doctors, lawyers, truck drivers—men I never would have guessed had feelings of attraction for the same sex. I had to broaden my view of bisexuals and homosexuals. Also, as I got to know them as people, their sexuality began to take on less importance.

Even in our worst moments, we had never lost the ability to suspend hostilities for periods of time and enjoy each other. I loved him despite everything. I liked to talk to him, about his values, what he stood for. I wanted very much to work out my relationship with Barry, but I didn't know whether it was possible. More than ever before, I was willing to accept his bisexuality as part of him. But I was still struggling with the issue of marital fidelity. I was no martyr, and I didn't want to suffer. Neither of us knew whether we would end up separating or staying together. Sometimes we'd plan for the future, and other times our every sentence was prefaced with the words "If we stay married..."

One day I went out to lunch with my friend Barbara. She had just separated from her husband. We had children the same age, and we had spent most of the early days of mothering together. Each of us had put a lot of energy into being good and proper wives and mothers. Now, however, she was a single woman again, dating, dressing up, enjoying her sex appeal, exploring what kind of life she wanted for herself.

I was in such a different place. My relationship with Barry went up and down; it was totally unpredictable. This particular day I felt miserable about my relationship with Barry. I felt unappealing and unattractive. I remember saying to Barbara very haltingly, "Do you think that if Barry and I separate, I'll find someone who will want me?" "Yes," she said with a smile.

It was New Year's Eve and as 1976 approached, the country was making plans to celebrate its two-hundredth year. In the pouring rain, final arrangements were being made to move the Liberty Bell from Independence Hall to its new site, a modern steel and glass building across the street. Depressed and discouraged, all I wanted to do that night was to go to sleep. Barry insisted we go to the Astral Plane and our friend Mimi also went along. I still was not completely comfortable there. I suspected that Barry had a relationship with one of the waiters, and I felt uneasy and uncomfortable with him and some of the others. But I went anyway. I wore an olive-drab corduroy jump suit, which exactly represented my mood.

The restaurant was vibrant with festivity. People were decked out, there were drugs, champagne, dancing. I looked over at a larger table near ours and was intrigued by an uninhibited group of people who were obviously celebrating. A few minutes later, I looked up again and one of the men from the group was standing next to our table. I looked at him, not particularly drawn to his appearance. He was short and stocky, kind of young-looking, but he had wonderful, magnetic blue eyes and a smile that was at once mischievous—smart-alecky was the word that came to mind—and all-knowing.

I wasn't even paying much attention to him, but he continued to stand there very calmly, just staring at our table. He took a gold cigarette case from his pocket and offered us a joint. A little later, he asked me to dance. I was shocked by his directness. It had been a long time since I had been asked to dance.

I immediately thought, "I don't know how to dance. What am I doing here? What should I say, I'm married?" Those were my thoughts, no matter what shape my marriage was in. I took a moment and then I said yes. There was nothing to do but say yes. That's what it was for me. We started to dance and it was fine and, all of a sudden, we began to really dance and it was wonderful. We danced for hours. He was the fantasy I had wanted in my darkest hours.

For the first time in my life, it seemed, I really let myself go. I forgot about what anyone thought. I didn't care. I had never danced with any man whose rhythm I so easily melted into, who led me so strongly or held me so tight. We didn't leave each other. About two hours after we had started to dance, we finally spoke.

He said, "What's your name?" I told him.

I said, "What's your name?"

He answered, "Robert."

A couple of minutes later, I said, "What do you do anyway?"

He said, "I'm a rolfer, do you know what that is?"

"Sort of," was what I said. "I've heard about rolfing but I'm not sure I really know what it is."

Two days later, I arranged to meet him at his house. Suddenly, I was introduced to a whole new way of thinking about life. It's not like he was just any man. He was the prophet from the West, the new consciousness incarnate. I was deeply drawn to him with an intensity I hadn't experienced for years. He questioned ideas of mine that I had never thought to question. I had lived in conflict so long that I had forgotten that there was any other way to live. I had given up the sense that I had any choice.

Robert forced me to see that I could either stay in my marriage and choose it as it was, or get out. He questioned my therapy. "Are you still paying that guy thirty-five bucks an hour?" I was so resigned that I had never questioned the notion that I could actually make the decision to leave therapy. What's more, he was smart and perceptive, and he made very significant observations about me, about my body, and the way I carried myself. He recognized the sexual part of me, and he also knew the olive-drab corduroy part.

Later Robert explained to me that a rolfer manipulates the body's structure to make it more vertical, lighter, more flexible and supported. In the process of straightening up, people generally experience a new centeredness and freedom. He encouraged me to get rolfed and I followed his advice two months later. As a result of rolfing, my posture not only improved, but I looked and felt more attractive, more relaxed and sexier. I had a new sense of the link between my physical and emotional well-being.

Robert fell in love with me and gave me a lot of reassurance at a time when I sorely needed it. He wanted me, and he was available. I was grappling with the alternative of having another relationship within my marriage, and I was also playing with the idea, which sometimes seemed much simpler, of leaving Barry and beginning a new relationship.

It was spring of 1976, and I was gearing up for a lot of big decisions. I knew I needed to go away without Barry. I wanted to do something for myself, and the only thing I could think of was sun. Friends of my parents lent me an apartment in Puerto Rico and I asked my friend Mimi to go along. Always when I traveled with Barry, he had made the arrangements. Just carrying my own suitcase was a new experience.

The vacation allowed me to get some distance from all the struggle, and having a separate experience gave me a chance to discover who I was apart from the marriage. Before I went on vacation with Mimi, I had been so confused and upset about the conflict in my relationship with Barry and my new relationship with Robert that I felt paralyzed. I didn't have the strength to make any decisions. The vacation gave me time to reflect, and it also gave me a greater sense of my own capability and independence. I had gone away wanting to escape, but I came back willing to try to resolve the situation.

Away from home I again got in touch with my love for Barry, how he was the one person in my life who consistently encouraged me to expand, to try new things, to open myself up, to experience adventures. Because I came home feeling so good about myself, I was willing to be generous and extend myself with Barry. A week after I returned to Philadelphia, I decided to give him a birthday party and to invite his gay friends, Tom and John, whom I had refused to have anything to do with before. Indirectly, I was saying, "It's your birthday. I acknowledge that bisexuality is a part of your life. If it's part of your life, then it's a part of mine." Before this time, I had spent all my energy resisting the truth. Now I was willing to face it. It was a good party. Tom and John mixed well with our other friends and I found to my surprise that I liked them.

Once I got back from Puerto Rico, however, my relationship with Robert grew even more intense. He wanted me to leave Barry and live with him. Again, I was in turmoil. About two months later, at the height of this confusion, Barry took control of the situation. He made up his mind in one day, booked plane reservations to Jamaica for a five-day vacation, and literally took me away. It was just what I needed. I was moved and excited by his directness, by his taking control at a time when I felt none.

A last step in making my peace with Barry's bisexuality was my willingness finally to read about it. It took me a couple of years to undertake my own process of education; I could have been spared a lot of confusion and misinformation and isolation had I read earlier on.

It's strange that it took me so long to search out books about homosexuality. I've always been a reader. On every other subject that concerned me over the years, I found it helpful to find out what the experts were saying. When I became interested in black people's struggles, I read every book I could find on the subject, from *Malcolm X* to *Manchild in the Promised Land*. I read everything on the women's movement. When I became pregnant, I immersed myself in books about pregnancy, nursing, child development. But in dealing with a subject as crucial to my own life as bisexuality, I avoided reading until the very end.

To some extent, my avoidance of educating myself may be attributed to my denial, my hope that bisexuality as an issue in my life would go away. I also think it was a function of my resistance to Barry, my stubborn refusal to feeling controlled by him, my anger at not experiencing any choice.

Next to my suntan lotion and bathing suit, I packed six books on homosexuality (there were no books available on bisexuality). In five days I read *Rubyfruit Jungle*, Merle Miller's *On Being Different*, a question-and-answer book about homosexuality, published by the New York Gay Activists Alliance, and a book of homosexual short stories. The books only served to validate my own experience and what Barry had been telling me all along, that there was nothing intrinsically wrong or deviant about feelings for the same sex. What was really happening for me was that for the first time I could see that there was nothing wrong about Barry, about me, or about our relationship. It was clear when I came back that my relationship with Robert, at least in the way it had been, was over.

Barry and I were both exhausted. We were tired of struggling, tired of living in uncertainty. It was a strange time. On the one hand, we wanted to get on with our life together, without all the unhappiness, and we did things like painting our house and planning for a month at the shore as if we'd be together always. Other times, our fights took so much out of us that we could see no rational reason for continuing to live together and we talked about dividing the furniture. I was still in therapy, not experiencing very much change or progress, thinking about terminating, but not doing anything about it.

Barry began to talk about taking a six-week trip by himself. We knew that we couldn't continue to stay married under these pressured conditions. Barry felt that going off alone to the Northwest where he had never been would provide some clarity. I didn't object. We needed a break from each other, and I also knew that I had to experience my own capacity to live without him, to care for Danny without his support, to make a life for myself. To be able to decide to live together, I had to know I could truly live alone. We never talked about it explicitly, but it was clear in my own mind that his trip to the Northwest was a trial separation for us.

I had married at twenty-one, moved from my parents' home to my husband's, and no matter how many interesting, expansive experiences Barry and I lived through together, I had never been completely on my own. This was the gift I was giving myself in staying home alone with Danny while Barry went away—to experience life alone, what it would be like for me to be single. I was nervous but I was ready. I had never gone to a movie alone, never handled bills completely on my own, never been totally responsible for the house, never handled Danny without consulting Barry, never had made my own social plans or travel arrangements, never slept alone for more than a few days.

We said good-bye to each other like two kids. "Have a good time," we both said, and we knew we were granting each other unspoken permission to do whatever we had to do in order to choose between staying in the marriage or getting out.

It was the Bicentennial summer, 1976, and except for a trash strike that dragged on interminably, the atmosphere in Philadelphia was festive. There were concerts on the Parkway, special events every day, and for me, not working, it was a chance to vacation in my own city. With Barry gone, pressures eased. Danny was in nursery school all day, and for the first time in years, I had long periods of time alone. Sometimes I got nervous about being alone and bustled around making plans for myself. But perhaps for the first time in my life, I didn't push myself to do anything. With no schedule and few responsibilities, I could respond to whatever presented itself.

After four years of pain and struggling, the summer apart provided the first respite—some breathing room, a chance to think free from the constant ups and downs, an opportunity to gain some perspective on our relationship at last.

Although I couldn't predict what would happen with my marriage when Barry returned from his vacation, I knew one thing for sure—I was ready to terminate my therapy and move on. The July day that I walked out of Dr. Green's office for the last time felt like a holiday. I was ready to live without analyzing my every motive, try new behavior without wondering whether I was "acting out." I wanted a vacation from figuring it out, from probing, from my head. My rolfing experience had made me much more willing to trust my body.

Friday afternoon of the second week Barry was away, I was alone in the house. It had been raining all day. A young man I knew only slightly, a waiter at a restaurant, stopped by unexpectedly and we sat down on the sofa to chat. He was only twenty-three and I had never given much thought to him as a person, although I liked him and thought he was attractive.

Maybe it was the rain outside or the closed-in atmosphere of the room. As we sat together talking, there was suddenly electricity between us. The idea of having sex with someone nine years younger than I seemed inconceivable. I was as surprised as anyone, and I had no idea of what to do with the feelings of attraction I was having. The sexual experiences I had had beforehand, and there hadn't been many, were always with people I knew intimately. Here was this young man I hardly knew, whom I had never spent time with and there he was sitting next to me, gazing at me intently, clearly aware of what was going on. Neither of us said anything for a few minutes.

Finally, I broke the silence. I said I was aware that I was feeling attracted to him. He said he was having the same feelings.

For a moment all the reasons "why not" passed through my mind. Then, I thought about how I had wanted this time away from Barry to serve as a chance for me to have new experiences. I wanted to begin to try things that I had avoided or denied myself before.

It was as if the movie projector stopped for an instant, something shifted inside me and I said to myself, "As much as I am able in my life, I am going to begin to say yes."

We went upstairs and had wonderfully hot sex together. He was sensual, direct, and eager. I was turned on to myself, the circumstances, the surprise of it all. Nothing had been planned, there had been no expectations, it was just saying "yes" to the moment. I was reminded of the "zipless fuck" I had read about a couple of months earlier in *Fear of Flying* by Erica Jong, the brief, anonymous sexual encounter that has traditionally been the territory of men, not women. No concern with propriety, no urge toward restraint, no fear of other people's criticism. Just doing what I wanted to do when I wanted to do it. I liked being accountable to no one. Sex was just part of my new-found freedom. After years of holding back, how liberating it was to do what I wanted to do and not to have to ask anyone's permission.

I was alone a lot too, and I saw that I could live with loneliness. I listened to records I hadn't listened to in years—show music especially—found I had a talent for making music tapes, began to sing and rediscovered I had a voice, reached out to friends, bought a new vibrator, and sometimes, late at night especially, I also missed Barry, missed him greatly. We talked on the phone once a week and wrote to each other, but as time passed, I saw that I was not missing him as a husband, not as someone I needed close-by to take care of me, but as a person I valued deeply, who could make me laugh, a man with whom I missed sharing the big and little moments of my life.

The question I had once asked my friend Barbara about whether I would be able to find someone else if Barry and I separated no longer concerned me. I realized that there were many people out there, and there was no scarcity of relationships available to me. Somehow, just knowing this made me look anew at Barry. I was not the inexperienced twenty-one-year-old whom he had married. By this time, I had had a number of the sexual and emotional involvements I always felt I missed earlier in my life.

When I compared Barry to the others, he was not diminished in my eyes. I recognized that he was still the one with whom I could make the deepest connection. Perhaps, I thought, some of his openness and willingness to share his deepest thoughts and feelings could be attributed to the very bisexuality that I had found so abhorrent for so long. Barry has great strength, but he is also a soft and gentle man, and it is those qualities—softness, sensitivity—that I have always been drawn to in all the men I know.

When Barry came home, I was very conscious of having made the choice to stay with him. Even though I was still not completely at ease with his bisexuality and the thought that he would be having sex with men, I could accept it. I realized that I had depleted so much useless energy worrying about what other people thought about us. And to be sure, once Barry had made peace with his bisexuality, had accepted himself, he blossomed. He had a new sense of directness and self-confidence. In essence, there was more of him there for me, and our relationship grew richer and more intimate.

I remember meeting him at the train when he came home that summer, in early August. He looked tall and lean and healthy, and as he came up the escalator at Thirtieth Street Station, I was very excited and a little shy. We'd never been away from each other for so long, and it was a celebration to be reunited. We went to dinner at the Astral Plane and he gave me a scrimshaw necklace he had brought back from the West.

We went to the shore for a couple of weeks. We played a lot, made a special dinner every night, spent time with Danny, invited friends to visit, relaxed in the sun, and talked endlessly. The happiness we had during those weeks made a very good beginning. It was hard to imagine, really, how much we had suffered.

We no longer saw each other as possessing each other in the way we had when we married. Rather, we were both independent people whose love and desire to make a life together were decisions freely chosen. There were still many unanswered questions—about how we would handle an open marriage, about my own bisexuality, how we would deal with the inevitable jealousy that would arise out of outside relationships. But after a long and stormy struggle, we celebrated our tenth anniversary, sure that we were committed— recommitted actually—to building a marriage based upon a very new set of assumptions.

Four

Can It Be Included?

Almost immediately after I told Alice that I had sex with a man, she suggested that we see a marriage counselor. I wasn't eager to begin therapy. I felt defeated that things had gotten so bad that we needed outside help, but a long time had passed, and I was still unable to sort out the confusion in my mind. Truly, I was willing to try anything in order to save our relationship.

We decided to talk to the psychoanalyst Alice's supervisor was seeing in therapy. When I finally got up the nerve to call him, he suggested that Alice and I see him separately for three exploratory sessions, following which we could all get together to discuss his recommendations for future treatment.

The analyst's office, a twenty-minute car or train ride out of the city limits, was located in a suburban office building, a singularly undistinguished structure, except that it towered above most of the buildings in the vicinity. It housed a veritable smorgasbord of doctors, dentists, psychiatrists, psychoanalysts, medical specialists of all kinds. That first morning I stood in the lobby for a while, just staring at the directory of offices and doctors posted in a glass-enclosed case on the wall, not quite believing I was actually standing there, about to see a psychiatrist. I had no idea what his reaction would be when he heard my story. All I could think about was that he would find that there was something basically wrong with me; there had to be, for me to be in such turmoil.

Little did I know that I would continue to enter that building, glance over at the names on the wall, and then step into one of the three waiting elevators, four times a week for the next four years. I didn't suspect that this early-hour appointment was only the first of many eight o'clock sessions I would have before rushing back to the city to my job as deputy attorney general. Nor did I guess how many lunch hours I would dash away from my office or from a meeting, jump in my car or catch a train, so that I would arrive on time for one of my regular appointments. I had no idea that for the next four years, this bland building, the middle-aged elevator lady with her bird's-nest hairdo, the corner office, would become the focus of my life.

Dr. Green looked exactly as I'd always imagined psycho-analysts—medium height, reserved, and distinguished, with dark hair graying at the temples. Conservatively dressed in a dark suit and tie, he was a handsome man, or at least he had been in his younger years; now he had a Lincolnesque quality that was at the same time a bit formidable, but also reassuring.

Books and papers were piled casually on his Danish-modern desk, and a modern couch covered with a tan burlaplike fabric sat at the other end of the room. A few light orange chairs were the only dashes of color in what was otherwise an office of neutral and subdued tones.

Alice told me much later than she always hated his office; she found it cold, lifeless, flat. It bothered her that except for the diplomas and certificates hanging on the wall behind the couch, the only painting was a small, geometric print of angular lines and shapes that she assumed represented the mind. I paid little attention to details of the surroundings as I sat across from his desk during those first interviews; I was far too preoccupied trying to judge and anticipate his reactions to me.

The pent-up secrets I had guarded so closely since I was a teenager came gushing forth as soon as I began to talk. Tearfully, I told the analyst about my history of adolescent encounters with boys, how I had repressed those feelings for ten years, and about my two recent sexual experiences with men. At last, I was telling another person the details about a part of myself that disgusted me, yet a part that seemed to be a driving force within me. Afraid of his criticism, I nonetheless found that it was an incredible relief just to let it all out, and I told him in no uncertain terms that I wanted to rid myself of my homosexual desires and save my marriage. I was convinced that I was sick, and I wanted to be cured.

As I look back, this first therapy session was the most productive and nurturing of any session during the entire four years I was in therapy. Opening up totally to another person, I experienced a calm that I hadn't felt in years. I watched Dr. Green's face very carefully as I talked, but he didn't appear shocked by anything I told him; in fact, he had a reassuring manner which made me feel comfortable. At last, I would have the opportunity to talk honestly with someone about feelings that I had kept hidden for so long.

After the third session, Alice and I met with Dr. Green, and he recommended that I enter psychoanalysis four times a week and that Alice begin psychotherapy on a twice-a-week basis. In order to cure myself of my homosexual feelings, he said, I would have to undergo full psychoanalytic treatment. I knew that I was committing myself to long-term therapy, but I felt it would be worth it if only I could be cured. I had heard doubts raised about whether therapy could cure homosexuality, but I was willing to give it everything I had to find out. I resolved to myself that I would follow my therapist's directions and that I would work very hard.

Looking back on this important decision, I realize that I knew very little about this analyst, a person with whom I would share a substantial part of my life during the next four years, and very little about the process of psychoanalysis itself. At the time, though, I wasn't even thinking about those questions. Finally, I was beginning to take some responsibility for my life and my future.

Shortly after entering therapy, the analyst asked Alice and me not to talk to one another about our therapy sessions. He said that if we shared the content of our work with him, we would dilute the intensity of the feelings that we were dealing with in therapy. While Alice and I reluctantly agreed to this request, we didn't realize the gap in communication and intimacy that it would cause in our relationship.

In some ways, not talking to each other was beneficial because it allowed us the time we needed to explore issues separately, to think our own thoughts, and to stop pressuring each other. During the next two and a half years, on my own initiative, I was able to expand my knowledge of bisexuality and homosexuality, something I needed to do in order to understand myself. But talking to each other, sharing our thoughts had always been basic to the way we related to each other. During this period, unfortunately, Alice and I were more distant from each other than at any time since we met.

Dr. Green followed what I thought was the orthodox method of psychoanalysis, which meant that I lay on a couch while he sat on a chair behind my head where I couldn't see him. I talked about anything that came into my mind. As I related the happenings of my current daily life, I was often reminded of childhood incidents, which I then went on to describe. Dr. Green said very little. Toward the end of a session, he usually gave me his interpretation of what I had talked about. I found the process interesting and eagerly looked forward to his few "gems of wisdom" at the end of an hour.

I know now that it was far from an orthodox position for a psychoanalyst to agree to see a husband and wife, and it's hard for me to evaluate the effects of his decision to see us concurrently. At the time, Alice was quite determined that we not see two different therapists and Dr. Green agreed, but only so long as Alice was in psychotherapy rather than analysis.

In the beginning phases of analysis, every time I talked about my homosexual desires, I felt guilty and depressed. Dr. Green's face remained impassive. He never made any explicitly negative statements about homosexuality or bisexuality, but rather, listened without comment.

My analysis began in September of 1972. During the first year, I also began "cruising" the streets of Philadelphia, picking up men on the street for anonymous sex. Each time I had sex with a man, I felt ashamed that I had given in to my impulses. I didn't tell Alice about these experiences, but she rarely left my thoughts. When I entered Dr. Green's office after an encounter, I'd reluctantly "confess" what I had done. It often seemed to me that Dr. Green was an invisible presence in bed beside me when I was having sex with a man.

There were two six-month periods during the next two years in which I gave up sex with men. Each of these times, I was thrilled because I thought that this was an indication that my analysis was working. Dr. Green subtly supported my enthusiastic interpretation of these periods, but was also quick to point out that these dormant times might or might not turn out to be permanent. However, as time went by, the drive to have sex with a man always returned, and I began cruising the streets again.

Sexuality was not the only subject I talked about in psychoanalysis. I talked about my childhood, problems and successes in my job, my relationship with Alice and my new son, Danny, and almost every other event that occurred in my life. It's difficult for me to now imagine how I managed to fill up four hours a week for four years just talking about myself.

On several occasions I asked Dr. Green whether he had ever cured a patient of homosexual feelings. He told me about one patient he had seen who decided that he wanted to be gay, but he never talked about anyone who had been cured. I began to think that probably he had not seen very many homosexual patients. When I would directly question him about his views about bisexuality, he was always evasive in answering, saying that my attraction for men was merely symptomatic of other problems. I remember him saying on a number of occasions that he viewed homosexuality as an "adjustment."

I had been in therapy for about a year when, in June 1973, I first made contact with people who felt positively about their homosexuality. Even though it happened through my work, it was a major breakthrough for me personally. In December of 1971 I had changed jobs, leaving Community Legal Services to become an attorney with a civil tensions and civil rights unit within the Pennsylvania Department of Justice. After six months I was promoted to deputy attorney general and director of the unit.

The Community Advocate Unit, as it was called, operated under a federal grant and used the power of the state—through negotiation, intervention with state agencies, programs and policies, and litigation—to enforce the rights of minorities—blacks, women, Puerto Ricans, and homosexuals. My first year as a deputy attorney general I concentrated my efforts on two major areas, police brutality and low income housing. My work with tenants toward reform of the state and local landlord-tenant laws and advocacy of the state's increased involvement in providing more low cost housing was really a continuation of my legal services experience. Police brutality was a new area of concern for me. Our unit had been started primarily to deal with increasing complaints from minority citizens about unlawful and unnecessary use of force by the Philadelphia police. However, even though our grant included discrimination against homosexuals, until this time the unit had handled only one such case.

When I first received a telephone call from a young man who wanted to talk about discrimination against homosexuals, I didn't know how to react. On the one hand, I knew that our unit had the responsibility for dealing with this kind of issue. However, the situation presented difficulties for me, considering that during this period I was trying to extricate myself from my own bisexual feelings through intensive analysis. Because of my personal hang-ups and self-hatred, I didn't see homosexuals as a minority whose rights were threatened. Rather, as I talked to this man on the phone, I thought to myself, "Why should we protect sick people? They need psychiatric treatment, not legal representation."

I decided, however, that my position with the state required that I listen, at least, to the kinds of discrimination that allegedly existed and make a decision about the appropriateness of our unit's involvement. Consistent with the way I handled other complaints of discrimination, I arranged a meeting with representatives of the eight existing politically active gay groups in Philadelphia.

Ten people attended the first evening meeting held at the Fellowship Commission on Fifteenth Street in Philadelphia. We spent several hours discussing a whole range of discriminatory practices which they believed were based on "affectional and sexual prefer-ence." These were new terms to me. I didn't exactly understand the affectional part because I had always viewed homosexuality as merely sexual. It took me a long time after this meeting in June 1973 to realize that homosexuality and bisexuality did not pertain only to sex—that my own feelings toward men were more than just sexual (no matter how I saw it at the time)—that the feelings I would have described as sexual, in reality, also involved a desire for closeness and intimacy. I coded these feelings of mine as being "only sexual," but in truth, they were affectional feelings also.

One thing I sensed about these men and women was that they felt different from the way I did about their same sex attractions. They viewed themselves as healthy and normal adults who wanted to live productive lives in the way they saw fit but were being unfairly discriminated against by many segments of society. I was not completely sold on the validity of their arguments, but, at the same time, I was attracted to their vitality, to the positive attitude they had about themselves.

I realized rather quickly that their complaints regarding discrimination were similar in many ways to the types of discrimina-tion suffered by other minority groups—discrimination in jobs and housing if their employer or landlord discovered that they were homosexual, and unequal treatment and harassment in the enforcement of the criminal code regarding solicitation and sodomy laws. They insisted that discrimination against them was intensified by the prevalence of many false stereotypes about homosexuality.

I was impressed by the fact that they were continually willing to go to the heart of the negative stereotypes generally used against homosexuals. For example, they said that many gay people were already teaching in schools, and had a right to do so, as much as heterosexual teachers. Research indicated that a child's sexual preference was determined at a very early age anyway, probably before four or five years old, and no school-age child could be persuaded to be homosexual any more than he could be convinced that he was heterosexual, if that was not the case. Furthermore, there was no evidence that gay teachers brought their sexual preference into the classroom any more than their heterosexual counterparts. And if such information did surface, it could only be a positive influence for students to see that gay people are educated and productive members of society. I was surprised to learn that FBI crime statistics show that 98 percent of sexual abuse of children occurs between an adult and child of the opposite sex, disproving the stereotype that gays are child molesters.

As an attorney, I began to see justification for their complaints of alleged sexual discrimination. As a person struggling with his own sexual identity, I resisted an objective evaluation of the situation. I left the meeting feeling personally confused, yet knowing that in all conscience I would have to follow up on their complaints.

After the second meeting of the group a few weeks later, I sought out one of the men whom I found attractive and personable. Tom Wilson's presence suggested a quiet power, and I learned that although he was young, he already had owned a camp, had opened Giovanni's Room, the first gay bookstore in the city, had helped found a local gay newspaper, and sold real estate on the side. Tom and I went to lunch together at a quiet bar across the street from the Fellowship Commission, the Westbury, and I opened up to him almost immediately telling him about my marriage, my attraction to men, and the sexual experiences I had had. He was encouraging and very sympathetic, listening quietly to what I had to say and then sharing several similar experiences in his life. I was very drawn to Tom, but he made it clear from the beginning of our talks that he had no interest in having a sexual relationship with me. Once I got over my initial disappointment and accepted the relationship on Tom's terms, he became my mentor and a kind of second therapist.

Over the next two years, Tom and I met several times a month for lunch, and I asked him every question I could think of about homosexuality. He gave me books to read and answered still more questions that came up as a result of my reading. Certainly, he had a positive bias toward the subject, but for the most part, his answers were objective, based on his own experiences and knowledge of people he knew.

One time we were sitting in the Spruce Restaurant, one of our regular places to have lunch together. I remember questioning Tom about the widely held stereotype that all homosexuals were just interested in having promiscuous sex rather than in establishing long-term relationships. He pointed out that he had been involved with his lover for three years and also told me about many other gay couples he knew who were in long-term relationships. One couple he told me about, whom I later met, had been together in a committed relationship for twenty-four years. He went on to explain that many gay people go through a lot of sexual experimentation in their twenties and thirties and have a variety of homosexual relationships because frequently they repressed these feelings when they were younger and didn't have as much opportunity to experiment. Therefore, he said, while sexual experimentation normally takes place in late adolescence, many gay people go through that type of adolescent experimentation at a later time in their lives.

Because I knew Tom would be empathic, I felt safe raising my doubts and fears about homosexuality in a way that I couldn't with my analyst. It didn't seem difficult for him to explain things to me or to understand my questions, because like many gay people, at one time he had held most of the same negative sterotypes that dominated my thinking. After our lunches, I'd return to my office and go on with my day. But, I spent hours mulling over in my mind the different points we had discussed. I began to think that my attraction to men just might not be weird or abnormal, after all, that perhaps it was an expression of something more positive.

I read the books Tom gave me and I bought other books I found. By 1974 hundreds of books had been published that took a positive view toward homosexuality. Books like *On Being Different* by Merle Miller, *Society and the Healthy Homosexual*, by George Weinberg, and *Rubyfruit Jungle* by Rita Mae Brown, spoke of homosexuality as healthy behavior and described the individual struggles that people had gone through in coming to accept their own homosexuality. The personal experiences related in these books and research and statistics compiled on the subject further supported my thinking about my own emotional, and sexual preference. I was moved by these books. They reflected my own experience, and even though I was reading about homosexuality rather than bisexuality, these books spoke to the part of me dealing with that issue.

I told Dr. Green about the discussions of bisexuality and homosexuality that I was beginning to have with Tom and the other gay activists I had met. He listened without comment. There was a new pride growing within me that I was a man capable of loving other men. It was no longer merely a sexual issue. Rather than feeling negative about these desires, I began to realize that when I was with other men who were sensitive, emotional, and loving, I felt the same way. My strength, my forthrightness, and my sensitivity began to expand as a result in all areas of my life—work, relationships, even in my day-to-day interactions with Alice.

Some of my changing attitudes about men as well as my own manhood can be attributed to the fact that I participated in a number of men's conferences during 1973 and 1974. Realizing that men as well as women were constricted by old-fashioned role definitions, some people were beginning to talk about the need for a "men's liberation movement," and these conferences were an outgrowth of this concern. When I decided to attend my first conference, however, I had no idea that discussion about men's sexuality would invariably deal with the issue of homosexuality.

It seemed that whenever a group of men got together and talked freely, sooner or later they began to discuss their emotional and sexual feelings for each other. Even those who defined themselves as totally straight eventually recognized that they had some measure of attraction for the same sex, even if they chose not to act on it. The accepting atmosphere of the group and perhaps the absence of women allowed many men to open up readily about these feelings without the pressure of proving their masculinity.

Many of the men who attended these conferences had been touched in one way or another by the women's movement. Some were married to women who had participated in women's consciousness-raising groups, while others had come in contact with feminists in college, work, or social situations. There was a good deal of dialogue about the way in which the changing role of women—increased independence, women returning to work and earning their own living, changing child-care arrangements, freer sexuality—was also altering the role of men in the society. Clearly, the times were changing, and many men were feeling the need to get together and talk about how these new developments were affecting their own lives.

Slowly, hesitantly at first, but increasingly after two and a half years of therapy, I began to let Dr. Green know that I was feeling better about my involvements with men and that I no longer wanted to make those feelings disappear. The first time I told him, I was shocked to hear myself utter the words. "Was this the same person who had come crying into his office two and a half years ago saying that he wanted to be cured?" I thought, as I listened to myself speak.

Certainly the changes that I was undergoing personally were not occurring in a vacuum. By 1974 it seemed to me that every time I picked up a newspaper or magazine, there was an article about gay activism. In Philadelphia publicity centered on efforts to persuade City Council to consider an amendment to the Human Relation laws that would prohibit discrimination against gay people, and similar actions were happening in most large cities. People of the calibre of Dr. Harold Brown, past New York City health commissioner in the Lindsay administration, were "coming out" on the front page of *The New York Times*.

I was moved and impressed by the courage of these people, their willingness to be open about their lives at a time when there was still enormous hatred and misunderstanding about homosexuality. Their pride touched me deeply because I knew they were fighting my battle too. And I knew by this time, knew intensely, that what they were saying was true—that people did not have to fear homosexuality, that gay people had the same problems and the same successes as everyone else, the same bills to pay at the end of the month. I also knew I wanted to stand by their side in this struggle for equality and recognition.

Within a few months, by February 1975, I felt much more certain about myself and about my decision not to cure myself of homosexual feelings. I still didn't know at this point whether I was homosexual or bisexual. What I did know was that my homosexual desires were an integral part of me, that I enjoyed my sexual and intimate experiences with men, and that I no longer viewed my physical attraction and loving feelings for men as sick or neurotic.

For so many years I had been saying to myself that loving men was wrong, even though it felt satisfying and natural. I was finally at a point where I could take a look at my own experience and separate it from what society said was correct. This was a giant step for me because it meant that I was going to make a decision about my life based upon my own values, rather than upon what I had been taught was right or wrong.

Certainly, there were still many questions to be answered. The number one question was the future of my marriage? How could my desire to have sex with men fit into a marriage? How could I love men and women? Could I continue to be married if I wanted to be what others called "unfaithful"? My frame of reference for thinking about marriage was very limited: marriage meant heterosexual monogamy.

It was clear to me soon after I began to accept my bisexual feelings as valid that I would have to tell Alice about this new stage in my development. A major shift had taken place; I had changed my goal in therapy from curing myself of attraction to men to wanting to integrate this part of me into my life. Alice had a right to know so that she could make some decisions about her own life based on more realistic understandings. Dr. Green discouraged me, though, saying that he felt my disclosure was premature and that it would serve no useful purpose. Over the spring months of 1975 I debated the advisability of telling Alice. It seemed like an impossible dilemma because I didn't know whether Alice could ever accept my bisexuality and whether our marriage would continue. It took me about six months more to make the decision to tell her the truth, and even then, I did not have my analyst's approval.

I knew I loved her. But could a marriage continue and include bisexuality? I didn't know. I was growing stronger. I felt confused about my future, but I knew that I would survive either way, with or without Alice. One major difference from the first disclosure a few years earlier was that now I was less isolated. I had several people to talk to about my problems. Most were homosexual friends who didn't have any answers for me, but they were willing to listen.

My conflict had transcended the question of sexuality. It had become an issue of integrity within myself and within the relationship. Lying, withholding, evading, repudiated my own standards of behavior. It was time to take the next step and tell Alice about my feelings in a straightforward way.

We were sitting on our living room couch on a Thursday night in May 1975 when I told her about the change in my attitude toward myself. It seemed different to me from the first time I had told Alice about my homosexual desires, because I was now less confused about my own feelings. By this time I had been through two and a half years of intensive soul-searching analysis, I had examined and discussed bisexuality and homosexuality to the point of boredom with Tom and many other gay activists, and I had read many books and articles about the subject. I didn't know what Alice's response would be, although I assumed that she would be very angry hearing that I had continued to have sex during those years and that I was no longer working to cure myself.

I remember examining the glass coffee table in front of us in minute detail as I told Alice that my attraction for men was an important part of me, something that couldn't be ignored, that I no longer wanted to ignore. I wanted her to know that I was beginning to feel good about loving men as well as women. I thought it meant I was bisexual because I was still attracted to her and other women. I had not yet met any other people who called themselves bisexual, so I was confused about this issue. I also told Alice that I loved her deeply and wanted to stay married to her.

Again, like the time I first told Alice, her reaction was erratic, changing from moment to moment. First anger, then sadness, then resignation, then anger again; it was as if all the emotions that had been bottled up for the two and a half years we were not talking about the subject came spilling forth. She felt that I was giving her an ultimatum, "Take me the way I am or leave me," and she was furious when she realized that I had deceived her for three years. How could I explain all the times I had wanted to tell her the truth but was afraid? We both cried when we realized that we loved each other but could not imagine our marriage continuing under present circumstances.

While this second revelation created turmoil in our lives, it also had the effect of bringing our relationship back to life. Our fighting, talking, and loving became more intense than we had experienced for a long while. With my secret out in the open, there were fewer barriers to our being able to communicate intimately with each other—all of it, the anger, the disappointment, the need, the love—not just through making love but with words and feelings. And, as we were to discover, this explosion gave us the impetus to look at our relationship anew.

Within three days of telling Alice the second time about the importance of my attraction to men, she told her mother and all our close friends. I would not have chosen to tell everyone as rapidly as Alice. I wasn't ready to announce my bisexuality to the world, yet I didn't have a choice. Alice had taken care of that.

It seemed to me that telling everyone so precipitously was a rash thing for Alice to do. I felt that she hadn't taken my feelings into consideration at all. Our life was in a lot of upheaval. It wasn't clear whether we would stay together or what would happen to us in the future. To tell her mother under those circumstances was inappropriate in my eyes, and I was angry that she had done so without consulting me. Much of my anger came from my fear of being rejected.

Alice said that the reason she had told her mother and our friends was that she really needed to know that she could count on their support. She had been living with the secret for a long time. Finally, there was no longer any reason not to let it out and deal with it directly. She didn't care at that point about the state of our marriage or how the revelation was going to affect me. Her telling was motivated by something else as well. Her own feelings were so raw that she wanted me to experience some of the same pain she was going through. It seemed to her that I should have to face the ultimate consequences of my behavior.

Alice's family had always been very important to me. In fact, part of my initial attraction to her was her warm and enveloping family life. My own family had always been in turmoil, and I longed for a family like Alice's. When we married, they immediately took me in as their own son and made me totally welcome.

There had been a standing joke in her family that if Alice and I ever separated, it would be Alice's fault. Alice was never a person to mince words. Because she generally expressed what was on her mind very directly, her family tended to see her as the potential troublemaker. They saw me as an easygoing person, full of equanimity and good will, with few faults. It must have been difficult and painful for Alice during that three year period to listen to her family talk about how wonderful I was knowing that the issue of my bisexuality could lead to the breakup of our marriage.

Once she had been told, Alice's mother called me almost immediately. Helen told me that she wanted me to know that she loved me, and that her love was something that would always be there regardless of the circumstances. But she wanted to talk to me, face to face. I went to the office where she worked and we had a talk.

Helen's major concern was that Alice and I would separate. She didn't want that to happen; she wanted us to stay together. I remember her repeating that she would always love me, and reminding me that they had always put me on a pedestal in her family. I knew this to be true. That was just the way they looked at me. Now she said, "You're not on the pedestal anymore; you're just like everybody else, and you have your problems too."

I felt much better after our conversation. Alice's parents, however, were perplexed. My bisexuality was a real mystery for them. They didn't understand why or where the need for male relationships was coming from.

Our friends too were shocked by the revelation about my bisexuality. They didn't know what to make of it, and they let me know that. For example, one day, shortly after Alice told our friend Barbara, I stopped by Barbara's house a few blocks from where we lived. She told me that she didn't understand why I would take a chance and ruin my marriage. She wanted to know what bisexuality meant to me because she had little understanding of it. That day, Barbara and I began the same kind of question-and-answer dialogue that I had experienced with Tom and that Alice had begun to go through with me. When Barbara first began to talk to me, she looked at bisexuality in purely sexual terms, similar to my own reaction when I first began to explore my own attraction for men. She asked me what homosexual sex was like, how it was different and the same as sex between men and women. Then slowly, we began to discuss the emotional side of relationships between two people of the same sex. I suggested several books for her to read that Alice and I had found helpful. She was very open to hearing about my life and the way I looked at sexuality.

There was never a question of anybody pulling away. From the moment our friends heard, there were continuous phone calls letting us know that they would not leave us, whatever we had to go through. We didn't realize that our friends would be intimately involved in the process with us and that their lives would be as affected by it as ours.

Alice's and my principal support has come from our friends. That doesn't mean that every one of them has always been encouraging all of the time, that they've always approved of our behavior, or been free from criticism. It does mean that we have been able to rely on them continually during our most painful periods of struggling, even during those times when we ourselves had given up all hope that our marriage could be saved.

Even after telling Alice, the issue of whether I was bisexual or homosexual was not clear for me. In fact, I had never met anyone who defined himself as bisexual. To my thinking, people were either straight or gay. Yet I realized that there were differences in the life experiences of my friend Tom and me. On a social level, Tom related almost exclusively to men, while I was married and had many close relationships with women. From my earliest memories, I had always been attracted to both sexes. Several times in talking with Tom I questioned him about differences between us and said that I thought that I was bisexual. I sensed an uneasiness in his reaction. Other gay people were more blatant in telling me that they did not believe in bisexuality. They saw bisexuality as an intermediate stage that a person passed through on the way to accepting his homosexuality.

I knew that I was attracted to men, that I had repressed those attractions for ten years, and that now I was feeling much more positive about these feelings. Yet, at the same time, I was still very attracted to Alice, and enjoyed having sex with her. In fact, our sexual times together were becoming more exciting now that I was not living a lie and was able to tell her more directly what I liked sexually.

Looking back, it's interesting that the two people with whom I was talking intensely about my sexual orientation—Dr. Green and Tom—represented opposite points of view. Neither of their positions left any room for bisexuality as a viable alternative to homosexuality or heterosexuality. I felt very alone; I didn't know where to turn and whether there were any other married people dealing with the question.

It was around this time, in January 1976, that Tony Silvestre, a man I met through my work with gay rights, told me about a support group of bisexual and gay married men that he had helped to start which was meeting weekly in State College, Pennsylvania. Tony was a graduate student at Penn State, a long time Gay activist, and is currently the Director of the Governor's Council for Sexual Minorities in Pennsylvania. I was astounded that such a group even existed, especially in a rural part of Pennsylvania. As soon as I was able to arrange my schedule, I traveled to State College to attend one of their noontime meetings.

When I arrived, the meeting had already started. The five men who were present were sitting around a table, eating lunch and talking very casually about the same kinds of problems that I had been painfully struggling with alone back in Philadelphia. To hear men sharing their feelings with openness and sincerity was deeply moving—it wasn't a way that I was accustomed to seeing men relate.

One time the discussion became more serious after one man related his wife's anger after he had stayed out until 3:00 A.M. Later the mood lightened, and there was light bantering back and forth about the bar scene in State College compared to Philadelphia's more active gay life. When the subject of bisexuality came up for discussion, a number of different views were expressed. Several men believed that they were bisexual, another was convinced that he was gay and married, and another was unwilling to label his behavior.

The meeting had a major impact on me. For the first time I knew that I was not alone. There were at least five other men dealing with the same issues as I was. Although I had already begun to change many of my negative views toward homosexuality from my involvement in the gay rights movement, I still had doubts about bisexuality and the workability of a marriage that included sexual relationships with men. All the people that I had met until that time who had been married now defined themselves as gay and were either separated or divorced. For the first time, however, I met men who wanted to expand their marriages to include their relationships with men and who firmly believed in the legitimacy of bisexuality as a way of life.

I began talking to Alice about my interest in forming a support group of bisexual or gay married men in Philadelphia. Initially, she was very angry and hostile about the idea. Extremely threatened, she saw it as one more way of my moving along the path of being open about bisexuality. She accused me of trying to embarrass her and wanting to use the group just to find sexual partners.

Even though I was eager to move ahead immediately, I had found a number of times in the past that if I was willing to wait a while and give Alice some time to adjust to my initiatives, she would eventually come around on her own instead of rebelling against what she felt was my domination. I waited five months, giving Alice a chance to get used to the idea. Meanwhile, she and I were doing a lot of talking. With time, her hostility lessened, although she was still anxious about the idea of the group. I arranged a meeting place where I thought people would feel comfortable being seen, and I advertised in an alternative newspaper, saying that a support group of bisexual or gay married men was forming. The ad read as follows:

> Bisexual or Gay Married Men will meet Fridays beginning May 7, noon to 2 p.m., for lunch and informal discussion in Rm. 22 of the Friend's Center, 15th and Cherry Sts., bring your own lunch. For more information call the Gay Switchboard at 928-1919.

On the day of the first meeting, I arrived early and spoke with the receptionist, explaining the delicacy of the meeting and the need for confidentiality and discretion. She understood and assured me that she would handle the situation with sensitivity. I waited nervously, not knowing if anyone would respond to the ad. Several minutes before noon, the first person arrived, and within a short time, there were nine men in the room. Two more arrived an hour later.

I began the discussion by sharing with the group a brief history of my relationship with Alice and with men, and my need to talk to other people in the same situation. Jim was the next person to speak. He had been happily married for two years to a woman ten years his senior; she had known about his attraction for men when they married, but was convinced that she could change him. Jim was a playwright, twenty-eight years old, about 5'11", with short curly hair. Echoing my own sentiments, Jim spoke eloquently about feeling isolated and needing to meet and talk with other people.

One by one, as each man told his story, I was amazed at the varied backgrounds and wide range of living arrangements. Some men were very circumspect, not willing at this early stage to reveal much of themselves; others were very open. Dan, for example, told about his thirty-five-year marriage, the last ten years of which had included sex with men. Now that he was separated from his wife he had again become involved with a woman.

Some people had never talked to their partners about their homosexuality, while others were completely open about it. One man, married for eleven years, had had a male lover for nine years. His lover lived one block away and had become part of the family, helping with food shopping and child care. Another talked about the possibility of him and his wife moving into a group marriage situation.

All of the men agreed that it was a tremendously positive experience to talk to other people. For most, it was the first time they had talked to anybody about this part of their private lives. We decided to meet weekly and continued to meet for the next year, with new men attending and some of the original members dropping out.

In time, the group became a very important source of support for me and the other men because it was the one place where we could safely expose the intimate aspects of our sexuality. Whether we talked about telling our wives, or supported someone who had decided to separate, or discussed where to meet men, the meetings were always emotionally moving to me. When I came home and told Alice the stories I was hearing about the men in the group and their wives, she too felt better, since she had been feeling as isolated as I.

Currently, there are four such groups of men meeting in Philadelphia, and several for women who are bisexual or gay. There also have been meetings of wives whose husbands are bisexual or gay. Similar groups have been started in Washington, D.C., New York, Portland, Oregon, and San Francisco. The people who attend these groups find that they take on a great deal of importance in their lives; experiencing total acceptance, perhaps for the first time, they grow more sure of themselves and more willing to take responsibility for their lives.

In the summer of 1976, after I started the men's group, I decided to take a leave of absence from my job to travel through parts of Washington and Oregon for six weeks. I don't know exactly what led me to make the decision to travel, but I know that I was influenced by a friend who told me what an opportunity traveling alone had given him to reflect on himself and his marriage. My personal struggle and the intensity of my relationship with Alice had left me exhausted and depleted. Just the idea of doing something completely different, away from my job, family, and friends, was tremendously exciting to me.

To my surprise, Alice agreed with the idea almost immediately. Now I understand that she too was looking forward to having some time alone to look at herself and evaluate the future of our marriage. Dr. Green was not as approving of my trip. I think he was afraid that I would not return to therapy if I left for that long a time. But he saw that there was little he could do because I was determined to go.

Before I left for my trip, Alice, Danny, and I spent a week together in Vermont. Since early in our marriage Vermont had become a kind of yearly retreat from the city for Alice and me. For the past ten years, with the exception of our years in the Peace Corps, we had returned to the same inn, located on beautiful Lake Morey in Fairlee, with its small rustic cottages in the heart of a rich rural valley. It's a place we've always gone to relax and unwind—rides through the countryside, water skiing, my early morning fishing, Alice's absorption in a good novel. We've always used our time together in Vermont—as we've used most of the vacations we've taken during our marriage—as a chance to get back in touch very directly with each other.

One rainy afternoon Alice and I sat on our beds in front of a fire and, for the first time, shared with each other our thoughts about therapy and Dr. Green. What we discovered was that just as I had been confronting Dr. Green on his views about bisexuality and homosexuality, Alice had been having similar arguments with him on a number of feminist issues. She hadn't felt supported returning to work, not being a full-time mother, and exploring outside relationships for herself. She sensed his unspoken pessimism about the future of our relationship if I continued to relate to men.

Although Dr. Green rarely presented his views directly, over four years Alice and I had learned his subtle ways of expressing them. For example, he never commented when I told him I had slept with a man. Instead he sat there with a blank expression on his face. However, if I told him about a satisfying sexual experience with Alice, he would usually smile and make a positive, supportive comment. Whenever I challenged him on his negative attitude toward homosexuality, he would say: "Did I ever say anything negative about homosexuality?" Of course, I had to say: "No." While I knew that his stony silence signaled his disapproval, it was difficult to challenge him about his negative attitudes because he never expressed them directly.

It did not take much discussion for Alice and me to decide to leave therapy because for a long time we had been realizing that Dr. Green was not the right person for us. At this point, he did not support our individual thinking and he seemed too far removed from the life-style we were considering. We didn't believe that it was our role to try to educate him about women's rights, bisexuality, or a whole range of other concerns we had. If therapy was going to be supportive, we wanted someone who shared our basic values and was open to alternative life-styles.

When I began my travels, I made an agreement with myself to explore my decision to continue analysis. I decided that I would make it a point to seek other opinions, and talk with other therapists along the way. As it turned out, I ended up living for a week in the home of a gay psychiatrist in Seattle. We talked about my therapy and whether I should continue and I also had some very enlightening conversations with a number of other therapists during my six weeks away. I began to realize that there were many points of view about the treatment of bisexuality held by members of the psychiatric profession and that ultimately the decision was mine as to whether I should continue my present psychiatric treatment.

It was wonderfully freeing to be away from therapy. Suddenly, I didn't have to report to anyone about my every move. I felt positively about myself and my encounters with people and situations, better than I had felt in many years. Away from Alice and Dr. Green, I no longer felt the need to prove that being attracted to someone of the same sex was natural; I just did what I wanted to do.

I also realized that some people, like my analyst, would always think that homosexual attractions were an aberration, but I didn't need to change their opinions in order to live my life. Shortly after I returned from my trip, I withdrew from therapy and wrote a letter to Dr. Green summarizing my thinking:

8/26/76

Dear Dr. Green,
I'm writing you this letter to tell you where I am regarding my future in therapy. I've always tried to be honest with you not because it was you but because I felt it was the way I would really change and get the most out of therapy. I will try to be honest in this letter too, because in ending my relationship with you I want you to understand how I've come to that decision and what part of it has to do with you and what has to do with me.

When Alice and I went to Vermont in early July, we shared for the first time our impressions of you on particular issues. I shared mine about homosexuality and she shared hers about feminist ones. We both knew prior to sharing them that your bias was against our point of view and that you professed neutrality in therapy, even though you had strong personal views on both subjects. But what we realized was that your personal views constantly came out in your therapy in subtle or not so subtle ways. When a person is in therapy with another person for four years, he can pick up how that person reacts to other subjects; I know that silence on your part regarding homosexuality is not really neutrality because of your reaction to other behavior which you get excited about or encourage, such as when I have good sex with Alice or a good experience in dealing with the Attorney General.

I'm sure this comes as no surprise to you because I know I've confronted you on numerous occasions over the past year about your attitude toward homosexuality. However, you always deny that your bias or predisposition is brought into your therapy with me. Well, I disagree and can cite many situations where it has.

I knew in Vermont that I could not return to therapy with you because of your view toward homosexuality. How many times have you told me that I have not changed your mind? Well, I do not see it as my job to change your mind in the therapy relationship. I want someone who at least comes to the relationship with that as a given. When I started my trip, I thought that before I went back into therapy I was going to seek out a non-homophobic analyst (if one exists). I talked to several people about my therapy while on my trip—some psychiatrists, counselors, and just lay people. I was reinforced in my views toward you but also began to question whether I needed or wanted to return to therapy at all. I knew that I was relating easily to people, that I was feeling good about myself, and that I was taking control of situations in a positive way when necessary. I've come to the decision that I don't want to continue therapy at this time. It's not that there isn't more for me to get into and learn about myself, but more that I'm not willing to put the energy into it at this time because I'm not feeling the need.

I originally thought I went into therapy because the issue of homosexuality was more than I could handle and it was threatening my relationship with Alice. I know now that there were many other issues and problems that were affecting my life and which you helped me get to involving my childhood. What I'm trying to say here is that you helped me get to many important things that have and will always affect my life. These revelations were real positives that cannot be set aside because of your views on homosexuality. I, therefore, will probably always feel mixed about you and our relationship. There were good things and bad and, at this point, I feel the positive far outweigh the bad. But also at this point in my development, I could not continue with you in therapy because of your views on homosexuality.

These are my views right now. I hope they are clear to you. I intend to see you the day after Labor Day as planned, but will not schedule any appointment thereafter.

Barry

In the time since I left therapy, I have further reevaluated my analytic experience. I know that many orthodox psychoanalysts see homosexuality as a perversion that can only be changed through intensive psychoanalysis. It is obvious to me that I chose the kind of therapy and therapist who represented my own point of view at that stage of my development. What I have learned is that people choose the type of therapy that best reflects their own conscious or unconscious view of themselves at that particular moment. When I began analysis, I had wanted to rid myself of my homosexual feelings; so I chose a therapist who would support my moving in that direction.

In the years since then, I have spoken to many other people who have had identical experiences. While some believed that they had been "cured," they inevitably found over a period of months and years that their desires for same-sex relationships returned. The timing varied—it might be a few months or years—but the result was always the same. Many of these people have never bothered to tell their former therapists about their reversion to bisexual or homosexual behavior. This lack of reporting back may account for why some therapists say they have cured people of homosexual attraction.

Leaving therapy marked a major shift in the way I viewed myself and bisexuality. It ended a sixteen-year period of self-hatred and struggle about my sexual orientation. For years I had thought that my struggle was about homosexuality—yet what emerged was my understanding that there was a part of my own sexuality, a valid sexual orientation, called bisexuality. As long as I could remember, bisexuality had been criticized, disparaged, misunderstood, not given attention, not even written about. Yet now I was meeting more and more people who acknowledged their attraction for both sexes. Even several people who had defined themselves as totally gay approached me to say that they were looking again at their orientation because of recurring fantasies and desires for the opposite sex.

I didn't realize at the time that this period also marked a beginning—a whole new part of myself was about to be discovered—a part that had been hidden from me, from Alice, and from my friends. It seems that my growing acceptance of myself released a new surge of energy. Until this time what had been used to repress my attraction for men was now available to nurture my personal creativity.

At the time I realized that I gained my understanding of bisexuality not only from my own experience but also from many other people who had been willing to share their lives with me in person or through their writings. I wanted to talk about my experience—what I had learned—to other people so that they wouldn't have to go through the painful struggle that I did. In the next year, I began to move away from practicing law and became more involved with sex education. I began speaking, along with Alice, at various sex education courses and conferences, devoted more time to expanding the bisexual and gay support groups in Philadelphia, and did phone or in-person counseling for three or four people a week who were struggling with the same issues in their own marriages. During this time, I realized the need for this book and decided to leave law and devote my full-time effort toward writing our story.

Five

Bisexuality Means Being a Sexual Person

When I compare the ten years during which I was denying my bisexual feelings with the past eight in which I have given myself the freedom to express my love for men and for women, I can see a phenomenal difference. My self-confidence, my ability to relate to people, and my creative energy in many areas have blossomed, positively shifting from one end of the spectrum to the other.

There were many years of denial in which I invested enormous amounts of energy in hiding the real me from my friends. I was so afraid of being found out that I curtailed my natural self-expression. I hid the fact that I liked to bake, that I sang well, and that I enjoyed listening to and helping people with their problems. My friends were unable to appreciate talents of mine which they have since come to love.

Many times when I was with Alice or my friends, and I had a thought about a man, I became distant, shutting myself off from them. Perhaps an attractive man would pass by and catch my eye, or one of my male friends would give me a hug. Whatever the circumstances, I was not willing to tell the people close to me many of my thoughts. How could I tell my friend Jeff that I felt weird when he hugged me? Instead, I'd hold back and give Jeff a tiny squeeze in return.

Whenever the issue of homosexuality was raised, even remotely, I froze, becoming immediately self-protective. Someone would say the word "homosexual" and I'd cringe, waiting for the roof to cave in. I'd look calm on the outside, but inside I was all butterflies. I'd clam up, shut myself out of the conversation, change the subject. Anything but that. My fears of being found out totally governed my behavior, and I spent a good deal of the time I was with people in a semiconscious state.

I remember becoming friendly with another lawyer from the Attorney General's Office. Many times when I had to make the trip to Harrisburg, the state capital, for a meeting with the Attorney General or some other business, we sat together during the two-hour train ride and talked. Over a period of time, Roy confided to me about some of the problems he was having with the woman he was living with. I longed to let him know that he was not alone, that I too was in conflict about my relationship with Alice, and, in fact, had entered into psychoanalysis in order to get some perspective on my problems. Instead, I said nothing. As a consequence of my withholding, I spent much of the train ride thinking about myself and my own problems rather than concentrating on listening to Roy. I worried that if he learned the truth about my sexuality, he'd never talk to me again or maybe he'd tell the Attorney General.

All that has changed now that our friends and family know the truth. It is much easier to have fun, to be spontaneous and genuine, when you don't have to be preoccupied with guarding a secret. The struggle of weeding through my own internal confusion to find out what I'm feeling or to make a decision has disappeared. Moreover, now I can talk about bisexuality and homosexuality without fear or self-consciousness. This is important to me, because for right now, a lot of my life is focused on these issues.

My friends have told me that there is a definite difference in my ability to talk to them now, compared to the way it used to be. Before, it seemed as if an impenetrable wall separated us. Yet, at the same time, I was totally unaware of how I distanced myself from people. When the barricade was lifted, I saw what was on the other side of my secrecy. I felt lighter, more spontaneous, and I participated more freely in all conversations, not just those having to do with sexuality. When I no longer had to be guarded and careful about what I said, I was more able to talk from my experience of the moment.

I can see now that as a child I had a natural talent which for some reason—perhaps connected to my sexuality and perhaps not—I felt I had to cover up later, the capacity to be understanding and to gain people's trust so that they felt comfortable talking intimately with me. A number of adults, my mother, my grandmother, the father of one of my friends, confided in me over a long period of time, pouring forth very personal details that they withheld from other people. They frequently told me how helpful it was just to talk to me. Yet, sometime in my late teens, I closed off access to this part of myself and became more withdrawn and cautious.

Now in my thirties, I was again experiencing my ability to listen and be supportive to people. Having gone through many years of keeping my sexuality secret and then finally letting the secret out, I was able to understand, in a very personal way, people's fears of being open. Certainly I had learned the value of talking honestly about one's feelings and I knew that the major obstacle that people faced in dealing with their problems was the willingness to talk with others. There was no doubt in my mind that once people were able to share what was on their minds solutions presented themselves. More and more, I found that people I knew intimately, casual acquaintances as well as people who contacted me for help in dealing with their bisexuality, sought me out for counsel.

Just recently my friend Jeff telephoned and asked me to come over because he was very upset about his lover Barbara's involvement with another man. He spoke quickly and sounded anxious and upset on the phone. I immediately went to his house. Over the next two hours, Jeff shared his deepest fears of losing Barbara and reexperienced the pain of old memories of situations similar to this one. At times he cried and his whole body shook with emotion. I did my best to comfort him as he poured out his hurt, holding, listening, and talking quietly to him. Eventually, his anger and fear subsided, and he felt calmer and more realistic. It was a very intimate and powerful experience for both of us to have shared, and one that could not have place prior to my "coming out."

Rediscovering my talent for encouraging people's natural abilities and helping them with their problems has made me feel that I have something unique to contribute to other people. Now that I have more of myself accessible to me, I find that I have more to share and other people look to me as a valuable source of comfort and advice. Besides counseling individuals and working with groups, I currently talk to over two hundred people a year on the telephone about bisexuality in marriage.

I receive on the average two or three referral calls a week from the Gay Switchboard and various counseling centers throughout Philadelphia. While no two calls are alike, many of them begin in a very similar way. First, the man or woman on the other end will ask for me and then ascertain it really is Barry Kohn he is talking to. From the anxious tone in the caller's voice, I immediately know that he is a person who is dealing with his bisexual or homosexual feelings.

For many callers, it's the first time that they've ever acknowledged to anyone else that bisexuality or homosexuality is an issue for them and they're often hesitant and unsure about how to begin. Having been there myself, I am patient because I know what they're going through.

Next I'm generally asked, "How can I be sure that you won't tell anybody else?" Most people are extremely concerned about confidentiality. Just recently a man called and started by saying, "I don't want anybody to know anything about it." I knew that for him calling me on the phone was a major step in his life, and he was fearful where it would all end. His voice was quivering. He worried about telling me things he wanted to tell me, and yet he had an overwhelming need to talk.

Many times I'm on the phone with callers for twenty minutes or more, for the most part just listening, thereby providing a positive atmosphere for them to express all their feelings—their attraction for men or women, their guilt for having had homosexual contacts and not telling their partners, or their total confusion. I do tell them that it's very natural for them to have all these conflicting feelings and thoughts and acknowledge their courage to reach out and seek help.

After they've told me the reason for their call, I give them a brief summary of my background and my own experience with bisexuality and marriage—that I've been a lawyer, that I've been married for thirteen years, that I have a child who is seven years old, and that I have relationships with both men and women. Frequently, they ask me questions. I don't have to say a great deal; just by letting them know that I'm coming from a similar place, it becomes safer for them to talk.

I know that there are many people out there who are married and who suffer because of bisexual feelings. Most of these people feel terrible about themselves and guilty about being married. They are frightened that if they allow themselves to experience the slightest feeling for a person of the same sex, they immediately will have to give up everything they value and declare themselves as gay. This fear keeps them trapped within themselves. I've talked to men who are sixty years old and have never mentioned the homosexual feelings they've carried with them for a lifetime. Although some have never acted on these feelings, when they begin to talk, it's as if a tremendous burden is lifted. It's then that I can let them know the options that do exist—people they can talk to, books to read, support groups, counseling.

Once my own bisexuality was no longer a secret, more energy was released to become involved in other interests as well. I began enjoying music again as I used to when I took singing lessons as a teenager. No longer did I limit my music appreciation to listening. Now I was willing to push myself to perform and be seen. I went dancing at local discos; I took weekly singing lessons, and I performed whenever I got a chance. Alice and I organized monthly musical get-togethers where friends could sing or play instruments.

During the fall of 1976, after I returned from my trip to the Northwest and even as I was still working for the Justice Department, I also started to bake pies and cakes for the Astral Plane restaurant one night a week. I had always loved to bake and had done quite a bit of it at home. Alice used to say that when she heard the sound of electric beaters, she knew something was up in my life. Even though I loved to bake and Alice loved to eat what I made, neither of us had been too eager for anyone to know about the baking and I surely had never given any thought to doing it professionally. It wasn't the customary male role, and there weren't many members of the Bar Association who doubled as bakers.

Early on Alice used to worry that once people knew I baked, everyone would assume I was gay. But the resolution of my personal life released enormous creative energy, a readiness to try the unconventional if that's what I decided I wanted to do, and baking for the restaurant that had been such an important backdrop to my life over the past few years appealed to me. Alice's concern about other people's judgments had diminished greatly during the time I was away on my trip, and she was readier to encourage me in exploring whatever directions I chose. After all those years of dealing with her resistance to what I wanted to do, it was amazing to do something with her backing. The first Friday that I baked for the Astral Plane, Alice and I decided to eat dinner there so that we could observe people's reactions when they ate my desserts. It was fun to overhear their positive comments.

Another major change in my life was that I started running about a year ago. For years my friend Oliver had urged me to take up running. Despite his testimonials about the physical and psychological benefits—he claimed that after a good run he could think much more clearly—I repeatedly refused to join him. I assured him that running held no interest for me.

During my visit to San Francisco, Oliver's words began to sink in. One afternoon, I accompanied him to the park for one of his runs. As I walked along the shore of the bay and looked at the runners, I was struck by the expressions on their faces; they radiated well-being and contentment.

In the past, every time I had considered running, I was reminded of all my painful childhood memories of being a nonathlete. I dreaded gym class. Even the D I got on my report card was a gift from the teacher. One of my worst memories is running in baseball games; as I rounded the bases, the other kids shouted comments and jeered at my slowness and awkwardness. The more they taunted me, the harder it was for me to run.

Yet here I was as an adult, ready to consider taking up the challenge of running. Something about that San Francisco experience had stuck with me. Back in Philadelphia, I found myself buying running shoes and clothing and working up the necessary enthusiasm to overcome my incredible resistance.

The first time I ran, I was very embarrassed. I was afraid of looking foolish and being spotted by one of my neighbors. It was hard to get out of the house, but I ran anyway a couple times around Rittenhouse Square and it turned out not to be so bad. In fact, I kind of liked it. After a couple of months, I was running about three miles every other day. In late July, my close friend Mark asked me if I wanted to train for the November Marathon in Philadelphia. I laughed at him and said "Me?" I didn't give him an answer for three weeks, even though each week he'd ask me again. "Could I actually train for a marathon, me a nonathlete?" Finally, I consented.

Immediately, we went into training. I surrendered completely to Mark; he became my trainer. By the time of the marathon, we were running about fifty miles a week. Mark was concerned that we were not well enough prepared and questioned whether or not we should enter the race. But, by this time, I was so looking forward to the day that nothing could keep me from running that marathon.

During the months of training, I had relived many of my childhood memories. Sometimes I felt I could not run another step. I would begin crying and relive all my past reluctance to participate in sports, the name-calling and anger at the world for asking me to play. Mark listened to my complaints and talked to me about other athletes who were constantly facing barriers and surmounting them. He never let me give in to my frustration.

Finally, the day of the marathon arrived. It was bitter cold with a steady wind. I was scared and determined. Would I be able to run twenty-six miles? I had told many of my friends about the marathon, yet I was still very surprised when so many of them showed up in bad weather to cheer me on. Oliver, too, was there. He had come from South Carolina just to run with me. My father, my brothers, and my sister showed up as well. My friend Jeff ran eight miles with me, another friend, David, ran the last sixteen miles, and several other friends ran shorter distances. My two brothers ran the last mile with me. All along the course, friends appeared in cars, on bikes, with water or Coke, urging me on. Each time I passed Mark, who was ahead of me in the race, he smiled and waved.

The race was grueling. I began to experience extreme fatigue around the twenty-first mile. My face was numb and distorted from the cold. As I got about a half mile from the finishing point, I began to hear shouts of "Go, Barry, go!" My friends were cheering for me. With all this support, I knew that there was no way that I would not complete the race. As I crossed the finish line I saw them all grouped together—about twenty-five of them clapping, smiling, and yelling for me. It was one of the most amazing and rewarding moments of my life. I had completed the marathon.

Becoming a more creative person and getting in touch with untapped sources of energy is one way in which "coming out" has expanded my life. The other relates more directly to who I am as a sexual person. During the years of repression, I was so preoccupied with the issue of homosexuality that my attraction for women was pretty much limited to Alice. Then, in the early months of accepting my homosexual feelings, I experienced such relief and release of built-up tension, that I became even more intent on experiencing all of my fantasies of sex with men.

Now that I've gained acceptance of my bisexual feelings, I have been able to get a better perspective on them. The issue of homosexuality has begun to lessen in intensity and importance, and I find my attention shifting. My thoughts and fantasies now are more equally divided between men and women.

I used to think of sex with men and women as very different. Men, I thought, were more genitally oriented, and much more open to experimentation. Women, in my view, were sensual, interested in being talked to and touched, but more restricted in their willingness to experiment. Many other men I have talked to about sex also have held this point of view. However, as I have had sex with more men and women, and talked about sex with many people, I find that these ideas are only stereotypes that more often than not have no validity. Just as I have met women who are eager to try anything in sex that can be imagined, I have met men who are very puritanical and held-back about sexual experimentation.

It seems that sexual inhibitions have more to do with past learnings, lack of education, unquestioned ideas about morality and embarrassment, than with gender. Most of us have grown up in a sexually repressed society, where sex is rarely talked about openly. When people hold back from even talking about a subject, it is difficult for change to occur. However, over the past five years I have seen many people more willing to discuss and explore sexuality. I believe that during the next decade we will see a major change in the way the culture views sexuality. We are moving away from old customs and limiting conventions toward a climate of increasing sexual freedom.

While I have had sex with other women and men, Alice pleases me more sexually than any other person. In the years since I have come out as bisexual, our sexual enjoyment has grown and expanded in ways that I never imagined possible. For me, the most satisfying and incredible addition to Alice's and my lovemaking has been anal sex. For years I fantasized about anal sex, but always I hesitated to mention it to Alice. I thought she would be disgusted and would refuse to become involved. I know many men who say that they turned to homosexuality either because they could not broach the topic of anal sex with their wives or because they did ask and were turned down. The irony is that although there's a widespread point of view that anal sex is a homosexual preoccupation, I now know that many heterosexual couples enjoy it, and the numbers are growing. When I finally overcame my embarrassment and fear and shared with Alice my fantasies and homosexual experiences with anal sex, I found that eventually she was willing to please me in this way. I have always loved intercourse with Alice. It's always been a way for us to break through whatever problems or tensions we may be feeling and make contact in a very direct way. Alice knows how to move her body in a way that totally arouses me. Knowing exactly what Alice liked, being able to talk about where we want to be touched, experiencing the familiar fit of our bodies—all these aspects of lovemaking make our sex together very special and it deepens the emotional commitment we feel for each other.

At times I found it difficult and embarrassing to be graphic about sexual fantasies with Alice. To do so required even more openness and trust—but once I experienced the use of dildoes, fingers, and hands to accomplish anal sex with men, and I realized that I could do any of these things with Alice, I did not want to exclude the possibility of sharing something so erotic with her.

Alice and I now include anal sex as a part of our lovemaking. While the initial mention of the subject may conjure up for many people images of feces and feelings of intense discomfort, anal sex has little to do with these things but rather deals with a part of the body that is extremely sensitive to touch and stimulation. Anal eroticism for me has been an important part of my sexual pleasure. More and more people I've talked to—not just gay people but heterosexual couples— are exploring this part of the body and finding it to be a very sensual erogenous zone.

Even though my experience with anal sex has shown me that sexual activity with men and women can be almost interchangeable, I am aware too that differences remain. I would not want to miss the unique experience of vaginal intercourse with a woman, any more than I would want to give up the pleasure of touching and losing myself in the largeness of a man's body and the power of his muscles. There is no need to limit the range of my sexual experience. I can't imagine ever giving up sexual and emotional intimacy with women or with men. To give up either would involve the loss of two different kinds of closeness that I enjoy, that satisfy a deep need in me, and that nurture my well-being and creativity. This is the way I like it. I am a sexual person. And the possibilities for pleasure are endless.

We are all sexual people, and our sexuality is revealed in broader terms than whom we sleep with. Sexuality includes a whole range of experiences, sensations, sexual behavior, fantasies, dreams, emotional attachments, and feelings of love and affinity for another person.

Buddies hugging one another, two women kissing hello, a man and a woman engaged in an animated discussion, a parent and child embracing—all are manifestations of sexuality.

Sexual labels, therefore, are deceiving because they distort the nature of sexual experience. Bisexuals, in our opinion, are not people who prefer men 50 percent of the time and women the other 50 percent. They are people who have the capacity to love men and women, in whatever form that love takes and in varying degrees—whether the attraction be emotional, physical, or a combination of the two.

Alfred Kinsey, who first published his hallmark research on male sexuality in 1948 and female sexuality in 1953, has had a major impact on our understanding of human sexuality. Kinsey presented a new way of looking at people's sexual attraction based not just upon overt sexual experiences but also upon erotic reactions (thoughts, fantasies, dreams, preoccupations). His findings are important because he discovered there are a large number of people who are attracted to or have sex with both sexes. Kinsey found that between 22 and 46 percent of all men are bisexual and about 17 percent of women are bisexual.

In some ways, it is astounding that this research was done more than thirty years ago, and yet the prevailing myth in our society is that there is no such thing as a bisexual person; that one is either heterosexual or homosexual. Kinsey's research shows that human sexuality must be viewed on a continuum, in terms of both sexual attraction and behavior.

In *Sexual Behavior in the Human Male*, Kinsey writes:

> The world is not to be divided into sheep and goats. Not all things are black not all things white. It is a fundamental of taxonomy that nature rarely deals with discrete categories. Only the human mind invents categories and tries to force facts into separated pigeonholes. The living world is a continuum in each and every one of its aspects. The sooner we learn this concerning human sexual behavior, the sooner we shall reach a sound understanding of the realities of sex.*

*Alfred Kinsey, *Sexual Behavior in the Human Male* (Philadelphia: W. B. Saunders Co., 1948), quoted in Fred Klein, M.D., *The Bisexual Option* (New York: Arbor House, 1978) p. 14.

In presenting his findings, Kinsey* classified people's sexuality along a seven-point scale, ranging from exclusively heterosexual (indicated by a 0) to exclusively homosexual (indicated by a 6). The categories in between showed a continuum of heterosexual and homosexual activity.

Exclusively heterosexual	0
Predominantly heterosexual with incidental homosexual activity	1
Predominantly heterosexual with more than incidental homosexual activity	2
Equally heterosexual and homosexual	3
Predominantly homosexual with more than incidental heterosexual activity	4
Predominantly homosexual with incidental heterosexual activity	5
Exclusively homosexual	6

It is significant to note that Kinsey's research showed that only about 5 percent of the male population fell into the categories designated equally heterosexual or homosexual. A much larger group, however, about 22 to 46 percent (depending on the period studied) were classified somewhere between 1 and 5. It is no wonder that so many people go through their lives worried and confused about the fact that they have attraction for both sexes. We live in a society that continues to assert that a person must be either straight or gay. Yet upwards of one-quarter to one-half the population has experienced attraction for or had actual experiences with both sexes.

One further observation needs to be made about Kinsey's finding that there is a much lower percentage of women than men who can be classified as bisexual. We know that as a result of the women's liberation movement, the accessibility of birth control, as well as more permissive sexual attitudes generally, only now is women's sexuality going through a major revolution. Over the past five years, there has been an explosion of literature on women's sexuality. Furthermore, widespread emergence of women's consciousness-raising and political activist groups has encouraged more women to talk openly about their sexual experiences and to assert their rights to determine their own sexual orientation and activities. In

*Ibid., p. 15.

my own circle of friends, I have seen a tremendous rise in women's awareness about their bodies and their sexual feelings. As a result, I believe that there has already been a sharp rise in the number of women who are becoming aware of and are willing to explore their bisexuality, compared to the early fifties when Kinsey examined women's sexual attitudes.

From my experience, people who are attracted to both sexes remain the most confused, ambivalent, and secretive about their sexual feelings. They have grown up believing that there is no such thing as bisexuality. They relate well to the opposite sex, and yet they are still attracted to people of the same sex. We all grew up with the subtle message that if you have to be one or the other, it's better to be straight. So that's what most people have chosen. If their same-sex feelings continue to surface, they feel guilty. Many have not yet had any personal contact with people who are comfortable with their bisexual feelings, and others, similar to our experience, are not ever aware that there is such a thing as bisexuality. Unlike gays and straights, there is still no bisexual subculture for people to turn to.

There has been virtually no literature on bisexuality. Frequently, I am asked to recommend books on the subject, and I am forced to use books on homosexuality as the next best alternative. Sometimes these books do more harm than good, because they argue against bisexuality as a legitimate sexual orientation.

One exception to this situation is a new book called *The Bisexual Option*, by Fred Klein. Dr. Klein is a psychiatrist and the director of the Institute of Sexual Behavior in New York. He uses his experiences as a therapist and researcher to describe bisexuality, as well as to discuss bisexual life-style, art, and history.

In a chapter entitled, "What Is Bisexuality?" Dr. Klein describes three different kinds of bisexuality: transitional, historical, and sequential. He defines these three categories as follows:

> A common view holds that all bisexuals are in a transitory stage—usually from heterosexuality to homosexuality. According to my findings and experience, this is true only for a small percentage of bisexuals. Bisexuality is used by such a person as a bridge to change his/her sexual orientation from one end of the continuum to the other. Within their lifetimes, some people can and do change their orientation by more

than one to two points on the Kinsey scale, but usually not in a short period of time. The change of emotions, ideals, and behavior necessary for such an alteration brings about, at times, the state of bisexuality. Often the bisexuality itself becomes the norm for that person, while a few people complete the swing to heterosexuality or homosexuality. For these few, this transitional bisexual period can be very short or can last for many years. It is also a two-way bridge—a person can travel the road from hetero to homosexuality or from homo to heterosexuality.

Historical bisexuality is demonstrated by the person who lives a predominantly hetero or homosexual life but in whose history there are other bisexual experiences and/or fantasies. Sometimes the bisexual history is extensive, sometimes minimal.

Sequential bisexuality is quite common. . . . In sequential bisexuality a person's sexual relationships are with only one gender at any given time. The frequency of gender change, of course, varies according to person and circumstance.*

Dr. Klein's classification of bisexuals is useful because it suggests that all bisexuals are not the same. In my contact with men and women over the past three years, I have met people whose life-styles and histories closely match those described by Dr. Klein.

I would say, however, that Dr. Klein's classifications are insufficient because they omit what we consider to be the largest group of bisexuals: those people, who, like Alice and me, are either aware of their attraction toward or are having relationships with both men and women concurrently. Most of the people that I counsel, whether individually, in groups, or by telephone, fall into this category. Many people do not see their bisexuality as temporary or limited, but rather are choosing to expand their emotional and sexual relationship with both sexes as an ongoing life-style.

The problem goes even beyond that of getting people to accept bisexuality as a legitimate life-style. The fact is that sexual labeling of any kind can be misleading and inaccurate. It establishes just one more box, one more pigeonhole, to categorize people's

*Fred Klein, M.D., *The Bisexual Option* (New York: Arbor House, 1978) p. 17.

behavior. The whole category of bisexuality does not account for attraction to one's self, to other objects, or to a higher universal spirit.

I am turned on by more than just men and women. I have wonderful times masturbating when no one else is around. Masturbation is an important part of many people's sexual activity. The traditional understanding of bisexuality does not include the autoerotic aspects of sexuality—setting up my room the way I want it, with "romantic" lighting and music and then making love to myself.

Nor does bisexuality include being turned on to animate or inanimate objects. For example, it is very common for people who live on farms to have sex with animals. Other people get turned on to motorcycles, leather, terry cloth, rubber, and many other things. Alice feels that taking a shower is a very sensual/sexual experience for her. None of these attractions are covered by the term "bisexuality," and yet there are millions of people who express part of their sexuality in this way.

A nationally known sex educator and counselor, Dr. William Stayton, has presented a more encompassing theory of human sexuality. Alice and I like his formulation because it speaks directly to our experience of sexuality and the experience of people we've talked to. His theory is simple yet wide-reaching in its ramifications. It is based on the belief not only that people have the capacity to be turned on to other people but also that part of being alive for people involves the potential to become aroused by anything in the universe. Dr. Stayton explains his theory in this way:

> As helpful as the Kinsey scale is, it is still limiting in considering potential sexual options. Earlier this year, in a discussion of this topic with a friend and colleague of mine, Dr. John A. Snyder of Philadelphia, he pointed out that Kinsey failed to take into account autoerotic experiences, and erotic experiences with nature, animals and inanimate objects. As I have thought about this, I have concluded that the entire universe may be our potential erotic turn-on. As I have read, heard and discussed with outstanding scholars and researchers in this field, such as John Money of Johns Hopkins and James Leslie McGary of the University of Houston, I am even more convinced that we are born "sexual" and the entire universe is, indeed, our potential

erotic turn-on. Nature's intention, God's creative act, is to produce persons who are sexual in the fullest sense of the word. "And God saw that His (Her) Creation was GOOD."*

In his human sexuality workshops, Dr. Stayton has come to know people whose experiences illustrate the multifaceted nature of human sexuality. He has met priests and nuns who have talked to him of being turned on to the point of orgasm from their meditation with God. He worked with a mathematician for whom math was a sexual experience; his greatest turn-on was a challenging math problem.

Some people will say that to be turned on by God is the ultimate blasphemy, and that sexual experiences with objects, one's self, or someone of the same sex are sick and neurotic. The conventionally accepted point of view about sex is that it is permissible with only one person of the opposite sex. Dr. Stayton puts forth the proposition that, if indeed we all have the potential to be turned on by an unlimited number of objects, then, on the contrary, what well may be neurotic is to limit sex to one person of the opposite sex only.

Alice and I are convinced that Dr. Stayton's theory of human sexuality opens a wider window on sexuality. It is based upon experience, feelings, and common sense rather than on long-standing myths which have little validity in people's lives. It permits the freedom to express love without shame or guilt. And it invites people to consider alternative life-styles, such as the one presented by this book, with interest rather than fear.

*William Stayton, Th.D., "New Thoughts About Sexual Orientation or What Really Turns You On," *Topics in Clinical Nursing*, Vol. I, No. 4, Dec. 1979 (Germantown, Md., an Aspen Publication).

Six

On Being an Independent Woman

As I look back on the experience I went through—the process that this book is about—it was and is much more than a reaction to learning about a husband's bisexuality. At first, it may have seemed like a process of dealing with Barry's behavior, but I soon realized that it was necessary that I, myself, grow up—as an individual, a woman, as a sexual person. So, in many ways, this book is about a kind of unfolding, which is still going on today.

I had no perspective on what was happening to me when I was going through it, but from this vantage point, I can see things more clearly. I know now from my own experience and from talking to others that the experience is describable, that it consists of specific stages, but like any process, people move back and forth between the stages or at any one time may demonstrate characteristics of several.

It's striking to what degree this experience parallels the mourning process described by Elisabeth Kübler-Ross in her book *On Death and Dying.** I've taken the liberty of borrowing the stages as she describes them. The way I see it, to change the expectations one has always held of marriage and one's partner truly involves a kind of mourning process, a "letting go."

I should say that even though what I've written here is directed toward women in particular, Barry and I have found that men

*Elisabeth Kübler-Ross, *On Death and Dying* (New York: MacMillan Publishing Co., Inc., 1969) pp. 38-137.

who are married to bisexual women go through a very similar process. For my purposes here, I will be referring to a woman dealing with a husband's bisexuality.

The first stage in the process is *denial and isolation*. When a woman first learns that her partner has been acting on his homosexual feelings, she experiences intense emotions of fear, sadness, rage, bitterness. The experience resembles losing a loved one. At this time the wife confronts giving up all the hopes and expectations she once had for her partner and for the marriage.

It is not surprising, then, that most women go through a period of denial. Generally, denial is expressed in the hope, "Maybe it can be cured." This was the time when Barry and I sought counseling. Many women I've talked to remember how they ignored all the hints and signs that their husbands had male involvements, no matter how obvious the indications should have been to them. I recall many nights during the time Barry and I stopped talking directly to each other, after we had started therapy, when Barry would leave the house at ten o'clock at night for a walk or some other excuse. Looking back I can see that I certainly had some sense that he might be meeting someone—especially since it had never before been his habit to go out for walks late at night—but I didn't allow myself to think about it.

Another variation of denial is the woman I know of whose husband finally revealed his outside involvement with men to her. She listened impassively and said nothing except that she never wanted to discuss the subject again. And they didn't. It's not at all unusual for many women to go along with their husbands' activities by passive acquiescence, a variation of denial; like many heterosexual couples in which one of the partners becomes involved extramaritally, they let the other know that he is free to do what he wishes, so long as he is discreet about it and keeps his outside life to himself.

Often, the bisexual partner is just as confused. Barry wanted to save the marriage and he would have done virtually anything, turn himself inside out, to keep the peace. Many people try to pretend, at least initially, that it just won't have to be an issue in the marriage.

For me and many women I've talked to, another expression of denial is keeping it a secret. During this period in my life, I had the hope that "If I don't talk about it, maybe it will go away." Telling even one other person makes the issue real, so there's a strong unwilling- ness to do so. It's also a question of pride and embarrassment, a fear that others could never understand, and a protectiveness of the bisexual partner. Although telling others is very difficult at this point, I found that not telling can be very isolating and lonely.

In time, there comes a point when denial is no longer feasible. That's the beginning of the next stage, *depression*. I knew that the problem was not going to disappear, and yet I saw no way of ever accommodating to a new definition of marriage. Barry was just as adamant in his position. There was a general feeling of hopelessness on both our parts.

The tendency is for most people to want to avoid this stage, to run from it. This approach doesn't work. There is no way of eliminating the experience of pain and sadness. This is a time when I thought about leaving the relationship. It is very natural to feel this way, and for some people, this is when the marriage is ended. Generally, however, Barry and I have found that this is not the time to pull out. There are too many issues unresolved. Anyone who has been married more than once, or who has had a series of relationships, knows that the same patterns, if not dealt with sufficiently, eventually repeat themselves in new relationships.

If the relationship holds together during the tough depression period, the process moves into the *bargaining* stage. By this time, I had acknowledged the existence of the problem and I was struggling to deal with it. There was still the hope that it would go away, but for the time being, at least, I knew that I would have to begin to consider a new marital agreement.

Barry and I used to spend hours discussing whether he could have relationships with men, and if so, when, how frequently, under what conditions, and with or without my agreement. When he eventually became more comfortable with himself, he began to want to tell other people. I was horrified. I wanted no one to know. This reluctance to go public began to be resolved in the next and final stage, acceptance.

Acceptance involves the willingness on the part of both partners to commit themselves to a new marital agreement based upon redefined needs. Some people never reach this point. Either they pull out of the relationship or they remain locked in one of the previous stages. No one can say for sure how long the struggle should go on. But, for me, I knew that if I couldn't eventually agree freely to a new kind of understanding in my marriage, then I'd continue to expend a lot of needless energy in resentment and anger.

Even if a couple is aware of all the stages of this process, there is still no way to avoid the tumultuousness of this period. A very important question begins to take shape from the moment a wife first learns the truth about her partner, and it is a refrain that will be expanded and developed with time. The question is, "What about me?" There is no doubt in my mind that this was the crucial question for me, and it is the question I encourage women I counsel to ask themselves.

I knew when I was honest with myself that I had unresolved issues in my own life, and that I could use this time as an opportunity for self-examination. The answers other women work out may be very different from mine, but there is a much wider range of possibilities than most women—who, at this point, are pretty beaten down and defeated—allow themselves to consider. It does not have to be an endless struggle without resolution or reward.

A woman can spend the rest of her life rebounding off her partner's actions, being a "poor me" and feeling no control, or she can start looking at herself. I tried to change Barry, but it didn't work. Then I had to decide whether I wanted to stay married to him and what kind of life I really wanted for myself.

Tony Silvestre, director of the Eromin Center, a Philadelphia counseling center for sexual minorities, has a great deal of experience in this matter. He has found that of the women who are dealing with the issue of bisexual or gay husbands, the ones with a greater sense of independence generally have an easier time working out a resolution. The less a woman has her identity tied up in being a wife, the easier it will be for her to accept her husband as he is.

It's only when a woman knows who she is that she can freely choose, that she can really give permission to her partner to be the way he is. Change, in our marriage, could take place when I no longer felt that I was an extension of Barry, and he of me. I had to know what life would be like for me alone before I could make the decision to live with him, and I had to fully accept the possibility that my marriage might break up. That's no easy matter.

It was also important for me to look at my own experience of the relationship. Did I experience tenderness and consideration from Barry? I had to answer for myself whether or not Barry still valued the relationship, if he was still willing to work to keep it together. I also had to evaluate whether or not Barry and I still got turned on to one another, or had the potential to.

When a person is in the depths of struggle, it is easy for her to lose perspective. It is helpful to keep in mind that dealing with a partner's bisexuality takes time, and that answers will not emerge right away. No one should feel compelled to make instantaneous decisions. I saw a young woman recently who is separated from her bisexual husband but desperately wants him back. Her family is urging her to divorce him, but she feels thoroughly confused. The most helpful advice I gave to her during our session together was to tell her she did not have to make an immediate decision. All the pain and pressure lifted from her. Like this woman, I know I needed to allow myself to feel exactly what I was feeling at any particular time without having to do anything about it. The only thing I learned to count on was that things would change; unlikely as it seemed, the way I felt right then was not the way I'd react in six months.

One very important rule a wife in this situation should follow is to ask questions when they arise. No matter how embarrassing the content of the question, it is crucial to ask it. When I'd ask Barry a question, I did not always get a direct answer, or sometimes I'd get an honest answer which I wouldn't believe. For example, when I held on to the belief that love equals monogamy, then it was difficult for me to believe that Barry still loved me and at the same time want to have relationships with others. Nevertheless, if the question is there, it should be asked, no matter how hard it seems to do so or how often it comes up.

It's important for a woman to respect her own internal process, her individual way of dealing with a problem, as well as trusting her ability to take whatever time she needs. Life is constantly changing, and people change as well. Too many couples get caught up in the initial hurt and anger and make decisions prematurely. It is not necessary to force a decision. As unlikely as it may seem, a resolution will emerge naturally. It is an essential, if trying, part of the process to be confused, and to sit with the confusion, ambiguity, and uncertainty for a while. The situation has to be dealt with gradually, a little at a time, handling only as much as is possible at any given moment.

Barry and I always tell couples to give themselves a year. This allows time to go through the process without the constant threat of imminent separation. When a woman is hurt and angry, she can easily forget all the traits she loves in her husband, as well as what is positive and nurturing about the relationship.

I thought of this time-out year as a gift I gave myself in which I didn't have to make any decisions I wasn't ready to make. I would deal with all the issues around bisexuality and fidelity as they presented themselves. But the most important thing I did was to place the primary focus on myself, not on my relationship or on Barry.

This was my chance to do things I'd never done and take some risks I knew I had to. I was scared to death. It's important to reach out anyway; if not, I would never have moved.

For some women, taking a risk might mean talking more directly with her partner, parents, or friends about what's going on in the marriage. It might mean getting a job, seeking job-training, working on developing some financial independence. Dance lessons, piano lessons, going out with friends, a vacation alone, a class—there are hundreds of ways to break new ground. One woman in my group had been working as a waitress to support her husband through dental school. She realized that what she really wanted to do was to be a nurse, so she decided to apply for nursing school.

Carving out one's own identity may begin with something as simple as going to the movies alone, a facial, a self-indulgent gift. Not everyone has to have an affair, but no one should rule it out. In any event, a woman should give more thought to her sexuality. If she's never discussed sex with anyone, she should start talking about it with friends.

This was a time when I began actively to explore my own sexuality, including my homosexuality. Perhaps it was a way of understanding Barry's involvements, although I suspect that his same-sex relationships tapped into a deep part of myself, a bisexual potential that I had not even been aware of before. In many ways, my entire sexuality began to blossom.

A person doesn't have to think about forming another relationship right away. To begin understanding herself and her own needs can be enough. She should take some time out of every day that's her private time. She can experiment with masturbation, read some sexy books, develop her ability to fantasize. In other words, she needs to get back in touch with herself as a sexual person. Sexuality does not necessarily have to do with a pretty face or a perfect body; it's a presence, an energy, generated from within.

Some women find it helpful to go into counseling, seek out women's groups, get involved in a personal growth experience. For me getting rolfed and taking the est training were extremely valuable. When it comes time to try something new, many people worry about being too old, or they're embarrassed or frightened. But generally, it's the embarrassment or fear or whatever that has kept them from looking at what they really want to do and then trying it.

The issues, questions, and struggles of the relationship will still be there. There will still be resentment, jealousy, and anger. There will be times when one of the partners will not want to take risks and work toward change. All of us have resistance to change. I still do. But if each partner becomes committed to developing individually and if that growth is shared within the relationship, the relationship issues gradually become clearer. The wife can get clarity about the relationship out of what she has learned about herself. And some of the problems in the relationship, her resentments about her partner, will clear up just from feeling better about herself.

Along with taking care of herself, the woman must focus anew on the marriage. Barry and I scheduled play times together, times when we consciously suspended the struggle, if only for a little while. Partners should touch each other, even if they don't want to make love. When Barry and I were in struggle, we got starved for each other's touch, for a comforting word or gesture, but didn't know how to ask each other for what we needed. It also helped us to arrange time together without our child, although it was equally important to maintain a sense of family and to plan trips and other family activities.

The ultimate in acceptance of any situation is the willingness to be open about it, to share one's life with others, to have them know. When I took the est training in 1977, I was struck by a phrase from est's founder, Werner Erhard, who said that it's the secrets of life that keep people stuck. I have found this to be true. The fewer secrets I have to guard, the more I can operate freely in the moment and be open to new possibilities.

I would hate to think that being married meant that I could never fall in love again. It's not that it happens all that often—it can be years between those experiences—but it's a very special part of being alive and I'd hate to screen it out. When someone is interested in me, I walk around with a heightened sense of my own sexuality and desirability. I rediscover a part of myself that I have forgotten or didn't even know existed.

For example, I met Bennett two years ago and have had a deep relationship with him ever since. It was late February and I had been spending the evening with my friend Linda. At eleven o'clock she suggested we go over to a local bar she'd been to a couple times.

They had live jazz and she wanted to introduce me to it. I hadn't been to many bars in my life, certainly not alone, and rarely with another woman. But Linda was not at all intimidated and felt at ease with the surroundings.

There was something special about the place from the moment I walked in. Maybe it was being able to hear live music on a Wednesday night. Maybe it was the "neighborhood" quality of it. It was dark, intimate, and mellow. People were friendly, but they didn't bother us.

We were sitting at a table close to the band, and we'd been there a while. Linda told me there was someone she wanted me to meet, the man she worked for. We went over to the section of the bar where he was standing. I'd actually met him before, and I knew he was a publisher. He was interested in literature, and owned an interesting, kind of forward-looking publishing house. Linda told me that he and his wife had recently separated.

He had a certain cool, "grown-up" quality that challenged me, and his appearance was interesting—sad eyes, a beard. I always look at faces first, and his face had depth.

I wanted to know more about him, but he had a guarded air. He was the most interesting man I'd seen in a while, casually dressed, but hip. After we were introduced, we talked for a few minutes. "I remember you," I said. "We met on Addison Street last year at my block party, but you look so much better now than you did then. You look, how can I put it, less depressed. The only thing is, you have to get rolfed." He was intrigued, and the attraction was mutual.

I've heard a lot of people say that they don't have the time or energy to pursue more than one relationship, that there's too much pain involved. There are times when I, too, have lost perspective or become confused, that I feel like a juggler balancing the different portions of my life. I think it just depends upon the kind of person you are. I've met people who can handle ten relationships and some who can't even deal with one. At this point in time, the less I keep my different involvements separate and secret, the more I have to give to each of them. And the more full my life becomes.

I know that I would not want to miss sitting on the leather sofa in Bennett's study listening to Tom Waits or Frank Sinatra or the Köln Concert by Keith Jarrett. Being with him calms me. I've known him for two years, and I still get excited when I see him. But we never make love right away. Our foreplay is talk. We sit near each other on the sofa, touch each other from time to time, and talk about books, feelings, money, business, us.

When we do make love, it is very erotic. He says he hates disco music, but when we have sex, I turn it on. I like the driving beat, the frivolousness of it, the absence of mind and intellect. Both of us enjoy the feeling of building up sexual tension—pulling back, coming together, turning on, turning off. It's exciting for me to watch him get slowly aroused by me. When we finally get together, the sex is sensual and very free. I'm a fairly controlled, contained person and so is he; when we let go, it's very direct and open.

I continue to have intimate friendships and sexual involvements with men, and I doubt that will ever change. Even though I am married to a man, I get a lot of pleasure from my relationships with other men as well. I make it a point from the beginning to be clear that my marriage is my primary relationship, that I'm committed to my life with Barry and I intend to keep it that way. I think any other person who becomes involved with me has a right to know this in order to be able to choose freely whether to become involved under the circumstances.

I grew up having very close relationships with men—my father, uncle, Howie, and Artie—and I know that being with men fills a deep need in me. I can express the aggressive, sharp-tongued, wheeler-dealer side of me and the very feminine, soft, and understanding part too. Talking about ideas, trading intelligences, is always a central part of the relationship. I like men who allow themselves to be vulnerable and are willing to be introspective, and I think I've always had a particular knack for bringing those qualities out in the men I care about. I can't imagine life without them anymore than I can do without the women I care about. I like the opportunity my life-style gives me to experience it all.

People ask me whether I would have gotten in touch with my own bisexuality had I not been married to Barry. I don't know. Exploration of my sexuality began even before Barry revealed his bisexual feelings to me. Certainly, though, his disclosure provided a major impetus to look at my feelings toward women. It wasn't until later that I realized that sexuality involves much more than physical contact. It has to do with coming to peace with oneself and acknowledging one's personal power and independence.

For me, homosexuality has two parts. The first is the ability to recognize that I am able to love other women and myself and identify the parts of me that are woman and feel good about those parts. The other is to feel erotic or sexual attraction for women. The latter is a much more recent development on my part. All my life I have had extremely close girl friends and have formed lasting, deep emotional ties with women. It is only recently, however, that I have been able to see where the attraction goes beyond something emotional and becomes physical or sexual in nature.

My stereotype of female homosexuality was that it was weird and deviant. Lesbians were masculine and didn't wear makeup. I didn't know there was such a thing as a pretty lesbian. Like most people I had incredibly erroneous myths about female homosexuals and could not identify myself with them. Actually, as I've gotten to know women more intimately, my standards have changed, and it's rare when I can't see the beauty that is in every woman.

I have recently become aware of a pattern of mine with other women that has been with me for a long time. When I see a woman who moves me, who I think is beautiful, or who has a body I admire, or some special quality, I immediately stare. In a split second, I look the woman over from head to toe. Usually what grabs me most about a woman is her face. I immediately compare myself to her. I look for flaws, and decide she is prettier than I am. Could I possibly compete? No, it's more that she wouldn't be interested, wouldn't want me, would not pay any attention to me. Immediately, I distance myself.

I suppose this is what people call attraction. For me, the words "being drawn to" describe the experience better. There's something about this woman that makes me sit up and take notice. It's not just a pretty face; it's her bearing, the way she conducts herself. It has to do with a kind of energy, the internal sense of self that she generates.

About a year ago, I was at a birthday party for a friend and a beautiful woman entered the room. She had just arrived from New York and a number of people who knew her made a fuss over her as soon as she came in. She was the star of a popular TV soap opera. I knew from my friend that she was also gay. I was attracted—she radiated a kind of presence and vitality that I always find intriguing in a woman—and I was also immediately jealous. Don't think I was going to join the crowd of admirers flocking around her!

Later in the evening, though, we began to talk. I liked her. We had a lot to talk about, including a mutual affection for soap operas. Suddenly, it was as if there was no one else in the room. Here was this wonderful woman who could have had her choice of anyone there, and the person she wanted to be with was me. I realized that for many years I had admired certain women but had not known what to do with these feelings.

We left the party together. Perhaps knowing that she was a lesbian and seeing that she obviously felt good about herself made it easier for me to think about sex with her. With the physical barriers lifted, there was an immediate openness between us. I had experienced seduction and attraction with men, but this was the first time I had encountered playfulness and enticement from a woman. I loved being the object of it. She was smart, sophisticated, and direct.

Exploring her body was like getting to know my own. Her openness allowed me to see her vulnerability and softness as well, and that, perhaps, is the element of any person that moves me the most. She had a thin body, similar to mine but with small, full breasts that had not gone through the process of nursing a baby. Because of this, her breasts seemed younger than mine and reminded me of my body some years earlier.

Her looks were very appealing. She had long silky hair and I liked to touch it. I've always admired women with beautiful, healthy looking hair. I liked her femininity. We spent a number of hours together, long, lazy hours full of talk and sharing. I rubbed her body; she rubbed mine. There would be moments when suddenly we got very aroused and would hold each other and hug and kiss. In the end, we put a vibrator between us and together we reached orgasm.

She went back to New York the next day and I haven't seen her since. But I have warm memories of our encounter. I expect that we will get together in the future. I don't know if we will still be attracted and want to be physical with each other. But I feel good about the intimacy we shared. I've tuned in occasionally to the soap opera in which she appears, and I smile to myself when I see her—a warm, private little memory.

For most of my life, I rarely touched another woman, even to hug or kiss. I find now that I like touching women. It's like getting to know myself. It would seem sad to me never to have touched another woman's breasts. The whole time I was growing up I never had the opportunity to do that. A lot of being with another woman is just to be able to touch her and to have her undivided attention. It's moving and very soft and tender. It makes me understand what men like about being with a woman. I also like it when I see the hard and aggressive side of women. There is often a natural kind of understanding. Often I am more direct. I play fewer games.

Saturday night I went to Brenda's; she has been a close friend of mine for several years. I had been working very hard and had no desire to go out anywhere. As soon as I walked into her living room, I felt comfortable. It was a woman's space, warm and safe. There were red roses in the vase on the coffee table. I like women who are in control of their own lives, who make their own money and know how to take care of themselves. It's exciting to see strength in a woman, and also to know the soft and vulnerable side of her as well.

Brenda was cooking dinner for me when I arrived. She knows how taken care of I feel when someone cooks for me. How special it is to be served by a woman, really served—it's a sense of being loved, cared for, nurtured. She made me lamb chops, a Greek salad, brownies and ice cream, and tea. After dinner, she suggested that I just relax on her bed and watch television. I drifted off to sleep, feeling warm and comfortable, and did not awaken until ten o'clock the next morning. No sex, hardly any physical touch, and yet a wonderful sense of being loved and pampered.

It's wonderful to feel generous and giving with a woman, to enjoy each other looking good, to contribute to it, to know that love is there for you. But to experience another woman's love, one must first be able to experience one's own. All the years that I kept my feelings for women bottled up, my relationships with them were much more stormy and conflictual—fights, grudges, feeling jealous of each other's accomplishments and victories, rather than proud. I unconsciously distanced myself and held back my natural feelings of warmth and respect. Now I take genuine delight in the fact that Brenda is a respected and competent psychologist, or that Barbara produces magnificent fabric art. Their achievements reflect upon and inspire me.

Holding back those feelings, by the way, did not just affect my female relationships. I was more cautious, careful, held-back with men too, with all people. My own sexual development is reminiscent of the process Barry describes. As I've become freer, more comfortable, about the homosexual part of me, I'm more able to express my total self. I'm looser, more comfortable, more demonstrative with people generally, and less scared.

My close women friends, the small group of six individuals

whom I've let into my life on the deepest level, are in many ways my lovers. They are also the sisters I never had. Each one is different, and they share many similarities with each other. I have been physical with all of them in varying degrees, over the years, and I have learned to trust them. There are other women in my life with whom I'm close, whom I consider to be friends, whom I love. But it is with these six women—Barbara, Brenda, Cheryl, Elaine, Mimi, and Paula—that in an ongoing way, I most intimately share my life.

I've known them all for a number of years, and we have a lot in common. They are deep women, intelligent, and sensitive; it's probably not coincidental that we all are trained psychotherapists, or that at one time we have all been married. My friends grew up with similar traditional upbringings, and they have respect for that tradition. At the same time they are each of them women who have the will to seek something more for themselves.

About a year ago, everyone except Cheryl and Barbara was able to arrange a week's vacation. We decided on the spur of the moment to travel to Mexico. We had never been away on vacation together before. We stayed in Puerto Vallarta, in three rooms surrounding a patio and swimming pool. Puerto Vallarta is a wonderful combination of sultry weather, beautiful beaches, interesting shopping, and fun night life. The five of us took advantage of all of it.

We had worked together. Some of us had gone to school together, others of us had raised our children together. But we had never spent seven days just being with each other—playing, hanging out, relaxing. We all had moments during our week together when we were out of sorts, feeling alone or unwanted, or thinking that everybody else was having a better time. But somehow there was an unspoken agreement to care for everyone's feelings and to make sure that no one went too long feeling cut off from the others.

By the second night, we had met four gay men to pal around with and have as escorts to the local disco. On our first visit to the disco, I got into a funk. Usually I love to dance, but this night, I was feeling tight and awkward. I felt like the odd one out, as if I were back at a junior high school dance where everyone had a partner except me. A string even broke on my pants. And as Elaine, who always takes care of me in moments like this, struggled to repair my pants, I began to cry. "I don't know the steps," I said.

"I don't know the steps" became a metaphor we jokingly used for the rest of the trip, whenever one of us was feeling left out. None of us liked having those feelings, nor did we want to let the others know about them. But this trip was not about keeping petty or insecure feelings to oneself and pretending that everything was fine. We were committed to being honest and vulnerable with one another. Keeping to that commitment made us feel very close. We pushed each other to talk about it when we were feeling sad, so we also learned how to get through the bad times very fast. I don't remember ever feeling as free on any vacation as I did in Puerto Vallarta.

Our photographs from the trip show the freedom and pleasure that we gave ourselves. We were playful with each other and extravagant, ordering room service constantly, shopping, buying presents. We were loving with each other, so instead of feeling competitive or jealous when we got dressed, we encouraged one another to look our best, trading clothes and jewelry, creating costumes. We were our own best audience. And the photos show that none of us had ever looked as beautiful.

There was something about being with other women intimately and supportively, that allowed us to reveal ourselves. Feeling turned on to ourselves and to each other, we created a very sexual, sensual experience that brought out our power, our vulnerability, our depth, and our beauty. We learned to take care of one another, to be generous and loving, and to appreciate the sexiness that is in all of us.

Sometimes the intensity of being with a woman scares me. Sometimes I just don't want it. There's a kind of merging that goes on with a woman that is absolutely wonderful but can also be engulfing. The experience transcends the sexual act; it is deeply emotional as well. Yet, at the same time, it's become increasingly clear to me that my personal power and ability, my creativity and my willingness to become involved in interests that I once would have considered "off limits" for me as a woman, have all been influenced by the part of me that is female-identified, that is capable of loving women.

In her book *Free and Female*, Barbara Seaman says, "The woman who fills the years of her life by raising a large brood of children will become an increasing rarity, for the social pressures are all against it now. Inevitably, women will rediscover the same outlets that men have long reserved unto themselves—creative work and sex. And women will be whores no more."*

For me, becoming a more sexual person has meant a change in the way I feel about myself, as well as how I relate to the world. I

*Barbara Seaman, *Free and Female* (Greenwich, Conn.: Fawcett Crest, 1972), p. 25.

am freer, more independent, less cautious. I am working with people, writing, singing—the things I've always wanted to do. I am more loving and compassionate. I care less about what others think. I have more energy and more self-confidence, and my increased feeling of competency permits me to be more nurturing in my relationships with friends, family, Barry, and Danny.

At times I still get pangs of fear that people will judge my behavior harshly, but when I have those worries, I also get angry. It is time for the old stereotypes of "whore" and "tramp" to disappear. It is possible to "be a lady" and like sex, to be a wife and like sex, to be a mother and like sex. To give oneself pleasure through masturbation or to experience the satisfaction of intimate sexual contact with another cannot be bad. And it's not even sex for sex that's the important issue here; it's the courage to break out of the restrictions of what was once considered appropriate for a good girl, for a wife.

A woman's power lies in both freeing up and getting connected to her sexuality, but it's sexuality broadly defined—the ability to love freely, to be intimate and caring, to be physical, to know one's own body, and to feel comfortable with it. How many times in the past I held back, waiting for someone else to express an opinion or ask for a date. Ironically, now I see that the more I assert and express myself, the more men are drawn to me, and so are women.

Sometimes I think there should be a new social movement in our country called "wives' liberation." There are a lot of women my age that married when they were as young as I, who have never given themselves the permission to explore their independent options within marriage, who have never even spent time away from husband and children. For too long, woman in general, and wives in particular, have been limited by outdated definitions of what is socially acceptable behavior. Women who are able to take their place alongside men in the marketplace are demanding and enjoying more choice, and are less willing to be constrained in the bedroom and in the home.

The choices I make today about how I want to live my life may change tomorrow. The important thing for me has always been that I not get attached to any one way of being, that I maintain an openness to life and a belief in myself. If I can do that, then I know that I will never give up being a fully expressive woman.

Seven

Telling the Truth

A person who is aware of his bisexuality but hides it from his partner continually puts himself through a private kind of torture. Preoccupation with hiding becomes a daily vigil. There's the ever-present fear of a slip, an unwanted revelation, the worry that his partner will find out from someone else. As much as someone may pretend otherwise or insist that it doesn't matter, the secret weighs heavily on the mind, grows with time, and gets in the way of spontaneity and intimacy in the marriage.

It's not that anyone necessarily wants to tell, or is wrong if he doesn't. We've just seen the costs of hiding—too many times, with too many people—subtle, insidious costs to the partner dealing with bisexuality, as well as costs to the relationship.

Most of us at one time or another have experienced the fun of a new relationship—the heightened sensations, the exciting closeness. It's not uncommon, for example, to spend the whole evening with someone and then want to call him or her the minute you get home to discuss another detail of the day. Yet when we live with another person for a long time and slip into the routines of life, it's easy to withdraw from each other, to stop sharing with as much frequency. We all become distracted with other matters, pressures build, children enter the picture and we hold back a little, deciding in advance what the reaction will be. Soon husband and wife forget to take time out to talk to one another.

When we were dating, Alice and I talked about our grandparents, about growing up, about our perceptions of life, about our dreams. I remember driving along, seeing a beautiful rural landscape, and wanting Alice to see it just the way I saw it. There were vacations when we were so happy to be together that every mishap, each adventure, was fun. The flow of our relationship, the way we were with people we met on the way, even the souvenirs we found, seemed perfect.

Gradually, distance sets in. We begin to censor our thoughts. The process of disengaging from one another in a relationship is usually a slow and subtle one. We constantly make instantaneous, private decisions about what is permissible to reveal and what is not. We hold back from expressing our thoughts, deciding that "It would be awkward to say that now," or "I can't be that vulnerable," or "That would embarrass him." Yet, every time we censor a thought or feeling, we are closing down a part of ourselves and limiting the relationship. It's as simple as that.

The drawbacks to sharing bisexuality often seem overwhelming. I've talked with people who are sure that their partner will have a mental breakdown. Some worry, "What kind of model am I setting for my kids?" A prominent pediatrician who has been married for fifteen years and is contemplating telling his wife that he is involved with another doctor at the hospital where he works said, "How can I do this to her? It's not fair to dump this problem on her, not after fifteen years and three kids."

Often people don't want to tell because they, themselves, are ashamed and disgusted, or else thoroughly confused. It's little wonder that they hesitate to let other people know. A man I know, Craig, is thirty-one, works for a large stock-brokerage firm in Philadelphia and has had an intimate relationship with a woman for four years. He is also aware of his attraction for men. He wrote to me about his conflicts and fears, and I think he captures quite poignantly the ambivalence that many people encounter when they begin to face the truth about themselves.

Dear Barry,

The thought of being a person who has sex with men, or even being a person who wants to, frightens me more than anything I can imagine. I feel I would rather die than be that way. At the same time, I know it's true that I have had sex with men, and that I have enjoyable fantasies about having sex with men. My most intimate and supportive relationships are with bisexual or gay men.

Last night, I slept with my friend Martin. We spent

the entire day together. In the morning we went for a long run. Then we sat in front of the fire and worked on our writing. Together, we had very intense personal conversations with my parents and also with a neighbor of mine, a man in his late forties who is gay but has not acknowledged it publicly.

After dinner we went for a long walk through the country. There was a full moon and we sat by the river and watched the moonlight rippling on the water.

All day I felt very safe. My experience was full. Looking forward to the rest of my life before me I was filled with gladness, glad to be alive.

When it was time for bed, I didn't feel like leaving Martin and going to sleep in another room. I felt that to leave him would cut into the rich and delicate fabric that we'd woven between us during the day.

Still, I was torn. Being in bed with a man seems like an unnatural act. I don't want to be queer. I don't want to face the scorn and ridicule of attractive women. I don't want other men to think I want to have sex with them and feel superior to me because they don't have that need or desire. I want to be seen as strong and irreproachably masculine.

Nevertheless, I got into bed with Martin, still wearing all my clothes.

When I was in boarding school, I had a roommate named Richard, and we slept in the same room for three years. At night we would lie in our separate beds and talk endlessly. We talked about our experiences and about other people, about the school and about things we liked or didn't like. The warmth and intimacy of those talks was very important to me. I don't know if I could have survived boarding school without them.

One thing Richard and I never talked about was our feelings for each other. Also, we never talked about sex. We never masturbated together or touched each other affectionately. But we wrestled together all the time. We were both State champions, and co-captains of the wrestling team. Often when we were in our room together, alone or with friends, we would rush at each other and begin to wrestle. On the bed, on the floor, all over the room. Our impromptu matches became famous and were even mentioned in a newspaper profile of Richard when he became a State football star.

I've never had a relationship with a man that was as profound or as important to me as that one with Richard. After boarding school, however, it was never the same. I missed him terribly at first and wrote letters to him and thought about him a great deal.

But whenever we got together it was somewhat uncomfortable. We acknowledged our importance to each other, but there wasn't the same experience of intimacy. We were too "grownup" to really enjoy wrestling, and we would never allow ourselves to touch each other, or even consider the possibility, And, or course, we both knew now that there was such a thing as homosexuality.

Last night when I got into bed with Martin, still wearing all my clothes, I felt very odd about it. But to leave him then, I knew would feel cold inside. An intense feeling of loss. Lying next to him, my discomfort disappeared. I felt the warmth of his body next to me, and allowed my body to touch his. He rubbed my back, and it felt very unnatural, but he was touching my shirt and not my skin. I got up and took off my clothes and put on a bathrobe, still unwilling to be fully undressed.

We lay together and touched each other, our arms and legs and back. It was a wonderful feeling. Touching Martin wasn't like touching a woman. There was much more to him, and his muscles were more clearly defined. Also, it wasn't like touching a man.

To me, touching a man is an awkward feeling, very formal and almost rough. Now I was touching Martin with the same affection and sensitivity that I experience in being with a woman. But it wasn't like touching a woman, and it wasn't like touching a man. Instead, it was like touching a sort of creature I had never met before, someone from another realm, a place full of magic and powerful feelings.

Martin asked me if he could touch my penis. In a way, I thought that would be very much to the point, very consistent with the rest of the experience. The feeling of warmth and pleasure running through my body seemed most intense in my groin, almost as though it started there and spread out through the rest of me.

Nevertheless, I said no. That part of my body is off bounds. I realize that I think of that part as being somehow different from the rest of my body. As though my cock isn't really part of me, but is a thing unto itself, separate and distinct. Moreover, I loathe and fear it.

What I have to say about my homosexuality is that even with what I've written here, and admitted here, I'm unwilling to admit to myself that I have homosexual feelings, that I have a need and desire to have sex with men.

Intellectually, I feel very strongly that there is nothing wrong with homosexuality. And I can say that my experience with Martin put me in touch with a part of myself that I rejoice in. A joyous part, that part of me that responds powerfully to beauty, to seas and rivers and storms and rainy days and flowers and music. It's the part of me that makes it necessary that I write and paint and dress well and live in a beautiful place.

I would have no hesitation in recommending to another man that he explore his homosexuality to its fullest extent. I could say with intense conviction that to do so would make his life more satisfying and complete, that he would become more creative and powerful and get more of what he wants from life.

Still, I know that I am not willing to do that. I would rather die than be homosexual. At the thought of it I feel nauseated and weak. There's a tightness in my throat, and I find it difficult to breathe....

Craig

In addition to the fears which Craig expressed, there is another fear, that the partner will force them to curtail their activities in order to stay in the marriage. This can often be a painful alternative. Karen, for example, a thirty-four-year-old mother of two who had been married to an attorney for twelve years, fell in love with a woman. That relationship became so important to her that she decided not to tell her husband because she couldn't risk the chance that she might not be able to continue the relationship that had come to mean so much to her.

We've talked to people who say that they have made the wrong choice in a marriage partner and pull out, rather than dealing with the effects of revealing the truth. We know a number of couples who have divorced without the partner ever having been told the truth about the bisexuality issue, and as a result, there always remained a sense of mystery and incompletion about the breakup.

There are risks involved in telling a partner. At the very least, the equilibrium of the relationship will be disturbed. Sometimes the consequences of this are positive, sometimes negative. Marriages do end, bisexual parents do lose custody battles, and people who consider themselves bisexual at first, eventually may decide that they are actually homosexual and do not want to be married any longer. For example, Nora, a social worker from the Midwest, describes the negative consequences that occurred after telling her husband about a previous relationship she had had with a woman:

> Jim was always so suspicious of my relationship with anybody but him, and he was particularly suspicious of my friend Sandy, whom I'd known since we were freshmen in college. He could see we had a special relationship, and he kept badgering me about her, saying, "What kind of hold does she have on you, anyway?" Three or four years after we had been living together he got on me about it one day and I finally said, "So I'm turned on to women, what do you want to know? Sandy and I used to be lovers."
>
> Well, he never let me forget it. Every six months or so, even sometimes when I hadn't had any sexual thoughts about women, and especially when we were trying to work out some issue which involved a lot of trust, he would bring it up again. He would bring it up when it didn't have any relevance to the situation. "I always knew you were a lesbian," he would shout. In the end he said he never wanted me to have his kids because of that.
>
> We're not together now, and my coming out to him is only one of the reasons. Mostly I view his response to this situation as absolutely consistent with his responses to other things. If he couldn't accept that part of me, if he had to use it against me as a defense against intimacy, then I knew, even though it took me another four years to admit it, that I didn't want to be with him.

And Judy, one of the first women to successfully complete an electrical apprenticeship course, describes her husband's negative reaction.

> Telling George about my love for women was like pushing a panic button in him. He got a lawyer immediately and started custody proceedings against me. I had no idea his reaction would be so violent. I know that lesbian mothers, which I'm not even sure I am anyway, haven't been doing too well in court these days, so I'm very fearful about losing my kids.

The decision to tell can never be made lightly, nor without awareness of the consequences. What we can say is that from our experience, those who make the decision to tell are ultimately more at peace with themselves as a result.

Howard, a thirty-six-year-old dentist who had been dealing with his homosexual feelings in psychoanalysis for fifteen years, finally came to the decision to talk to his wife after attending several sessions of a support group.

> I don't regret telling Marie even though it caused a tremendous amount of disruption and turmoil in our marriage. At first it seemed that we would separate, but eventually she decided to stick by me. Since I told her, the skin condition I've had since dental school disappeared, and she's told me I'm considerably calmer and less irritable. For the first time in my marriage, I'm not living a lie.

Some people think they can withhold one part of themselves from their partner and then expect the rest of the relationship to be open and free. But the lie, the thing we can't talk about, is always there. It doesn't go away or diminish in importance, and it always occupies a place in our consciousness. Actually, the more we hold on to it, the more it grows.

Most people have conflicting desires to develop themselves and at the same time to remain unchanged. When a relationship has been closed down for a while, when it's stagnant, the need to grow may be buried. But it's still there. When one person begins to open up, it produces a reaction in the other which, although not always pleasant, nonetheless forces some movement within the relationship.

Alice says that although she didn't feel this way at the time, she now is grateful to me for telling her about my bisexual feelings when I did:

> I knew something was wrong, but I couldn't figure it out. He was distant and preoccupied. Both of us were depressed and withdrawn. We weren't being open with other people either. Before, we used to love going out on weekends. But during this period of secrecy, I remember endless Saturday nights that we sat home together, side by side on the sofa, watching the Saturday night lineup of situation comedies: *All in the Family*, Mary Tyler Moore, *The Bob Newhart Show*, and Carol Burnett. We were not enthusiastic about ourselves, each other, or other people.

As much as it may not seem so at the time, for many people, telling can lead to greater closeness. About two years ago, we received an anonymous letter from a woman, married to a bisexual husband, who wrote about what it's like for her to know about her husband's bisexuality.

> I was also lucky enough to have a husband who was willing to let me share in a part of his life. I have gone out with him to the places he goes when he's alone. It was hard in the beginning, especially knowing what would happen if I weren't with him, but now I don't mind because he's not hiding anything from me. This is who he is and I must learn to understand. It has also brought us closer, because in these places he is himself, more relaxed. He gives me more attention here than he ever does in a normal, straight place.
>
> To me, lying shows a lack of trust, Being honest with each other will bring you closer together. I know I've hurt him or got him mad at times saying what I think, but I feel someone you really love is entitled to the truth. Being married is hard enough without wondering what's the right thing to say. I think he really wants to hear the truth anyway.

Telling your partner the truth makes the issue real and gives both partners the opportunity to determine what they want from the marriage. Perhaps even the boredom of a stagnant relationship seems preferable to the rocky course ahead. By not telling the truth people avoid the extremes—the lows, the rages, the fights—but they miss out on the joy as well.

Some of the closest times Alice and I have experienced have followed on the heels of an angry and bitter quarrel. Typically, Alice would provoke me with questions like, "How do you know you're not strictly homosexual?" or hurl an accusation such as, "You don't value our life together." The fights that ensued were unpleasant and wrenching, absolutely exhausting. Yet somehow, after we had emptied ourselves of all our hurt and rage and bitterness, we usually made a very intense connection. Sex was never better, freer, and more experimental than it was at those times.

Often when a partner finally tells the truth, the couple quickly gets back in touch with the foundations of the relationship, what brought them together in the first place. They experience very directly what their commitment was when they got married, and what it is now. In the midst of the turmoil, that experience can be very affirming. Alice says:

> It wasn't until I faced the possible dissolution of my relationship with Barry that I realized with clarity how very much I loved him and wanted to stay married to him. For the first time in a long time, there was no doubt in my mind that I cared deeply for Barry and didn't want to lose him. This realization that I loved him was not an intellectualization or an evaluation; it was a very direct and simple experience. I got immediately in touch with how deep and rich our relationship had always been, aside from any problems we had. Experiencing how much value our marriage held for me came directly out of his telling me that he had bisexual inclinations, that he wasn't going to change, and that he loved me and wanted to remain married.

Another result of telling Alice was that I stopped feeling guilty about lying to her. As much as I rationalized that not telling came from a desire not to hurt her, I knew that the withholding, the half-truths, and the innuendos still equaled dishonesty. I was lying. Deep down inside, I knew it wasn't fair to Alice, and it felt terrible to me. When I was keeping my secret from Alice, I walked around cautious, worried, self-protective. Sometimes I blamed Alice for making me feel guilty so I was less loving toward her. After I told her, it became possible to talk about feeling guilty rather than having to work so hard to repress the guilt.

Sometime after I told Alice, however, I experienced a new kind of guilt—that which comes from having to watch someone you love suffer. I thought to myself, "It's not fair that she should have to deal with this. I'm selfish. It's more than she bargained for when she married me. Why did I do this to her; I should have handled it myself." Yet, as the days, months, and years have passed, I am convinced by Alice's growth and the deepening of our relationship that the decision to tell the truth was a crucial one for us.

Not everyone shares Alice's and my opinion about the issue of lying. Some people decide that they are willing to trade off the closeness, rather than face the possible dissolution of their marriage and a life-style that they have worked hard for. Stephen, a prominent New Yorker, who has been married for over twenty years, explains why he has not told his wife the truth about himself:

> Since my gay urges are strong and their gratification cannot be denied, it has been hard to continue concealment. Like other men in my situation, I have had moments when I thought I could not go on with the sham. And I have had moments when I hated my wife—not for anything she did or said, but just because I felt trapped.
>
> But even in my most desperate hours I have never come close to confessing the truth. One reason is that a tranquil married life is attractive to me, and on balance it outweighs the lure of gay life. I have several children whom I dearly love, many interests in common with my wife, a pleasant place to live, an active social life with congenial friends. I hesitate to jeopardize all this.
>
> Lucy, though understanding, broad-minded, and in many respects sophisticated, nevertheless has strong and unassailable notions about the sanctity of marriage. She fervently supports monogamy. She insists that the partners in a marriage belong to each other, until death parts them. She thinks that marriage should entail sharing of everything, including one's thoughts. Since I have never challenged these notions, she justifiably believes that I accept them as the basis of our marriage. The revelation after all these years, that I

have not belonged exclusively to her, that I had a secret life of my own, and that I took the marriage vows with my fingers crossed, would hurt her deeply. She could forgive my being gay, but she could not forgive the deception. I cannot bear the thought of the turmoil.

And there is another reason. *If* I had the courage to tell, and *if* we survived the emotional stress, Lucy would most certainly expect me to renounce my gay life (such as it is). I am unwilling to do this, and until I am willing, I certainly do not want to tip my hand. Now, because she is unsuspecting, I can stay out on "business arrangements" or "work late at the plant," and indulge my other nature. I could no longer get away with these lies and excuses if she knew the truth.

Truly, duplicity and concealment become such second nature to the married gay man that he does not know how to be honest.

There is nothing intrinsically at fault with Stephen's decision; it's certainly a choice every person has to make for himself based upon his own assessment of the circumstances. But there's little doubt that some intimacy is sacrificed. In our view, intimacy involves an ongoing intensity of sharing. There are marriages, many of long duration, that do not place a high value on intimacy as we are defining it. Whatever arrangement is chosen, however, it's hard to deny that honesty creates intimacy and dishonesty creates distance.

People come out to their partners at various stages of the process of dealing with their own bisexuality. Generally, we have found that people under thirty-five are more likely to reveal their bisexuality than people over thirty-five. Certainly the longer a secret is kept and the more elaborate and complicated the lies, the harder it becomes to tell the truth. We know a number of older men who have been married twenty-five or thirty years, whose children are grown, and see no possibility of ever discussing their bisexual feelings with their wives.

Younger people do not necessarily have an easier time coming to the decision to tell or dealing with the ramifications of telling. However, there seems to be more tolerance and societal support for a wider range of marital options among younger people. Although no less painful when it happens, there is also a more permissive attitude toward separation and divorce among those under thirty-five. As younger people look to the years ahead, they do not seem to be as willing as some older people to live a life of withholding and evasion.

Many people try to "test the waters" to determine how their partners will react. They drop every possible hint, such as commenting on a particular news item about homosexuality and then waiting to see how their partner will react, leaving books on homosexuality around the house, or talking about other liberal subjects such as abortion or women's rights. What's missing from all these "tests" is that they have little relevance to the personal lives of the people involved. The closest test is to talk about another couple dealing with bisexuality in their marriage. Even then, however, when someone else's marriage is involved, the issue will not affect the partner in a way that accurately reveals the partner's attitudes or beliefs about bisexuality.

One of the things that will defintely ease the tension is patience and understanding. It is important to remember that this disclosure may be shocking, and the partner most likely needs more support now than ever in dealing with this emotional crisis. Usually the partner coming out is feeling needy and uncertain as well, so it may be difficult to provide this understanding, especially in the face of recriminations and conflict. Using other people as supports—a friend, a therapist, a self-help group—may enable each partner to extend himself beyond what he might have imagined possible.

It is not necessary to tell every detail at once. Most partners will make it known how much information they want to hear. Some are curious about every intimate detail, including how much sex, with whom, and what it's like. Others want to know almost nothing. The questions being asked are a guide to how much to reveal. A commitment to being truthful does not mean overwhelming the other person with details all at once. In telling Alice, I spoke about my one adult sexual experience with Timmy and then went on to describe some of the experiences I had had as a teenager. I did not reveal every fantasy, nor did I tell her about the experience I had had with the doctor a couple of months earlier. She was in such shock about what I did tell her that I saw no reason to let her know everything at once. In the months that followed, she gradually asked me additional questions about other experiences, and I answered truthfully.

Those who have already spent some time exploring the whole issue of bisexuality for themselves tend to find it easier to help their partners through the initial adjustment. Exploration may include reading books about homosexuality and bisexuality as well as talking to people who feel good about this part of themselves. It cannot be said too often that the partner will have an easier time accepting bisexuality if the person coming out is himself comfortable with his own sexuality and has already evaluated the negative stereotypes and myths. My own knowledge and certainty were tremendously helpful to Alice:

> I asked Barry endless questions about homosexuality and bisexuality. I just had never given it much thought before. It seemed foreign and bizarre to me, abnormal, and I certainly had never heard of anyone who was gay and married. My questions ranged from "What do homosexuals do in bed?" to "Is it a perversion?" Sometimes I wanted to ignore the whole subject and preferred to put it away and deny it. At other times I was filled with great curiosity. Barry knew a lot. Plus, by this time he had a definite point of view that bisexuality was not unhealthy, and he could argue it in a way that I could understand. He had educated himself, and now he was educating me.

Sometimes a crisis forces the revelation. For example, Jerome, a middle-aged, quite respectable-looking businessman, married for twenty years and the father of two children, first told his wife about his history of bisexuality after being arrested in the movie section of an adult book store for "solicitation to commit voluntary deviant sexual intercourse" (still a crime in Pennsylvania, although nineteen other states have repealed their sodomy statutes). He was booked, detained all night at police headquarters, and then released on his own recognizance. Early in the morning, he arrived home, haggard and exhausted from his ordeal, and when his wife asked him where he had been all night and why he looked so upset, he just broke down, then and there, and told her.

We know of many situations where men have been arrested at rest stops, adult bookstores, public rest rooms, with no recourse but to tell their wives the truth. In Jerome's case, he and his wife eventually worked out their relationship and are still married today. But in many cases, public disclosure puts incredible pressures on a relationship, and many marriages break up after an arrest.

It is essential to point out, however, that no matter how extensive the preparation, the moment of telling the truth is likely to be explosive. Vee, a forty-five-year-old, attractive, educated mother of two, grew up in Europe and met her husband there. She was married twelve years before he told her the truth about himself:

> He just came out and told me in a very open, almost brutal way. I was beginning to be suspicious just before the thing broke out, because it seemed he was dropping very large hints. Later, he said in his opinion, he thought I knew, but the way he told me, well, you can't be kind about this sort of thing, you can't say it in a polite way.
>
> It's as if the whole house came crashing down around my head, and it almost made a noise, and I was feeling the pieces tinkling and falling to the ground. I knew that things would never be the same again and that we'd have to start a new thing, and that was the way it was.

Only repeated and loving reassurance can soften the blows. Alice recalls:

> At the point that Barry told me, it was incomprehensible to me that he could have feelings for anyone else, let alone a man, and still maintain his love for me. In my mind, that was the biggest blow, that he must not love me anymore. Because he kept assuring me that he loved me and was still attracted to me, I had to begin to fit the information about his bisexuality into a new context. I would yell at him, "You're lying. You are really gay. You're not telling the truth when you say that you are attracted to me." He would ask me to look into my own experience as to whether he still loved me, and when I thought about the way he was with me I could see that he was telling the truth. I was not yet ready to let into my value system that you could still love someone and have needs for others, but my own experience that he still loved me made me broaden my point of view to allow that the possibility could exist.

It was one thing finally to tell Alice about my bisexuality and to deal with her reaction. But then there was the rest of the world—parents, aunts, uncles, cousins, brothers, sister, neighbors, and friends. Did I want them to know? Was it necessary for them to know? If I decided to be open, how would I begin to tell them?

It was not easy to arrive at a decision to tell the truth. For a long time, Alice and I had many fears about people finding out. We would not even consider the possibility of sharing our secret. I asked myself, "Why bother?" Why risk having to deal with people's criticism and rejection? And indeed, many people say they are unwilling to have their sexual lives become a matter of public discussion. Other couples feel that the important thing is whether they have worked out their own relationship; they have no interest in dealing with the judgments of others. Sometimes, one partner wants to tell and the other doesn't. And just as there are people who go through a lifetime never discussing their bisexuality with their partners, there are couples who never talk about it with anyone else.

The decision to share the truth about our lives has been a gradual, unfolding one. It was marked by a lot of struggle, and Alice and I did not always see eye to eye on it. At some point, it just became clearer to us that the costs of holding on to the secret were greater than the benefits. As we grew more comfortable with ourselves, more convinced that there was nothing wrong with the life we had chosen to lead, it came down to a question of integrity. Why hide parts of ourselves and a way of life that we considered valid? Although we tried to rationalize withholding the truth, we became increasingly aware of the detrimental effects the deception was having on the relationships we most valued.

For example, for the past year, Alice and I had been aware of the need to tell my aunt and uncle, Herb and Elaine. They had always been important people to us during our marriage, and we had kept up a constant relationship with them. Herb is only ten years older than I, and we have been close since I was a child. However, over the last two years we saw them less and less. When we did get together, the visits were not pleasant because when we were with them, we were not ourselves, and avoided sharing aspects of our life.

By not talking to Herb and Elaine about bisexuality and our marriage, we distanced ourselves from these people we loved. Instead, we expended energy that could have contributed to building the relationship in maintaining a secret. Until recently, in order to avoid the discomfort and awkwardness, we rarely visited them. In other words, it is we who cut off the relationship.

There have been times—too many to remember—when I was with people I cared about and the conversation turned to sexuality or some allusion was made to homosexuality, and I held back the truth. I am amazed now that I have been willing to sit through dozens of these scenes, feeling uncomfortable, rather than to tell the person that I am bisexual.

Most people who know Alice and me now know that we are bisexual and that we have relationships outside our marriage. We have told our friends and parents. My father's immediate family found out at a funeral, Alice's aunt was told by one of her co-workers who knows me, and our neighbors on the block have heard by word of mouth. And yet, with all the people who do know, at times we still come up against our fears of rejection in telling the next person. We wonder sometimes why this should still be a problem for us when most of our world already knows. There just seems to be an automatic response of fear and embarrassment when we first consider telling anyone about our relationship. Let's face it. Talking about one's private life can be embarrassing. Most people are not accustomed to discussing sexuality openly, let alone revealing the intimate details of their sexual lives. It gets easier each time, and I've learned not to wait so long to tell, but I still go through the same initial resistance.

I remember the first time that I shared my secret with a friend. In July 1972, shortly after I had told Alice that I had sex with a man, we spent a day at the seashore with my old friend Joe and his wife. Joe and I had developed a close relationship the last two years I was in college, and he had also dated Alice before I began to go out with her. Another bond was that Joe had participated along with us in the Bethel, Maine, group dynamics experience. At the time, he was my closest male friend, although recently he had married and moved to Massachusetts. This made it difficult for us to talk as frequently as we once had.

I had thought about telling Joe about my bisexual feelings for over a year, but I was wary about his reaction. Since he was a tolerant person and a psychotherapist, I thought he might be understanding. That day we took a walk. As we strolled down the beach, I thought to myself, "This is the time; it's time I let him know what I've been going through." There was an empty feeling in the pit of my stomach and I was short of breath. I debated with myself, should I or shouldn't I? What will he say? I took a deep breath and told him that I was in therapy, and I was there because I was attracted to men. His response was short and abrupt, "God, you're really sick, I'm glad you are in therapy."

I displayed no outward reaction, but inside I felt crushed. I wanted to cry, run away from him, and take back my words. The severity of his negative response shocked me. Why had I exposed myself? Joe confirmed all my fears of what people would think about me if they found out. I didn't talk to Joe about my reaction to his words, but instead, hid them and felt sorry for myself. His words gave me renewed impetus to work hard in therapy and to rid myself of these feelings.

Joe's response illustrates one of the major reasons why most people fear telling others about their bisexual or homosexual feelings. No one wants to hear that other people think he is sick if he, himself, is concerned about that issue. It conjures up rejection and ostracism. No one wants to take the chance of losing the love of friends or family. Rather than taking that risk, people live their whole lives guarding their secret.

We have heard hundreds of people articulate the reasons that they fear telling. People don't tell their parents because they believe that parents are too set in their ways and could never understand; they don't tell friends because relationships that have taken so long to develop will be threatened; they don't tell their boss or co-workers because of the fear that they will be fired or excluded; and they don't tell neighbors because they fear their kids will be deprived of playmates. A therapist we know who lives in the South and supports herself with a private practice told me that she was afraid of losing her clients and being forced to leave town if people learned about her bisexuality.

Each time I've told someone about my bisexuality, it has been more than a question of simply declaring my sexual orientation. I am married. There is another person who is directly affected by any decision I make to share the details of our relationship. If I tell anyone about my bisexuality, I am allowing that person into a very private part of my marriage.

In June 1975 I remember coming home and telling Alice that I had just told a close friend from work about my bisexual feelings. Alice became furious. She said, "You don't have a right to tell anyone because your telling affects me too. I feel as if I don't have any control over who knows about my life. You make the decision to talk about your bisexuality and I'm stuck with it, whether I want that person to know or not."

At first, I didn't understand Alice's complaint. I felt that I was just talking about my own life and concerns. I didn't see why I should have to get Alice's permission to talk about my own bisexuality. However that summer, when Alice started telling people about my bisexuality without first asking me, I understood her earlier response. It was my turn to feel "done to." It seemed to me that Alice had acted rashly, that she was not taking my feelings into consideration. I worried about what would happen to my relationships with the people she told.

After all, a bisexual marriage implies a nonmonogamous relationship, and, for many people, that fact alone is a shock. No matter how couples behave in reality, most people still hold on to the expectation of a monogamous marriage for themselves and others. When two people openly question that tradition, the tendency is to look for flaws in the relationship. Open marriages are still suspect, and the added bisexual element brings into account an additional set of questions. It doesn't matter that most marriages deal at some time or another with one or both partners having an extramarital relationship. No one could grow up in our culture without having a strong stake in monogamy.

What Alice and I realized was that most people were willing to accept the existence of a bisexual orientation in a single person, but were less sure about how it could be incorporated into a marriage. Marriage, with all its problems, still has a certain sanctity to it. The generally held point of view toward marriage does not include bisexuality or any kind of infidelity for that matter. To hear other people's questions about monogamy, at a time when we were still unsure about what we wanted, was unsettling. We found that their doubts mirrored our own, and we certainly knew no easy answers.

Within two weeks of telling Alice that my bisexuality was an important part of me and that I no longer wanted to change, she told almost all our friends, as well as her mother. At first discussion about bisexuality among our friends was constant. But as time went by, and everyone had heard all our stories and problems, there came a point when there was nothing more on the subject to talk about. As a result of our sharing our secret, some of our friends began to talk with us about the secrets in their lives. One friend told us about the sexual problems she was having with her husband; another told us about the boredom he experienced in his primary relationship. It seems sad to me that all of us suffer so with our little secrets, when sharing them with friends makes them so much less formidable.

Telling friends, however, can sometimes lead to strain and disappointment. On at least one occasion, I remember how my decision to tell a friend caused an irrevocable strain on our relationship. The difficulty came from the fact that I told my friend Susan before I had told Alice, and I asked her to keep my revelation a secret. I was naïve not to realize how much pressure this placed on Susan.

From 1972 to 1975, Susan, Alice, and I had grown to be very close friends. Alice had first developed a friendship with Susan while working in her second year field placement under Susan's supervision. During three summer vacations, Susan and I became constant fishing companions and also developed a close friendship. About four months before I talked to Alice about my bisexuality, I went out to dinner with Susan and told her. Shortly afterward, Susan stopped visiting us almost entirely. I didn't understand why she no longer stopped by and was unavailable to spend time with us. For a long time I thought she disapproved of my bisexuality.

Many months later she told me that it was more the issue of having to preserve my secret than the bisexuality itself that had kept her away. Now it was Susan who had to hold onto the secret, and it had a decided negative effect on her relationship with Alice and me.

Unlike Susan, other friends not only drew closer, but a number of them began to undergo their own changes. One of the major surprises that came from telling our friends was the way in which many of them gradually came to describe themselves as bisexual.

When we first talked about bisexuality, most of our friends were totally naïve about the subject. But with the two of us dealing with our sexuality so intensely, they couldn't stay distant from the issue and remain intimate with us. Most would have defined themselves as unquestionably heterosexual. Slowly they began to ask us all the large and small questions about bisexuality and homosexuality that most people have, and began expressing their fears and concerns as well.

For the most part, they asked the same kinds of questions that we had wondered about when we were first looking at our own sexuality. "Don't you think there is something wrong with a person who has feelings for someone of the same-sex?" "If you are attracted to one sex, does it mean you are no longer attracted to the other?" "What do you do sexually?" By now we were experienced at answering such questions. Once the subject was demystified, our friends were interested in looking at whether they were aware of any bisexual feelings.

Some of our friends have experimented with same-sex relations and then decided that it was not for them. Others have moved toward acknowledging their bisexuality. But the shift that has taken place for them is in not being afraid or put off by the idea of homosexual experiences. The fear about what it would mean in their lives to have a same-sex relationship has lessened, as has the concern about the negative judgments of others. They are now more comfortable both in talking about sexuality and in choosing their own individual expression of it.

Sometimes coming to terms with bisexuality for them has been preceded by a period of intense discomfort. When this has been the case, our friends have pulled away from us temporarily, using this time to more clearly assess the impact of our lives on theirs. During these times, Alice and I have worried that our fears of rejection were coming true, but it has never taken too long a time for our friends and us to get back together. It seems that as long as we are unwilling to stop talking to one another, our relationships with friends continue to grow, no matter what is going on in our individual lives.

After Alice told her parents about my bisexuality, our relationship with her mother and her father (who died two years ago) deepened rather than moved apart. Alice's mother has also known about Alice's bisexuality for some time. Perhaps the reason for the increased closeness was not only because they knew the facts about our marriage but also because we had shared a private part of our life with them. Alice was freer, more spontaneous, less withholding with them than she had ever been before, and they were aware of that.

Over the past three years I have told both my parents. Neither of my parents was thrilled about our bisexuality or our other outside relationships. They have told us that the way we live is not the way they envision marriage.

To tell my parents represented the ultimate confrontation with disapproval for me. On some level, we all want to please our parents, and therefore it's their criticism that we fear the most. The expectation both of hurting them and of encountering their opposition causes many people to decide that telling the truth is not worth it.

I told my father by writing him a letter. I wanted him to know, and yet I could not face telling him directly. At the end of the letter, I invited him to discuss the issue with me at any time. He never talked about it and a year passed before I was sure that he had even received the letter. During that interim period, he never mentioned the letter, and neither did I. In fact, his second wife, Dottie, was the one who finally told me that they had received the letter.

Ultimately, it was I who first spoke in person with my father about the subject. I used our book as a way of breaking the ice. My father seemed eager to hear about the book's progress. For him, talking about our marriage from a more objective point of view was an easier and more natural way for him to acknowledge and legitimize our choice of life-style than to talk about it directly. Since that first conversation, I have talked more directly with him about our marriage and our bisexuality. He is always very straightforward in saying, "Whatever makes you happy is all right with me."

Last year, Alice and I attended a workshop in Norfolk, Virginia, that was organized by parents of gay children. These parents were giving advice to gay persons about how to deal with their parents. One of the major points they made was that after you have told your parents about your sexual orientation, it's important to give them some time to integrate this new information into their way of thinking without continuing to dwell on it. In the meantime, they stressed that children should be willing to continue to share other parts of their life with their parents. They felt it was important for parents to see that their children were living full, satisfying lives— including work, family, friends, special interests—and that their lives did not revolve around sex.

Some people I know have wanted immediate, unconditional acceptance of their sexual orientation from their families. In fact, they have made such an issue of it that when their parents say they cannot accept it, they were the ones who cut off all communication. Such an extreme action is unnecessary. For example, I have seen that just by giving my father time to think about the issue, and by his continuing relationship with Alice, Danny, and me, he has been able to handle the changes and to accept our life-style.

This does not mean that it has been easy either for him or for any of our parents. Telling our parents began a process of tremendous questioning and reevaluation for them. We were prepared for negative reactions, anger, threats, and there were certainly conversations that took place in which they expressed their disapproval. Yet we were surprised to experience genuine compassion and kindness from them. There was no way to anticipate their reactions. I found that when I was able to allow them to express openly whatever they were feeling at the time and not argue with them or try to persuade them about anything, they inevitably reached a new level of understanding and acceptance.

Most of all, what parents want is for their children to be productive and satisfied people. They want to protect us; often they think they know what is best for us and sometimes they do. Other times, it is a matter of new learning on their parts. In our case, allowing our parents to share in our lives has given them the opportunity to see that we are not suffering. Their own experience of our relationship has made it easier for them to accept us and our marriage.

When I first told Alice about my bisexuality, she was very concerned that someone on our block might find out and that we would be ostracized. Her worst fear was that a particular neighbor, who likes to talk about everybody's problems, would find out and then everyone on the block would know.

In fact, one of our biggest fights involved Alice's fear about our neighbors finding out. One night the weekend after Thanksgiving in 1975, I told Alice that I had been going to gay bars. It obviously was a symbol to her of my increasing willingness to be open about my sexuality. She told me that she didn't want me to go to these bars and when I refused, she became hysterical, yelling and hitting me and demanding that I leave the house. "What if one of our neighbors sees you walking into one of these bars? They will think that I am a fool," she cried. That was Alice's major worry. She didn't want to be embarrassed or pitied by anyone, especially by our neighbors.

However, as Alice and I began telling friends and family, the fears about neighbor's reactions also diminished. One day in the spring of 1976, Alice told me that *she* had told one of the neighbors. I was really surprised that she had taken that step. The result was similar to experiences with other people we have told. The neighbor began to confide in Alice about some of the problems that she was having in her marriage. Since then, Alice or I have shared our relationship with several other neighbors. Each time, our fears of being rejected were not realized. In fact, the opposite has occurred. Each time we have confided in a neighbor, our relationship has intensified as that neighbor felt free to share some aspect of his private life with us.

We are not sure how the word got out originally, but we do know that most of the neighbors at this point know about our bisexuality and our marriage. We have been told by one couple that we are discussed from time to time when the neighbors are gathered on someone's stoop. Alice used to be concerned about their gossip, but has come around to my point of view: that there is just so much that can be said, and then it is yesterday's news.

I have always been active in our block association and served as president of the club for two years. I know most of my neighbors and value their friendship. They, in turn, know that I'm a responsible person and my life involves more than sex. They continue to be friendly; they always say hello, and their kids and mine are in and out of one another's homes. If anything, more couples have opened up to us about their marriages since they found out, and we have even learned of a few other couples on our street and a number in our area who are dealing with the same issue of bisexuality within their marriages.

Whether or not people decide to tell their neighbors depends on a number of different factors. Certainly a primary consideration is how comfortable people feel about their marriage and the issue of bisexuality. It may depend also on where they live, what kind of people live around them, and the quality of their relationships with these people. Alice and I have talked to couples who have tremendous fears that their neighbors will find out, even though they live in a city location where more open and accepting attitudes about alternate life-styles exist. Other couples have been able to share their life-style in a suburban or more rural setting where one would think that attitudes are more conservative.

The paradoxical nature of this situation underlines the fact that it is the couple themselves who create acceptance or rejection of their life-style. If they are unsure or nonaccepting of themselves, then they generally invoke a similar response from others. Others find us as acceptable as we find ourselves.

To tell the truth does not destroy relationships, but rather builds them. Part of being open entails becoming "known." Now that the word is out, we often meet people for the first time who have already heard about us from others and know our story. We find that being public actually uncomplicates our lives. We don't have to deal with the preliminaries, the detailed explanations. When people have questions, they usually let us know what they are either directly or indirectly. And often, when we least expect it, people willingly reveal their own bisexuality to us. We still have fears and hesitation about telling sometimes. However, where once we feared rejection, we now look forward to the warm, direct contacts we are able to have with people. We have found that when we share who we are, more people reach out and make contact with us.

Eight

A Family Portrait

Living in center city Philadelphia is like living in a small town. Many people who live in our area, west of Broad Street, know each other, either personally or by reputation. This is true especially of families with young children. The business districts and tall city buildings are interspersed with scores of small residential streets, shops, and restaurants. Our street is a bit south of the major shopping area and not far from Rittenhouse Square, a small and elegant city park surrounded by exclusive apartment buildings.

Addison Street, where we have lived for almost nine years, is a small, quaint, treelined street of multicolored, three-story town houses that were built in the 1860s. The homes were built as a development to house the servants who worked in the grander homes on Spruce Street and Delancey Place. Many of the homes on Addison Street had been in disrepair until about fifteen years ago, when a growing influx of people began moving back to the city. During the last fifteen years, most of the homes have been renovated and have soared in value.

When we moved onto the street in 1971, there were very few families with small children, and generally, they tended to move to the suburbs by the time their children reached school age. This has changed. There are a number of families now on our street with children Danny's age who intend to stay in the city and raise their children here. And our neighbors have been prolific. In the sixty-some houses on Addison and neighboring Lombard Street, there are at least twenty-five children.

These days people tend to stay on Addison Street a long time; nobody moves very often. While there are some houses and apart-

ments that are rented, the homes, for the most part, are owner
occupied.

From early spring to late fall there is an active street life on
the block, neighbors come out of their houses, and the pace of life
relaxes. It is hard to feel alone on Addison Street. Sitting on our stoop
in the early evening, we watch our kids riding their Big Wheels, chat
with people arriving home from work, and visit back and forth.

There are private people on Addison Street, people we don't
know, but, by and large, people are friendly and talk to one another.
There's vitality and a sense of community on the block, noise and
laughter, familiarity bred by raising children together. It's also
characteristic of the block that when doors are closed, privacy is
respected.

Our home sits toward the end of the block. It's a white stucco
house with the door and shutters painted black. Like many of our
neighbors, we have window boxes which we keep filled with flowers
and plants. Every year the neighbors paint the curbs white and hang
Christmas tree lights on the trees. These extra signs of care are a
source of pride to Addison Street residents.

The most dramatic part of our house is the third floor. It's one
large room with a beamed cathedral ceiling, a loft, a fireplace, and lots
of built-in bookshelves. The room serves as both our bedroom and an
office for Alice. A king-size platform bed surrounded by plants sits
diagonally on a large area rug in the middle of the room.

Danny's room is one floor below us. Peruvian embroidered
pictures on burlap and a Panamanian mola, brought back from our
time in the Peace Corps, hang on his walls. It's a cheeful red, white,
and blue room, with a trundle bed and shelves that hold his books,
toys, and collectibles.

The other rooms in the house are small. Another bedroom on
the second floor doubles as a guest room and Barry's study. He uses it
for meetings of the groups he runs for gay and bisexual married men.
There's a spinet piano against one wall which serves as a focal point for
our musical get-togethers with friends.

The living room downstairs is warm and colorful. It's an
inviting room and people like to sit there. There are mementos—some
tacky, some valuable—photographs, and art we've collected over the
years. A handsome mahogany grandfather clock, which once belonged to Alice's grandmother, Anna, sits by the door. There's the

inevitable teak table of the late sixties, but other family antiques give the room a sense of history. Both of us grew up having close relationships with our grandparents, and we like to feel their presence in our home.

We wonder sometimes whether there is such a thing as an average family, anyway. We see a lot of families around us who, from the outside at least, look as if they've stepped out of the pages of *Ladies' Home Journal*. And yet, on closer look, the husband turns out to be an alcoholic, or the wife sits at home all day bored and dissatisfied, or the parents are too harassed by financial pressures to pay much attention to the children. It's not that families don't exist who lead regular lives without great trauma or adversity. But most of us have our skeletons, and unfortunately, we feel worse about our problems than we need to because of some idealized, mythical picture we've grown up with about the way American family life is supposed to be.

Actually, then, even though Alice and I define ourselves as bisexual, and we have outside relationships and we spend a lot of time pursuing interests independent of the family, we still see our home as offering all of us qualities we consider vital to our well-being— security, constancy, and love. We don't think that anyone, child psychologists included, has found the formula for successful child rearing and satisfying family life. We're not saying that we've come up with any definitive answers either. But we have found this to be true about relationships generally, and family interactions are no exception: self-denial doesn't work. Children are nurtured by knowing their parents are complete human beings, that they are leading lives they consider fulfilling, and that their parents are willing to share with them their own satisfaction with life.

Alice and I are no different from other parents. We want our child to be happy, to encounter as few conflicts and as little guilt as possible, and to be able to contribute something of himself to others. Toward this end, we can provide a home in which Danny knows his needs will be taken care of (meals on time, regular bedtimes, family rituals), and we also encourage him to experience his own power to provide for himself.

Danny is a "city kid." He walks home from school every day, he's comfortable operating in stores and is more at ease with the traffic and hustle-bustle of the city than many adults who come in occasionally from the suburbs. But when he arrives home from school, he never has to question that he'll find a loving adult present—one of us, his grandmother, or a baby-sitter that he knows well. Ironically, Danny is one of the few kids among his friends who take for granted being part of a nuclear family, with a mother and father still married and living together.

Danny is an only child, but he has a large "extended family." When Alice and I speak of our extended family, we are including our close friends as well as our blood relatives. That's the way it is for us. Over the last few years, increasingly, our close group of friends have become as intimate and ongoing a part of our life as our relatives; we share each other's dreams and secrets, we celebrate special occasions together, our children think of each other as cousins.

Most of our close friends are well established in their fields— therapists, social workers, psychologists, psychiatrists, a physician, one is an artist, several have written books, and more than a few have Ph.Ds—and they are respected people in the community. Although we can be quite frivolous and party together, we also spend a lot of our time discussing ideas and talking about our work. We devote a great deal of energy to personal support of one another; we trust one another's judgment and are willing to take more and more risks toward greater honesty and openness and not holding things back. For example, our friend Mimi has served as a marriage counselor for us at times, and we've also been available to talk to friends when they have problems.

Many of our friends live within a mile of one another so the kids are used to playing together after school and sleeping at one another's houses on school or weekend nights. Danny's closest friend, Rick, who is three weeks older than Danny, is the son of our friend Barbara. He lives only several blocks away, and he and Danny have played together since they were three months old. Every Tuesday night Danny sleeps at Rick's and on Thursday nights, Rick sleeps at our house. He has grown up a lot from spending one night a week with another family. He knows that they have different rules and he accepts that he must conduct himself according to the expectations of their household.

At the same time, Alice and I both are very close to our families, who also live in Philadelphia. Danny is the firstborn grandchild on both sides of the family, so he receives a lot of attention and affection. Frequently, he spends a night or weekend with one of his grandparents, which also gives us some time alone. That's very important to us. There's something about letting go of the roles of Mom and Dad, even for just a little while, and reexperiencing ourselves as a man and a woman that always revitalizes our relationship. And it's a comfort knowing that Danny is having his own separate good times and is developing a sense of belonging to his family.

We have good times with our friends—parties, potluck suppers, vacations, musical get-togethers. Just as in a relationship, memories of the good times can carry you over the problematic periods; it's the many good times we have with our friends that bind us together over time. As we've all gotten older, we've come to appreciate the importance of establishing rituals and marking holiday celebrations. For example, it's grown to be a tradition with us that every Thanksgiving, our friends and their children gather at Paula and Jeff's home in Swarthmore, a handsome college town on the outskirts of Philadelphia. We generally celebrate birthdays and other special events together. We have a lot of parties among us, cooperative ventures in which we all prepare a dish or provide some other contribution. It's expected that New Year's Eve will be celebrated at our house. I usually bake something special for these events and Alice's contribution is a cassette disco tape for dancing that she spends a couple days preparing.

Alice and I usually get away in the winter for a week by ourselves, but we also plan family vacations as well. Two years ago, the three of us camped in New England for a couple of weeks. It's also grown to be a ten-year tradition that we spend a week over July 4th on a lake in Vermont. We've taken Danny there since he was seven months old, and he loves the spot. Barry and I spent a good part of our childhoods at the Jersey shore and we still return there every summer during August. Our life is intense, busy, and involved in the city, so we find that we need these times away for replenishment and quiet.

Probably one of the major differences in our life-style compared to other families we know is that over time, Alice and I have spent more time apart from each other than many couples—and it's not even time to be with other people. We enjoy having time to be alone. Even where bisexuality is not the issue, in any long term relationship, it's easy to become enmeshed inside each other, and you can lose track of who you used to be as a separate person.

In my case, my favorite solitary pursuit is to be in the outdoors, preferably a wilderness area, and I have taken a number of canoe trips and Sierra Club hikes. Ever since I went to the Northwest for six weeks in 1976, Alice has taken delight in having our house completely to herself. Sometimes, when I am away, Danny stays with her mother and Alice has a few days alone in Philadelphia. She says the experience always intensifies her sense that she can handle things on her own, and she likes to leave as much of her time unstructured as possible so she can respond to whatever presents itself.

We are out of the house several nights a week so we often rely on baby-sitters. It has always been important to us to have quality child care for Danny. Alice has a special knack for finding talented and warm baby-sitters, people who are comfortable with our life-style, and who relate well to Danny. Recently, Barbara came to live with us. She was a student at a nearby art school, and in exchange for room and board, she was available for baby-sitting and some light housework. Danny was very fond of Barbara, and especially liked to visit her nearby studio, where she put him to work drawing or involved him in a variety of art projects. Through his contact with Barbara, Danny gained a sense of himself as a creative person, and his friends enjoyed spending time with her as well.

We are convinced that the time Danny spends with our families, friends, and baby-sitters greatly enriches his life. At the same time, we are aware that he enjoys spending time with us and he needs to have his parents around. We would not want to be absent to such a degree that we would miss the daily pleasures and struggles of watching him grow up. We do think that he profits from being exposed to many different kinds of people. We like to think that as Danny matures, he will incorporate into his philosophy of life an openness to all kinds of people and an ability to reach out and communicate with them.

For the past two years, Alice and I have shared responsibility for Danny's care in a "coparenting" type of arrangement. Each of us has primary responsibility for Danny half the week. The decision to switch to coparenting was made as a result of other changes in our life-style. It was a choice based partly on convenience and partly on a newly developed philosophy of child care. As we began to lead more independent lives, it became obvious that it would greatly simplify our days and nights to have agreed beforehand who was in charge. We also became more and more aware of the positive effect on Danny of knowing that at any given moment, only one parent was responsible for decisions, discipline, or helping, and that the parent in charge was much more consciously focused on Danny's needs. Rather than being only "half there" all the time, we found that we could be "all there" some of the time.

In making our decision to coparent, Alice and I were influenced by several of our close friends who chose a coparenting arrangement following their separation or divorce. In one situation, Josh, who is nine years old, lives half the time with his mother and the other half with his father. I was very critical of this arrangement when Josh's father, Jeff, first told me about it. I believed that a child should have one home, and that it would be confusing and unhealthy for Josh to be split between his parents.

After seeing how well it worked for both Josh and his parents, however, I reevaluated my criticism. We began to think about how we could incorporate into our own family some of the benefits of coparenting without having to be separated or divorced. Josh's mother, our friend Miriam Galper, has since written a book called *Co-Parenting: A Source Book for the Separated and Divorced Family* in which she describes her own experience. She talks about the advantages and disadvantages of this arrangement, and makes many helpful suggestions about how to put together a successful coparenting arrangement. We are convinced that coparenting can have tremendous benefit within the intact family as well.

When Danny was first born, Alice and I shared a commitment of being involved parents. We thought that this meant doing things as a family—all together. What we failed to realize, however, was that always being together deprived us of two things—first, individual time with Danny and, second, time alone.

In the years when Alice and I worked full-time, we would frequently arrive home exhausted, not ready for the immediate responsibility of caring for Danny. How unnecessary it now seems for both of us to have shouldered the strain of turning to Danny the moment we walked through the door. Now that we alternate that responsibility, it has changed from a chore to a time of parent-child connectedness. For the "off-duty parent," it is a welcome time of retreat, a breathing space for attention to one's own needs—perhaps a nap, a visit with a friend, an early movie. We had forgotten that the time from 5:00 to 9:00 P.M. was actually available to us, but it now has the potential for being a favorite part of our day.

With coparenting, the question of time and schedules has taken on a new meaning. Somehow, in being part of a family unit, we had lost track of our own personal rhythms. Alice does her most creative work not from nine to five, but late at night. She hates doing things on schedule, and would much prefer eating dinner when she is hungry than at 6. Our current arrangement provides for a compromise, so that on some days she can retain her spur-of-the-moment habits, and on others she is ready and willing to conform to the kind of schedule that works best for raising a child.

It's has been two years since Alice and I first began to share parenting responsibility equally within our marriage. We have a regular schedule of responsibility, but it's important to say that we operate more flexibly than is presented here. On the days that I have primary responsibility for Danny, I get up with him in the morning, make his breakfast, see that he gets to school, and attend to any dentist or doctor appointments, other after-school activities, dinner, bedtime, and evening baby-sitting if necessary. Alice is free to participate or not, as she sees fit. The same arrangement holds for the days when Alice is in charge. Each of us has one weekend a month totally free, and the other two weekends are split up with one of us responsible for Saturday and the other for Sunday.

Dividing child-care responsibilities in this way has been wonderful for all three of us. For one thing, it has removed the tension that used to arise when, for example, it was 7:30 in the evening and both of us felt too tired to give Danny a bath. Now that this task is clearly defined, there is no arguing and no resentment as a result of "giving in." Obviously the elimination of these struggles means a much more positive, loving atmosphere for Danny. Rather than seeing two parents argue about being with him, he experiences predictability and acceptance of his right to be taken care of.

Coparenting within marriage has done more, however, than simply to facilitate our daily caretaking of Danny. It has given us the freedom and time to pursue relationships and interests and still feel confident that Danny's needs are being met. This is an important point, because many couples have asked us how we arrange to do all we do and still raise a child. If we did not have a coparenting arrangement, it would necessitate our engaging a baby-sitter every time we wanted to go out, and we would worry about whether Danny was getting enough attention and love from us. With coparenting, our times away from Danny engender little if any guilt or concern, since we know that most of the time he is being cared for by one of us.

I look forward to the time I spend with Danny. We have our special activities that we enjoy doing together. During the winter, we frequently go ice skating at the University of Pennsylvania indoor rink. In the summer, Danny becomes my fishing and crabbing partner. I'm always amazed at Danny's capacity for amusing himself on our small motorboat. For hours, he plays with the minnows, reels his line in and out to check his bait, or puts together some mechanical contraption out of string and other odds and ends that he finds. When he catches a fish or a crab, I get a lot of pleasure from seeing the expression on his face and hearing the excitement in his voice. I love to see him having fun. For me, it's one of the major rewards of being a parent.

When it is Alice's turn to be with Danny, she is more likely to take him to a children's movie and then to his favorite restaurant, Levis' Hot Dogs. Levis' is a Philadelphia tradition. The restaurant has been at the same location, serving hot dogs, since the late 1880s. On the walls are names of people who have frequented the restaurant for fifty years or more. Danny often asks Alice how many more years he has to wait before he can have his name on the wall.

Alice and Danny spend a lot of time just talking. I am often amazed at the details she knows about his everyday life and his interests. She has a unique way of being with him and focusing in on what he has to say. I admire the deep sense of respect she conveys for who he is as a person. As a result, Danny trusts her and is very open with her.

Although each one of us is primarily responsible for Danny only half the time, we also believe that it is important to arrange for "family times." About four evenings a week, we eat dinner together. On most of these occasions, Danny clears the table, and Alice washes the dishes. Danny likes our family meals and participates actively in the dinner conversations. Weekends, too, provide opportunities for family times. Often it is our preference to be together rather than

apart. We enjoy taking trips to our home in Avalon on the southern
New Jersey shore or just staying around our house on Addison Street
and being in the same place while carrying on separate activities.

The major question that Alice and I are asked almost every
time people hear that we are bisexual and married is "How do we deal
with our child?" People want to know whether Danny is aware of our
bisexuality, what we have told him, whether we are worried that our
bisexuality will have a negative effect on him, and whether we care if
he turns out to be bisexual.

We have only one child, and he is still very young. While we
have discussed certain aspects of our life with him, because of his age,
our talks have been limited. We still have not had what we consider to
be any kind of in-depth discussion about bisexuality. Danny's education is a practical one, grounded in his experience of living with us,
seeing how we relate to each other and to other people. We have
interviewed and talked to many other people whose children are older,
and they have dealt with their children in a variety of different ways.

Our approach on most issues, including sex, has been to
answer his questions when he asks them.

For example, when Danny was about four years old, he asked
us many questions about how babies were born. The degree of
complexity in our answers matched that of the questions. Also, we
bought him a children's book on the subject. His curiosity about
childbirth seems to have waned since that time, and he has not
brought the subject up for discussion again. We do know, however,
that he has talked about it with our friend, Barbara. It seems that at
this stage of his development, he feels more comfortable asking his
questions of someone other than his parents. Barbara has told us that
Danny sees sex as nothing more than a way to have children. He does
not yet have a concept of sex for pleasure, nor does he seem to be
aware of the differences between homosexual sex and sex between a
man and woman.

As we have become more comfortable with the issue of
bisexuality within our marriage, we have steadily increased the extent
to which we are willing to talk directly about it to Danny and allow
him to see us with other people. It's a common occurrence for him to
witness a show of affection, hugging or kissing, among our friends. At
our parties, he has watched the women dancing with women and men
dancing with men.

Alice and I have on different occasions stayed over at another person's house and then come home in the morning. Danny is accustomed to this, and he rarely asks where we've been. If he does, we tell him the truth. From his perspective, it's quite natural that sometimes one of his parents sleeps home and sometimes Mom or Dad sleeps out. One of us is always there, however, when he wakes up to attend to his needs, and if the other walks in a little later, he can see that neither of us is uncomfortable with the situation. Generally, we have seen that children can be satisfied with any living arrangement, so long as their parents are comfortable with it.

In the beginning, we made sure that if someone stayed overnight with one of us, he or she would leave in the morning, before Danny woke up, or if the person stayed later in the morning, we made sure that Danny did not come up to our bedroom. Our decision was based mainly upon our own discomfort with the situation. Recently we have become much more relaxed in our thinking about this issue. Danny usually does not see us in bed with other people—it's been rare, at least in the past year that another person has slept here—but we don't think it's harmful for Danny to know that we have intimate relationships with other people, or that it's fun to sleep with them. He has never seen us having sex with each other or with anyone else, and we do not intend for that to happen.

While Danny knows that we both sleep with other people, he does not yet understand that we have sex with some of them. We asked our friend Barbara to interview Danny about his life. During one portion of the interview he told her that what we do in bed with other people is to "have a little chat" just like he has with his friend Rick, when they have a sleep-over date. He mentioned the names of specific friends of ours who he knows have slept here and he seemed very comfortable with that knowledge. Danny never appears surprised or perplexed when he sees me in bed with someone other than Alice. For one thing he knows my friends, and he has his own relationship with each of them.

When Barbara asked Danny the meaning of the words "homosexual" and "heterosexual," he claimed not to know what those words meant. He was vague about the definition of bisexuality: "I think I know what that means. I think it's two women living together. I know two men, Tom and John, are living together. It would almost be the same thing like two women living together."

Barbara then asked Danny what the difference was between two men living together and his Mom and Dad living together. Danny replied: "Well, Tom and John are just friends, and Mom and Dad are married. Tom and John don't have a girl. My Dad is married with Alice, who is a girl." Then Barbara asked what is the same about their living together. Danny said: "Both have men, and my Mom and Dad and me love each other, and Tom and John love each other." When Barbara asked whether he thought Tom and John kissed each other, Danny answered: "No, I think they may shake hands and hug each other. Because I think kissing is for Mom to kiss me, or my Mom and Dad to kiss each other or my Dad to kiss me."

Danny has always been reluctant to kiss us or other people. While he likes to hug more now than when he was younger, he is still very selective about his kisses. He told Barbara in the interview that he didn't like kissing because it left a "little wet spot" and also because people kissed him whom "he didn't particularly like that much." Danny seems comfortable with the idea of girls kissing or hugging, but he was more ambivalent about men doing the same. While he had no objection to men kissing, he did not want to be there to see it.

It is difficult to know whether Danny's reaction to the sight of men kissing is related to his feelings about our life-style, or whether it is a result of the same socialization process to which I was exposed as a child. At seven, Danny spends the majority of his waking hours away from our home—either in school, at the homes of friends, or at some special event like a movie. We cannot prevent his coming into contact with the prejudices and stereotypes that continue to be associated with homosexuality and bisexuality, and we do worry about what effect the outside world will have on him. We try to provide as nurturing and accepting an environment as possible for Danny both at home and in our choice of Danny's school.

Danny attends the Philadelphia School, a private school in the city that has a progressive, open-classroom philosophy of teaching. The children proceed at their own rate of learning and there is a good deal of individual attention and love between teacher and child.

Most of the school staff know about our life-style. While some of the teachers may not agree with our kind of marriage, it is comforting to know that they, at least, support our right to choose our own values, and that they do not allow any difference of opinion to interfere with their treatment of Danny. Furthermore, since more than a third of the school's children come from homes where the parents are divorced or separated, the teachers are used to dealing with a variety of parenting arrangements. Coparenting is not unusual at the school. Consequently, many of Danny's friends live in more than one home. The fact that there is such a range of family experiences for children at Danny's school makes his own family seem less unusual. The fact is there does not seem to be one family that could be considered more typical than another, and we believe that this works to our advantage.

Of course, the fact that Danny's school environment does not promote stereotypes of the "ideal family" does not mean that he lacks exposure to the American mythology of the family. In our home, as in most American homes today, TV is an important companion to Danny, especially given the fact that he is an only child. Danny's favorite television program is *The Brady Bunch*, a prime example of the idealized American family—the handsome, successful father, the beautiful mother and housewife, the *House Beautiful* home, the six adorable kids, and the wise, devoted housekeeper. Every problem has a solution; love reigns supreme.

We intend to tell Danny more about marriage and bisexuality as he gets older. It may be that we should be telling him more now, but we are going along with our instincts about how and when to give him information.

George, a forty-year-old writer and teacher, who is married and also has a male lover, told his children about his bisexuality when they were very young. He shared the following conversation that his five-year-old daughter, Ingrid, had with another adult who lives in their house.

> The television show included a flurry of excitement because of who was "sleeping with" whom. Ingrid asked John as he put her to bed why people would be upset about sleeping arrangements. John explained: "What they really mean by 'sleeping with' was 'having sex with.'"
>
> "What kind of sex were they talking about?" Ingrid asked.
>
> "What do you mean, 'what kind'?" John responded, "What kind of sex do you know about?"
>
> "There are three kinds of sex," Ingrid stated matter-of-factly. "Men with men, women with women, and men with women."

When I first talked to George about his bisexual life-style, I was aware that he was far more open with his children than I was with Danny. In fact, I remember being kind of shocked at the time that he would allow his children to see him in bed with another man. Today, I see George's honesty with his children as a natural outgrowth of his honesty with his wife. For several years now, George and his wife have dealt openly with the issue of his bisexuality, and their level of comfort with the subject has grown enormously. It is reflected in the ease with which his child talks about bisexuality.

While Danny's questions have yet to shock us, George, more than once, has faced some pretty provocative questions from his daughter.

> Ingrid seemed intent on eating her breakfast, but suddenly addressed me and my friend who had slept over the previous night.
>
> "Daddy, you and Brent are lovers, right?"
>
> "Yes," I replied between gulps of orange juice. "Why?"
>
> "Well, then," she continued, "why don't we call you Mommy and Daddy?"
>
> The question wasn't easy to answer. The outside world presents loving to her as an activity between mommies and daddies. If Brent and I are lovers, we must be a mommy and daddy.
>
> I explained as best I could, and realized again that my three children had to do a lot of thinking to try to figure out what it means to have a bisexual father. I am committed to giving them information and in other ways supporting them, hoping that they will grow up without much of the homophobia which has oppressed me.... What I mainly want to share with my children is that gay love is delightful.

Some parents have decided not to tell their children about their bisexuality because they are afraid that it will have a harmful effect on their relationship. They fear rejection, and the loss of their children's affection. In the same way that revealing one's bisexuality to a partner does not have a predictable consequence, so too, telling a child may have unexpected results. A man from Portland, Oregon, who had been married nineteen years and has a seventeen-year-old boy and a fourteen-year-old girl, told me that his children reacted very negatively to the news that their father had homosexual feelings. "My son has said that he would destroy me personally and professionally if I'm gay. My daughter says that gayness is gross."

Some parents, fearing exactly this kind of reaction, choose not to tell their children about their "other life." A minister, the father of three children, shared the following sentiments on "not telling":

> My chief motivation and interest in life are our three children (ages eighteen, twenty, and twenty-three), one girl and two boys. I love them dearly and I have always had a very good relationship with them even since leaving my home three years ago. I have no indication that they know of my sexual preferences, and maybe it would not make a large difference to them if they did know. I don't think my wife would tell them, for like me, I believe she may think it would hurt them and possibly turn them against her for having told them.
>
> My children confide in me and we can talk freely about many things. We take trips together, play sports, go to shows, and go out to dinner, and I try to take them on a vacation trip each year. But I am unable to confide completely in them about myself. Although I have mixed emotions about this, for I am continuing the "game of deception," I am unwilling to take the risk of being rejected again or of hurting them in any way. I have a good relationship with them. I cannot presently see how telling them of my bisexuality would enhance our relationship.
>
> The "relief" of being this honest with them about my private life—if "relief" it would be—would not compensate for the possible breach in our relationship that it might cause.
>
> Perhaps as they mature, as I "come out" more, and as I become more able to talk to them more openly about the sexual expressions of love, the risks in love, marriage, and other relationships, perhaps then I will be able to tell them, and be glad I have. Perhaps I lack faith. I am basically a rather insecure person with a facade of being an overly friendly person. Perhaps I lack faith in my children's love for me and their own maturity.

Another father who told his children of his bisexuality still felt that there was a lack of communication between them one year after he had told them. He shared this letter which he wrote to his children in an attempt to regain some of the lost intimacy.

> Dear Children:
> Somehow that greeting doesn't seem right. I don't really think of you as children anymore. You're growing up so fast.
>
> I'm writing this letter because we don't seem to have the opportunity to talk as much as I would like, and when we are together I don't always want to use our time talking about heavy things. Another reason is that when we talk, things we mean to say don't always come out the way we mean them. I hope I can do better with a pen.
>
> I want to tell you something about my feelings. For starters—I don't think you could ever know how difficult it was for me to tell your mother and then you kids about my bisexuality. I felt that in opening the subject I was risking every material thing I had in life, but even more importantly I realized that it could threaten the very foundations of our relationships. On the other hand, my homosexual interests were something that I had to deal with. I finally decided that in fairness to your mother and in an attempt to find some personal peace in being open and honest, I would be open with you.
>
> Almost a year has gone by since I told you. I know that in many ways it has been a difficult year for you. I certainly wouldn't count it as one of my better years either. Frankly the one thing that has been the hardest for me has been the lack of real contact that we've had. Sometimes I think, "Oh, God, I wish they would tell me what they are thinking." Sometimes I think, "Do they care one way or the other?"
>
> You know, a father's role is unique in the family. For a period of time children need their parents. This need nurtures love. Women often have a need for their children. A man's need for children is much less strong. Therefore, I feel that whatever love he has for his children is much more honest because it isn't based on his needs. If this love exists (and it isn't automatic) it is based on a more personal relationship that has developed over the years. In my case, I knew I loved you, as I've taken more time to really think about it, I never knew that I loved you as much as I do.

Talking about thinking, I want to tell you something about the bisexual men's group I've been attending and how it has affected my thinking. Someone who was not familiar with the group would probably think that we get together either because misery loves company or because we are looking for sexually stimulating conversation. Believe me, if that were the case we would have run out of things to talk about long ago. The men in this group have all gone through very difficult emotional upheavals in their lives. The basic reason is simple. Life for a bisexual is much more complicated.

Psychiatrists generally agree that there is a wide range in people's sexuality. Some people are completely heterosexual or completely homosexual, so choosing sexual partners is relatively easy and natural for them and their relationships tend to be less complicated. There is a larger group of our population, probably a majority, that fall somewhere in the gray area of sexuality between a pure heterosexual and a pure homosexual. Many of these people are close enough to one end or the other of the sexual spectrum so that it is relatively easy for them to conform to either heterosexual or homosexual life-styles. The person in the middle, the bisexual, has unique problems since by the very definition bisexuals are sexually attracted to both sexes.

Getting back to the group, we all realize that our sexuality has brought unhappiness to some extent in the relationships we have had with others.

We have found that we all have been lost in the muck of these painful relationships. But instead of saying "Stop the world, I want to get off," we are helping each other build better self-images based on real worth. And we have found that there is considerable worth within all of us.

Every person on this earth is a complicated creature. Too many people try to oversimplify their fellowman and want to put him into easy-to-understand categories. But there isn't any real reason to divide the world into Asians, heterosexuals, nonsmokers, hippies, Republicans, etc. There's good and bad qualities within any so-called category. I've been thinking a lot about how important it is to try to judge each person as a unique individual. Likewise, I don't want to be judged in a category. I might be a bald man, a bisexual, a

boss, or a white man. It's true I'm all of these, but the total
me is something quite different, something unique. Judge me
on the combination.

I feel that I've grown because of the group, and that all the
conversations, laughs, and even tears that we've shared have
eased me out of a cumbersome shell that I've worn for years.
Being out has allowed me to think more about and care more
about others. Which brings me back to an earlier point in this
letter. I'm glad that I've had a chance to realize how much I do
love you. Unfortunately, realizing this makes me even more
frustrated in our relationship as it exists now.

In closing, I'm not going to ask that you love me or even
care about me. I would like to be loved and cared about, but
I'm not asking you to tell me what I want to hear. What I do
want is honest communication between us. I know it's not
always easy for kids to tell their dads what they really think.
God only knows, it's not easy for a dad to tell his kids what he
really thinks. But I'm trying. I hope you will too.

Love,
Dad

I recently spoke to the man who wrote this letter and asked him where
things are now. He told me that he hardly sees his children at all
anymore, and blames his wife for the distance. He believes that she
has influenced the children not to talk to him. His approach is to stay
away and give the situation some time. He is not happy with the way
things are, and yet when I asked him whether he regretted having told
his children, he said that he was not sorry at all. He feels that he had
no choice but to tell, because he was unwilling to live a life of lies,
especially in the presence of those he loved.

Sometimes the telling happens quite naturally. Allen, a man I
met in San Francisco, is married and has a ten-year-old daughter. He
shared with me the story of how three years ago his daughter Sarah
learned about his bisexuality:

> It's just that the stuff I was doing in the community and the
> people we know are nearly all gay. So we just openly talked
> about it. I remember my daughter started asking questions
> like, "What is a lesbian?" "What does it mean to be gay?"

> stuff like that. And that's when we answered her questions. I
> don't think there was any time when we sat down and said,
> "Hey, Sarah, Daddy is gay."

Sarah has told some of her friends, but her father says that she is
careful to tell only people she can trust.

> Last week she had a friend over at the house and I came in the
> kitchen and the friend said to me, "Sarah said that you're gay,
> is that true?" And I said, "Yes." And the friend sort of looked
> at Sarah and, you know, did a little smile kind of thing and
> that was all.
>
> I notice that Sarah tells the people she feels comfortable
> with. I think kids have this sense of someone who is not going
> to agree with them or hurt them or make fun of it. Just the
> way I wouldn't go on the bus and shout that I'm gay.

To think that we can protect children from the reactions of others in
this area of their lives, any more than we can shelter them from other
painful realities, is an illusion. It also does children a disservice, we
believe, to deprive them of the opportunity to handle the truth.
Children are strong beings, and the more we show our faith in their
ability to manage their lives, the stronger they become. It is the
withholding of information that makes children uncertain and interferes with their natural capacity for adjustment.

We do not know what Danny's sexual preference will turn out
to be, although his gender identity (sense of himself as a male or
female) is clearly masculine. We believe that the choice of a partner is
his, and his alone. From all that we have read, it seems obvious that
we as parents don't have a whole lot to say about it. After all, most
homosexuals are products of heterosexual parents. In May 1979
Masters and Johnson said on the Phil Donahue show that for all the
extensive studies, research, and laboratory testing on sexuality, what
we really know about people's sexuality comes down to two basic
facts: We are born a man or a woman, and we are sexual.

As far as we are concerned Danny will be whatever he will
be; we hope, though, that he will not have to go through the guilt,
ignorance, and conflict about expressing his sexuality that we did. As
Danny begins to indicate his sexual preference, our reaction to him

will hopefully follow the advice of Harry S Truman: "I have found the best way to give advice to your children is to find out what they want and then advise them to do it." In the long run, we believe that this book and others like it will contribute to further freeing Danny and his generation from limiting sexual stereotypes.

We know that as long as Danny is able to experience the loving and commitment that characterize our marriage, the truth can only draw him closer to us. If we are comfortable with the life we lead, Danny will be too.

Alice says that in her work as a family therapist, she has seen that it is the lies, never the truth, that destroy families. When children cannot reconcile their actual experience with what they are told, they begin to mistrust their parents. In families where trust is in question, the entire family structure and sense of security is undermined.

We do not lie to Danny. He may have some hard times ahead of him, and if he does, it will be painful for us to witness his struggles. Yet we also know that the greatest gift we can give Danny is our loving support to be proud of who he is and to share that pride with the world.

Nine

What We've Learned About Relationships

As we write the final chapter of our book, Barry and I once again ask ourselves why our marriage has lasted. Why has our relationship flourished when those of so many of our friends and contemporaries have failed? Certainly, it would appear that the issue of bisexuality within a marriage has the potential to be far more dramatic and threatening than many of the factors that typically spark separation and divorce. How is it that, for us, bisexuality has led not to breakdown, but to greater satisfaction?

The problems we have encountered over the years we have lived together are really not so different from the problems of many other people; we've had easier times than some and harder times than others. Along the way, we have discovered certain basic principles that have helped us to maintain a proper perspective on what we were going through. I can't emphasize how vital it's been for us to have had for all these years, guiding principles, ways of understanding what relationships need and how they work, ground rules about living inside a relationship. Some we started with and some have developed with time and experience. These principles come from a number of places. The first writer to influence us was Carl Rogers, the humanistic psychologist and author of *On Becoming a Person*. Rogers believed that people could be guided in their lives by certain principles, rather than be forced to "muddle through life" as generations before them had done.

Rogers' principles are as valid today as they were when he wrote them in 1961. Rogers urges people to rely upon their own experience, on their internal sense of what's appropriate for them. His writings have supported us in bucking what was conventionally acceptable and living our own way. He says:

> *I can trust my experience.* One of the basic things which I was a long time in realizing and which I am still learning, is that when an activity *feels* as though it is valuable or worth doing, it *is* worth doing ... the more I am simply willing to be myself, in all this complexity of life and the more I am willing to understand and accept the realities in myself and in the other person, the more change seems to be stirred up. It is a very paradoxical thing—that to the degree that each one of us is willing to be himself, then he finds not only himself changing; but he finds that other people to whom he relates are also changing.*

In addition to Rogers, Barry and I were influenced by the liberation movements of blacks, women, and gay people that served as a kind of backdrop, but also an influence for our marriage during the last thirteen years. Like the work of Rogers, these movements are based on principles of self-expression and human rights and are grounded in the belief that everyone benefits when all people are freed from personal and political restraints.

There's a new movement in the late seventies; a movement for sexual liberation. People are beginning to affirm their right to sexual self-determination, freeing themselves from antiquated myths and stereotypes and outdated information. When women began talking to one another about sex, they realized how out of touch they were with knowing and loving their own bodies. Men are no longer satisfied to live according to narrow expectations of masculine behavior. Gays have openly come out to the public stating bluntly and directly that they will no longer tolerate being subjected to oppressive laws that prohibit their right to love a person of the same sex.

Within this atmosphere of change, more and more people are talking about bisexuality. Rarely a day goes by when Barry or I are

*Carl R. Rogers, *On Becoming a Person* (Boston: Houghton Mifflin Company, 1961) p. 22.

not contacted in person or on the phone by people, both women and men, who want more information about bisexuality. Support groups for bisexuals are springing up from coast to coast. More articles and books have been written about bisexuality in the last five years than ever before, and Kinsey's original findings in 1948 showing that there's a large population who could be classified as bisexual are being independently validated by other researchers. Two such prominent sex researchers, John Money and Patricia Tucker, in their book *Sexual Signatures* acknowledge the large numbers of people who are bisexuals:

> When it comes to sexual behavior, the bipolar fiction of what is masculine and what is feminine posits a purely heterosexual man and woman on one side of the dividing line, and an equally imaginary purely homosexual man and woman—pure transsexuals—on the other side. In reality, people are infinitely varied along the spectrum in between, all capable of bisexual behavior. In fact, it is safe to say that every adult human being has, in fantasy, engaged in some form of bisexual behavior, if not physical contact, to some degree at some time in his or her life. "Ambisexual" describes the human race more accurately than "heterosexual," "homosexual," or even "bisexual," although the degree of ambisexuality varies in intensity from one person to the next.*

Among the books contributing to the human potential movement, *Open Marriage*, by Nena and George O'Neill, had an impact upon us. When we read the book in 1972, we were just beginning to feel the restrictions of a monogamous relationship. Because we felt insecure and tentative about our feelings, it was very reassuring to find encouragement from this often misunderstood though widely read book. The O'Neills emphasize the importance of the two partners in a marriage encouraging their own and each other's individuality and not settling in to what they call "the couple front."

> The meaning in marriage today must be independently forged by a man and a woman who have the freedom to find their own reasons for being, and for being together. Marriage

*John Money and Patricia Tucker, *Sexual Signatures: On Being a Man or a Woman* (Boston-Toronto: Little, Brown and Company, 1975) p. 16.

> must be based on a new openness—an openness to one's self,
> an openness to another's self and an openness to the world.
> ... Open marriage is expanded monogamy, retaining the
> fulfilling and rewarding aspects of an intimate, in-depth
> relationship with another, yet eliminating the restrictions we
> were formerly led to believe were an integral part of
> monogamy.*

The other major influence on our thinking more recently has been the
est training, created in 1971 by Werner Erhard. In the est training, we
realized that our marriage and our sexuality had not "happened to us"
but that we had continually shaped ourselves and our preferences
according to both our needs. We saw that we could separate the
"points of view" and "positions" that we held about the way a
marriage should be—the values we held in 1966 when we married—
from the way our marriage actually did look in the present. We
became aware of how as Erhard puts it, "our judgments and
evaluations" had limited us and kept us from appreciating how
satisfying our relationship really was. We used this insight to validate
our sense of the worth of our marriage, despite the prevailing opinions
about sexuality and monogamy which would contradict our own
sense of what was appropriate for us.

In his biography of Werner Erhard, William Bartley quotes
Erhard on the subject of using these insights to provide a model for
others. He says:

> Our culture does not encourage people to be philosophers,
> and this is perhaps the most devastating denial of freedom in
> our lives. My own aim is to open to people, through
> philosophical reflection, a mastery of the philosophical con-
> texts, the ground of being, the presuppositions and models,
> from which their lives spring. This in turn opens mastery of
> life.†

*Nena O'Neill and George O'Neill, *Open Marriage* (New York: M. Evans and
Company, 1972) p. 43.

†William Warren Bartley, *Werner Erhard: The Transformation of a Man, The
Founding of est* (New York: Clarkson N. Potter, Inc., 1978) p. 184.

This is, in part, what our book aims to do, to offer our ow, philosophy of marriage and sexuality. Gaining mastery over our relationship has freed us to contribute what we've learned to others so that they, like us, can lead more creative and open lives.

Letting Go of the Myths

People enter into relationships assuming that they know instinctively how to develop intimacy and closeness. We expect our partner to know exactly what to do in order to make us happy. Unfortunately, the truth is that most of us know very little about long-term relationships; we've been taught almost nothing, and we operate mainly from trial and error.

I remember when I was young and thought that someday I would meet that special person who would make me happy for the rest of my life. I had no appreciation then of the complexity of a relationship, of the never-ending process of learning to live with another person. Songs popular in the late 1950s—Johnny Mathis singing "Heavenly" and "Chances Are"—gave one the dreamy impression that love was carefree and that passion would last forever.

There is a myth that we should not have to work at a relationship if we are really in love. We have found that like plants, relationships need nurturing. Nurturing can mean just taking a good look at the relationship once in a while. Sometimes, people are afraid to look at their relationships too closely, fearing that there will be no solution if they discover problems.

Barry's friend John runs a greenhouse. He has seen time and time again that if a plant doesn't look good, people *stop* taking care of it. They become discouraged and think that it's beyond their power to restore the plant's vitality. John says that it is just when a plant is in that condition that it needs extra care.

The same is true of relationships. When there are problems in a relationship, people begin to think they cannot do anything about it. "It's hopeless," they decide. Maybe, they think, if the problems are ignored, they will get better on their own, or maybe they'll just go away. Instead, what happens is that the problems intensify and seem even more unresolvable.

We've found that being willing to say that something is wrong in the relationship is the first step toward improving it. This may mean discussing one's feelings with one's partner or else with a friend or counselor. For Barry and me, this process often begins with nothing more than a feeling of discontent. We're not even sure what's wrong. Barry might say, "Something doesn't feel good to me and I don't know what it is." Somehow, just putting it into words seems to mark a change in attitude.

Aloneness

While a relationship can enrich one's life and provide intimacy and companionship, it cannot be used as a shield against the basic fact that, ultimately, each one of us is alone in the world, no matter how many people we relate to. When I was in high school, I read a book called *Captain Newman, M.D.*, by Leo Rosten. There was a passage in that book that made a deep impression on me. I carried a copy of it in my wallet for years. It read:

> I learned that everyone is lonely, at bottom, and cries to be understood; but we can never entirely understand someone else, no matter how much we try, or want to; and each of us remains part stranger even to those who love us.*

The life that we have chosen to lead, being bisexual and married, frequently puts us in a position of confronting our basic isolation. It forces us to be self-reliant and to resist the tendency to expect the other person to take care of us.

Barry and I have lived with each other for thirteen years, we have many friends, we have lovers, we have a child, we have many interests. But, when we shut our eyes at night, even though we are sharing the same bed, we are alone. Neither of us can help the other go to sleep, neither of us can make the nightmares go away or create pleasant dreams for the other. Nobody cares about Barry's hopes or fears quite as much as he does. Nobody thinks about my next day in the same detail as I do.

---

*Leo Rosten, *Captain Newman, M.D.* (Greenwich, Conn.: Fawcett Publication, 1956) p. 269.

The person we choose to develop a lifetime relationship with is the person who we think will *most* understand what life looks like through our eyes. No matter how close and intimate the relationship, however, we can never totally lose sight of the fact that ultimately we go through life separately.

People who are independent and willing to be alone can bring more power, energy, input into the relationship. Knowing they can exist without a partner frees them to involve themselves freely in a relationship. Contrary to those who see their individual well-being linked to the continuation of the relationship as it is, people who maintain a separate identity are not invested in keeping things the way they are. They are not threatened by change, but rather see it as an opportunity to take a critical look at their own lives.

Jealousy

There is no doubt that the kind of life we lead has demanded that Barry and I come to grips with jealousy. It's not that jealousy has disappeared from our lives completely, but that we are willing to handle it when it comes up. We've learned that there's value in confronting it directly, but that we don't need to base major life decisions on something that feels so terrible.

Sometimes I can tell I'm jealous by my body reactions before I know it in my head. It's as if the air has been knocked out of me. There's a burning in the pit of my stomach, and it's hard to breathe. I flash back to an experience when I was ten years old.

When I was a kid, I loved to play baseball with my cousins and their friends. They were all boys, and because I was a good hitter, I was the only girl allowed to play. It was a thrill to be the only girl in the game. I felt special and singled out. It meant that I could have an easy intimacy with boys that I was drawn to, that I had crushes on. The other girls in my class had crushes on Richard Greenberg and Steven Patterson, but only I was allowed to play in their game.

One time I was the catcher when Richard Greenberg was batting. My cousin Artie was pitching. It was a tense moment in the game, and I liked being right up where the action was. Artie pitched the ball in my direction, but it went high, and I had to stand up and reach for it. At that very moment Richard swung the bat backward to gain full momentum before he moved to meet the ball. The backward thrust of the baseball bat whopped me with a thud right to the stomach. The pain was awful, and I fell to the ground, all the air knocked out of me. The shock of it was overwhelming. For a few moments that seemed interminable, I was bowled over, unable to catch my breath. I didn't know where I was or what had hit me.

Jealousy strikes me just like that. It is sudden, unexpected, and devastating. Every time I feel that way, it's as if Richard Greenberg has just swung a baseball bat into my stomach. The intensity of it is so strong at the moment when it happens that I don't know whether I'll ever be able to regain my breath again.

Jealousy is such an intense feeling because it's not only a reaction of the present moment, but taps into so many similar experiences we had when we were young. Feeling jealous evokes every other time in my life when I felt left out. Jealousy does seem directly related to exclusion; I hate being excluded; I feel like Cinderella gazing in at the ball. As irrational as it may be, I am convinced that in the end I will be the person no one will want.

Jealousy relates to very old fears of abandonment, and almost everyone experiences jealousy as a very basic and primitive threat to his or her survival. In response, we will do anything to fight back. The fear and the pain are so intense that it seems as if they cannot be tolerated for too long. There are no rational words, no explanations, no understandings, that can be called up at the moment to assuage the anxiety.

Sometimes what I want to call jealousy is really sadness. It is difficult to accept that the other person doesn't want to be with me at the same moment that I so intensely want to be with him. I hate not being chosen. It's a feeling of rejection, a thought that if I could only be with the other person, I might be able to fill up the emptiness I feel.

Jealousy is here to stay, but we don't believe that it has to be the debilitating, wrenching experience it often is. We have found that it helps to talk directly, just admit straight out that we're jealous, and then examine what the jealousy is all about. Merely to say "I'm jealous" doesn't get to the roots of the experience, what the component parts of it are. For instance, I might say that I feel abandoned, that I am afraid he is going to leave me, that I am angry or sad or that I have tension in the back of my head. When I can actually put into words the truth of my experience, I gain some control over it.

Jealousy is similar to fear. If we stopped ourselves from trying new experiences every time we were afraid, we'd end up in a room somewhere underneath the covers. Most of us have learned that it's important to keep going even if we are afraid, and we feel good about ourselves when we do that, in spite of the fear.

Too often, we cut ourselves off from new relationships or other opportunities that present themselves, and we object when our partners reach out because we don't think we can handle jealousy—our own or our partner's. But we are all a lot stronger and more resilient than we give ourselves credit for, and there's a wider world out there to experience than we allow ourselves to know.

I have come to realize that ultimately it's my responsibility to work out my jealous feelings. I used to assume that if I were unhappy or insecure or uneasy about the relationship, the onus was on Barry to make me feel better. Now I have come to recognize that all of us are basically on our own, even within our relationships. If we try to construct our relationships as fortresses against separateness and isolation, we are expecting too much of ourselves and each other.

When I feel jealous, I am not afraid that Barry will leave me physically, because I know that it would take a lot for him not to want to live with me. My fear is that even as we are living together, he will withdraw his emotional energy. I begin to see the existence of Barry's other relationship as an either/or proposition; it's either the other person he'll choose, or me. I feel protective of myself, sure that he won't have any time left for me.

When I feel vulnerable and raw, and jealousy sweeps over me like a wave, I know that the truth is that I am feeling uncertain about myself. For example, not too long ago, Barry came home after having spent an afternoon with Peter. It was clear when he came in the door that he was feeling good. He had picked up some red snapper, fresh broccoli, and salad makings and was all set to prepare dinner for us. I shouted at him, "I don't want to have dinner at home. I'm tired of having dinner at home. I thought we would go out and grab a sandwich. You didn't even ask me what I wanted to do."

Looking back now, it is obvious to me that I was not angry about having fish for dinner. What I was really angry about was the fact that Barry had gone out and had a good time while I was feeling lonely and incapable of doing very much for myself. I was jealous of his energy and burdened with worry about my own work. It felt like an intrusion to have to deal with his happiness and enthusiasm when I was feeling so miserable. At the time I was too upset to be reasonable. Even in the midst of being very upset, I knew that Peter and Barry don't have the same kind of relationship that Barry and I do. However, because I felt so lousy about myself, I temporarily lost sight of this truth.

I had to get out of the house. As soon as I left, I walked down Addison Street and knew that I was not the same person who had walked down our street five years ago. First of all, at that time I never would have left the house. I would have been scared to walk down a city street at night. Had I managed to get to the street, I would have been so involved in my own unhappiness that I would not have noticed the beautiful, clear sky and bright moon. And I certainly would not have headed for the Astral Plane.

Walking into the Astral Plane is not like walking into just any bar or restaurant; for me, it is entering a safe environment where I know I am always welcome, and where I can escape for a little while. I sat down at the bar, ordered white wine, and for a few minutes I was not a wife and I was not a mother. I was Alice, a separate person.

My way of handling jealousy in the incident just described was to get out and do something for myself. I needed to experience myself as a separate individual, not as Barry's wife or Danny's mother. It was necessary to rise above the belief that my entire survival was dependent upon Barry and our relationship.

On other occasions, I have gone to see a friend, or taken a long car ride with the radio blaring. There is something about being behind the wheel of a car that makes me feel stronger. Sometimes, I just like being in my own house alone, staying up late, singing alone at the top of my lungs. I get reacquainted with my sense of my own rhythms, a sense that I often lose when Barry is around all the time. Jealousy disappears when I begin enjoying myself.

While encouraging myself to feel strong and independent is one way to cope with jealousy, I am not always able to respond to feelings of vulnerability with such decisive action. When I am feeling vulnerable, a little tenderness can go a long way. Sometimes when I'm angry with Barry, I resist his overtures, but I know I need them, and I'm happy when he breaks through my initial resistance.

A few mornings ago he came home after having spent the night with Mark. It's not that I really minded the fact that he had been with someone else. I woke up feeling alone and tense, independent of him. As I sat bent over my desk, intent on my work, Barry walked up behind me and stood there with his hands on my shoulders. For a few minutes, no words were spoken and he just rubbed my neck and shoulders. There was something I got from being touched that made words unnecessary.

Many of us risk losing the person we are jealous of by making sure we don't have any good times together. This is easy to do when we're feeling petty and afraid. When I am not liking myself too much, when I am not feeling strong and potent, I don't set up too many opportunities for pleasure. I become withholding, resentful, whiny. Nothing Barry does is enough to prove to me that he cares, and I cut myself off from any comfort or tenderness he wants to give me.

When I am jealous, my fear is that Barry will prefer Person X to me, that he will achieve greater heights of delight, pleasure, and fulfillment than he has within our marriage. The reality for some couples is that one partner does find another person more interesting, although this is often temporary, and primarily due to the thrill of getting to know someone new.

Psychiatrist Spurgeon English, writing in *The New Sexuality* about outside relationships, concurs, saying the other relationship "could be a *different* experience than she has had with him, but would not be very different, and certainly unlikely to be any better. It is only his sense of inferiority that causes him to see his rival as achieving or receiving so much more with her. 'Differentness' contains no guarantee of better."*

Certainly this is true for Barry and me. I am the one Barry goes home with, and I am the one he most shares his life with. All I have to do is to get outside myself and my own fears to take a look, and I recognize that it's true. What I see is that he's not going anywhere. By this time I also have a backlog of relationships with other people and of activities and involvements separate from Barry. The fact is that I'm still with him. That doesn't mean that we both don't have thoughts and fantasies about the way life would be with someone else. Every time I meet someone whom I find very appealing, I think, "What would life be like with ———?" And yet I always choose to stay where I am.

*O. Spurgeon English, M.D., "Positive Values of the Affair," ed. by Herbert A. Otto, *The New Sexuality* (Palo Alto, California: Science and Behavior Books, Inc., 1971) p. 187.

When I am feeling expansive, when I can grant him the freedom to do what he wants to do, I know that he could never find what he has with me with anybody else. My experience of our good times, the specialness of the relationship we have together, convinces me.

We are often asked whether jealousy is different depending on whether the other one is involved with a man or with a woman. For both of us, there may be subtle differences, but basically, jealousy is jealousy. It certainly carries more social acceptability if the involvement is with someone of the opposite sex. However, the feeling and emotions of jealousy seem to be the same. This has also been the experience of people Barry and I know from the groups we have been in. Almost without exception, partners are as threatened when the person they love is involved in a same-sex or an opposite-sex relationship.

We have found that it helps to get to know each other's friends and lovers. As unlikely as this may sound, it has made everyone more comfortable in the long run. At one time I would have thought it would be impossible, that I could never handle it. For sure, it hasn't always been easy. But it's been critical for both of us to push ourselves to do this despite our reluctance, because it takes the mystery out of who the friend or lover actually is and allows communication between people who ordinarily would not meet. This has been especially important for me, since I used to disparage each new person Barry became involved with. Occasionally, I still respond this way but once I get to know them I have found without exception that Barry doesn't choose people unless they have something unique to offer.

For example, when I met Wayne, I didn't pay much attention to him. He was just another one of the waiters to whom I had very little to say. He seemed a particular favorite of Barry's, and that made me uneasy. Later when I learned that Barry had been having a sexual relationship with him, I could barely glance his way. Part of it was embarrassment. What's the "appropriate" way to behave toward a man you know is having sex with your husband?

It wasn't so much a question of seeing Wayne as a threat. I knew Barry had no intention of leaving me for him. But at the time he represented the side of Barry I was reluctant to look at. It was also uncomfortable to be at the restaurant and to know that everyone there knew that Barry and Wayne had a relationship and I had been the last to know.

So long as I knew Wayne only through Barry and had no separate relationship with him, I knew I would always feel uneasy. As Barry and I began to resolve the struggles between us, and I felt more comfortable with myself, I was more willing to get to know Wayne. Now he and I have become good friends. He stops by the house regularly and we like to talk. Not too long ago when I was sick, he drove me to the doctor's office. When I enter the Astral Plane now, Wayne makes me feel special. He has become a human being to me, not an ogre. The relationship I have with Wayne adds to my life, separate and apart from Barry's relationship with him.

We have interviewed a number of people who say that they don't experience jealousy, and it does seem that some people are more constitutionally prone to the disease than others. Over time jealousy occurs with lessening frequency in my life; and the more I don't avoid it, the more I am willing to deal with it directly, it has actually begun to disappear. For someone whose life was ruled by it at one time, this is truly amazing.

Monogamy Is a Choice

Yesterday I had a phone call from my old friend Betsy who lives in a very traditional marriage—three kids, religious, stable; she and her husband are both hardworking professionals. She reminds me of myself during the early years of our marriage. I always tell her she is my "normal" person. I asked her whether she ever gets jealous of her husband. She said that they have discussed what would happen if either of them ever got involved with someone else. She thinks her gut reaction would be to want to kill her husband or the other person; rationally she knows they would probably sit down and talk about it, and she would ask herself what was or wasn't happening at home to provoke him to look outward. In her opinion both of them get enough from one another that they don't need to get involved with someone else.

Betsy's response represents a widespread point of view about getting involved in a relationship outside of marriage. There's an

assumption that people get involved extramaritally because the primary relationship is not meeting enough of their needs. If one or both
partners get involved, it is because they are looking outward rather
than dealing directly with each other. Betsy sees a healthy relationship
as one in which both partners do not experience the need or the desire
to be intimate with anyone else.

We believe that no one is naturally monogamous, either by
biology or by destiny. In reality, there's no instinct, no drive, that
makes people want to limit their attentions to one other person only.
Rather, it's a question of socialization and of choice. Our society
differs from others, both historical and contemporary, in its emphasis
on maintaining monogamy as a standard in marriage. In such a
society, feelings of jealousy are intensified and made more severe.
Unlike other cultures where exclusivity in marriage was or is less
strictly defined, we are taught to place great emphasis on the values of
loyalty and faithfulness to a partner. Many people never think to
question the basic assumption of monogamy. It carries a religious
sanctity, even for those who, in practice, violate its tenets.

We think it's important to distinguish between monogamy
and fidelity. They are not the same, although unfortunately, the two
words are often used interchangeably. We are not monogamous, yet
fidelity is extremely important to us. In our marriage fidelity implies
ongoing trust and a commitment freely given; the fidelity between us
is deeper than whom we have sex with outside the marriage.

We know that our marriage has to come first. We put a lot of
energy into keeping it alive. This means making sure that we do not
fail to nurture our own relationship. We need time to be together as a
couple and as a family, time to work together, and time to play. We are
conscious of creating a family history which enriches our lives and
binds us to one another.

At the same time, Barry and I knew when we married that
we wanted to experience life as fully as we could. Part of experiencing
life for us includes relationships with others. I know that Barry will
get things from other people that I cannot give him, that he will have
good times without me. I also know that the other relationships will
not equal the depth, history, and devotion that we have together; we
stay together because each of us meets the widest constellation of the
other's needs.

Fighting in a Relationship

Over the years we became aware of a pattern of fighting. After a certain period of time, we reach a plateau. Everything is going well—good talks, good sex, a feeling of warmth and closeness. After a while, we begin feeling more distant. We might bicker, feel less attracted to one another, find ourselves having routine sex. This period used to last several weeks, after which we generally had a big fight. At this point it's rare that we are angry for more than a few hours.

We don't hold back when we fight. We tell to one another all the things we haven't said, no matter how painful, insulting, or embarrassing they may seem. The more explicit we are able to be, the more quickly the urge to fight disappears. Over the years we have become more and more direct and honest in our fighting. We have learned that if we don't get it all out, the anger will not disappear.

We know that fighting is not necessarily bad for a relationship. In fact, the willingness to continually challenge one another can be a sign of deep commitment. Fighting can be very healthy for a relationship, especially when we don't spend all our time blaming the other but are willing to be introspective and find out what is really bothering us.

During the last year, we've been able to avoid the intensity of the eruptions by setting time aside each day to talk, even if the talks last only a few minutes apiece. We use that time to say how we are feeling at that moment, as well as to clear up any misunderstandings that may have accumulated since we last talked. In this way, we do not lose touch with one another, and we avoid having little concerns fester into big problems. As a result of these daily talks, our relationship feels more stable. We avoid the tendency to withdraw in the face of small annoyances because we have a built-in commitment to air our grievances.

I want to stress, as well, that the feelings expressed during our scheduled talks are not always negative. This is also a time for us to express our love and appreciation of one another, and usually it's the good feelings that are left once the anger is expressed. Other people, to whom we've recommended this kind of sharing, report a similar reduction in tension and an increase in intimacy, trust, and caring. We have seen time and time again that when we hold back our thoughts and feelings, we permit them to grow in significance and they can destroy a relationship.

Communication About Sex

Communication about sex is perhaps the most essential and problematic area in relationships. I grew up with the idea my lover would arrive at the door and with no help from me, be the perfect sex partner. He'd know instinctively how to please me, what to say to turn me on, and where and how to touch me. Only it doesn't happen that way.

Barry recalls:

> I remember my surprise when Alice confided in me, after close to a year of marriage, that she had never reached orgasm. We had not talked about orgasm until then. I just assumed that she was getting the same kind of sexual enjoyment as I. What I saw from that experience was how little Alice and I had talked about sex.

At a very young age, most of us learn that sex is a forbidden topic. As a child, it has a mysterious quality about it. Barry remembers how his grandmother would cut in whenever one of his uncles would tell a dirty joke. "Not in front of the kinder," she would say. All discussions would cease until the children left the room.

It's amazing how sex, one of our basic needs, is kept so hidden. Other human needs, such as food, clothing, and shelter, are freely discussed. We can talk about how to prepare a particular recipe, right down to the most minute detail, without embarrassment or discomfort. And yet, even among couples who have been married many years, and who know almost every other intimate detail of their partner's lives, often there is little discussion about sex.

One of the major obstacles in talking about sex is embarrassment. All of us want to be seen as good lovers without any limitations. For about a six-month period, Barry had a continual problem of losing his erection during sex. This had never happened to him before. He had always been very confident sexually. Every time it happened, he would get very embarrassed and upset, but he couldn't bring himself to talk about it.

Rather than talking about my limp penis, I would try to get my erection again. I was never willing just to say, "Listen, Alice, I've lost my erection. I'm upset and I'm still very turned on to you." Eventually we would talk about it, but by that time we were both frustrated and we would end up fighting and accusing one another of not being willing to communicate.

I worried about what would happen to my sex life with Alice if this problem continued. Then I began having the same problem with men. However, when I was with a man it seemed easier for me to talk about it, and then I would stop worrying about what the other person was thinking. Within a short time I would find that my erection had returned. Finally, I realized that I would have to talk to Alice each time the problem reappeared, even if I was embarrassed. As soon as I was willing to talk to her, I no longer had the problem.

I've been in the same position with Barry when I'm not sexually aroused. We have gone through the same process of "trying to get me excited" that Barry went through. Usually it doesn't work. Rather, if we take a minute and talk about whatever is worrying me at that moment, the problem clears up.

Barry and I have come a long way in our willingness to talk about sex. What constantly surprises me is that when I tell him what I want, he tries to please me. Barry wants to satisfy me in sex and he is able to do that better when I talk to him and tell him my wishes or fantasies directly.

Sometimes I wish I didn't have to tell him. I hope he will naturally know what I want him to do without my asking. I find myself thinking, "If he really loved and cared for me I wouldn't have to tell him, it would just flow out of our natural energies." Yet I know from my own and other people's experiences that really satisfying sex rarely occurs without communication. Barry comments:

Many men I talk to assume that their wives would not be willing to perform certain sex acts, and that is why they have turned to men. For example, John, an insurance salesman in his late forties, told me that he had wanted his wife to have oral sex with him. He had wanted her to do this throughout their twenty years of marriage, but because he thought she was very prudish about sex, he never asked her. Finally he told her about his sexual relationship with men, and what about sex with men turned him on. Their marriage went through the expected tailspin after he told her, and then their sexual activities changed drastically. Not only was John's wife willing to perform oral sex with him, but she began to want much more sex for herself. It seemed that John's willingness to talk to his wife allowed her to vocalize many of the fantasies that she had been ashamed to talk about throughout their marriage.

John's situation is not unique. We are all sexual people with fantasies and desires for many different kinds of sexual experiences. Yet if we keep our desires secret, we may be closing off the possibility of ever satisfying them.

It is almost as if there is some delicate magical spell that we are afraid to interfere with during sex. However, I have found that whenever I hold back from saying something it interferes with my pleasure. Instead of being in the "here and now" with my partner, I am thinking other thoughts or having fantasies that separate me from that person. The more quickly I am able to say what is on my mind, the faster I can totally involve myself in making love.

Most marital sex is not good. That may seem like a strong statement, but from my observation over the years, from working with families in agencies and mental health centers, from Barry's involvement with men's groups, from our years of experience in sensitivity groups, est seminars, consciousness-raising groups, and from friends, we continually hear the same complaint of unsatisfying sexual relationships in many marriages. Some couples complain about not having sex for several years or infrequent sex every few months, or they find that sex becomes unpleasant because of sexual dysfunctions such as frigidity, premature ejaculation, or loss of erection. At the very least, they complain that sex has just become routine and boring.

Barry and I believe that a good sexual relationship is the cornerstone of an alive marriage. It's certainly a basic way in which the two of us connect. We have seen one marriage after another fail as the sex became limited or nonexistent. Obviously, it's not possible to judge a marriage totally on the kind of sex that the couple is having.

But usually, the sexual relationship is indicative of other problems that are occurring in the relationship.

Commitment to a Relationship

Webster defines "commit" in the following way: "to bind as by a promise; to pledge." As the dictionary definition indicates, there is nothing abstract or magical about commitment. It is a simple and straightforward agreement. In the case of a relationship, it is a promise to see things through, to hang in there when the going gets rough and not to bail out at the first sign of trouble.

There are plenty of times when I look at Barry and ask myself, "This is the one?" I am not always in touch with my experience of being in love. But I have committed myself to him and to our relationship out of my sense that he meets the widest range of my needs and that his personal goals are worthy of supporting. Commitment is the anchor that binds me to him. It involves a process of choosing and rechoosing, and it is a pledge that must be given freely.

Sometimes, the original assumptions upon which the relationship was based may no longer be appropriate. Rather than discarding the person and the relationship, it is possible to agree upon new guidelines. A process of renegotiation can take place, and along with that renegotiation comes a recommitment to the relationship. Such periodic reevaluation and recommitment can keep a relationship from becoming stale and unexciting. It is also a statement of faith that good times will return again.

Barry and I believe that there is value in continuing a relationship over a long period of time. We have a history together that greatly enriches our lives. Whether it is talking about our Peace Corps experience or revisiting the apartment we lived in eight years ago, we find great comfort in knowing that there is someone else who cares as much as we do about those experiences. While we encourage, indeed insist upon, one another's separateness and individuality, we also appreciate the life we have as a couple.

More than anything else, as a result of our thirteen years together, we have come to know one another very intimately. We know the fears, the self-doubts, the strengths, and the accomplishments. We have an appreciation of how we have matured, and we have fun thinking about what lies ahead.

Bisexuality in Perspective

In a recent conversation with his friend Mark, Barry gave some thought to where our relationship is today and how bisexuality fits into our lives:

Mark and I ran yesterday afternoon. It was one of those very special late March spring days. The temperature was about seventy degrees and the sun was shining brightly. Along the Schuylkill River the weeping willow trees were green, showing the first leaves of spring. We were nearing the end of an eight-mile run when Mark brought up the subject of bisexuality.

Mark said that he knows he gets a tingling feeling in his chest when he sees a beautiful woman. He'll want to hold her and make love to her. He told me about talking to a woman earlier that afternoon at his apartment house. She was everything he wants in a woman: beautiful, athletic, refined. A model, she was on the crew team in high school and came from a good family on the Main Line. He knew that he wanted to make love to her.

With a man, his feelings are different. When he is with a man with whom he knows sex is a possibility, rather than a warm, romantic feeling, he feels a kind of tension in his body.

We were doing our warm-down exercises on a patio that overlooks a waterfall on the river. There was charged energy between us as we continued to talk quietly. I thought to myself, "It's not easy to be different, yet the rewards of being who I am are visible just by the setting I am in and kind of conversation I am having."

I told Mark that since I've been close to him over the last year, my desire to be with other men has diminished. I don't find myself having sex with as many men as I once did. And, on occasion, when I do have sex with another man, I often fantasize about Mark. "I am totally drawn to you," I told him. "I love our talks, our runs, and just spending time with you." With Mark and me, sex is a very small part of our interactions. There is a need he fills in me just to be close and intimate with another man. He is physically strong and dynamic, and yet he has been willing to let me in to the soft and tender parts of himself.

I thought to myself, "He is a beautiful man. I love his clear blue eyes, his straight brown hair, and the broad smile which sweeps over his face. Our relationship is really special."

I then told Mark that I've never been attracted to another woman as much as I am to Alice. She was the first woman I had ever loved in that way and I still adore her. I'm amazed that I get sexually aroused morning and night when I'm with her; I'm attracted to her body, to the way she dresses, to her style, to the fact that she loves to indulge herself by having a manicure a week. a facial every two months, and fresh flowers in our living room. I love her when we fight (although I don't like it when she's angry at me), and I love to spend high times with her. My deepest commitment to another person is to Alice.

I also get attracted to other women all the time. Sometimes when I'm running in the park or walking in town, I pass a beautiful woman who will take my breath away. I still favor blondes, with long, slender bodies. From time to time I make love to another woman, but I've never met a woman who has come close to matching Alice—her talent, her wit, her ability to sexually arouse me, her overall femininity. She is just the woman for me.

As we walked silently back to the car, I knew that I've said the same things to Mark before, but for some reason this time he seemed to have a deeper appreciation of what I was saying.

The older I get, the less I seem to need the approval of others for the way I live. I know that people talk about me and make judgments about my life-style. That will always be true. What matters for me, above all else, is my integrity, and the way I use that integrity to enrich my own and other people's lives. Through my relationships with people, both sexual and nonsexual, I express who I am. Sharing with people, touching them and being close to them, adds beauty and fullness to my life.

As I look at my own life, my feelings closely parallel Barry's thoughts. Recently I walked through Rittenhouse Square. It was a warm, sunny, December morning, unusually warm for this time of year in Philadelphia. I thought about how many times I had gone through the park in bleaker periods of my life, walking my baby in his carriage.

The square was always beautiful, but I was hardly able to notice it then, I was so preoccupied with my thoughts. I wasn't just worried about Barry and me in those days. It seems as if I was always worrying about something—where I was going next, what was going to happen, what I wanted from life.

My life is more open than it ever was then. People know who I am, and they know about my life, and yet I have little concern about whether they are saying anything critical about me. I must confess that sometimes I even enjoy the notoriety. I feel very free, expectant, and alive. The thirties are a wonderful age, young enough to be vital, old enough to have gained some wisdom and independence, and my options, which once seemed so limited, now appear endless.

Why do I choose to be with Barry? I suppose because after all these years, he is still the most interesting person I know. I can talk to Barry. He has deep reservoirs of understanding, and he's the person who most intimately shares my life. Barry really is a visionary kind of thinker—he dreams great dreams, and he believes in himself. And through it all, we have fun. He has taught me a lot.

I spent so many years being afraid of I don't know what— always cautious, concerned, careful. I love feeling at home in the city. I love feeling at home with my life. I have chosen to live as I do; it wasn't forced on me, and I could have gotten out. But I didn't. I like it. I learned that there was something beyond all the pain and torment, something on the other side. A life awaited me that was more full and rich and exciting than I could have guessed, a sense of personal power and mastery that I didn't know before.

There is a touch of irony in the fact that my own liberation was so much spurred on by Barry's coming out. And yet, in a way, it seems a very appropriate comment on the need to do away with rigid sex roles that Barry's struggles with bisexuality did so much to put me in touch with my own sexuality. What my experience with Barry has shown me is that one's sexual identity and feelings about self are never static; that each of us is in a process from birth, through childhood, adolescence, adulthood, and old age. That process of sexual exploration allows us to discover who we are and what we value.

BIBLIOGRAPHY

Anobile, Ulla and Richard J. *Beyond Open Marriage*. New York: A and W Publishers, Inc., 1979.

Babcox, Deborah, and Belkin, Madeline. *Liberation Now!* New York: Dell Publishing Co., Inc., 1971.

Barbach, Lonnie Garfield. *For Yourself: The Fulfillment of Female Sexuality, A Guide to Orgasmic Response*. Garden City: Doubleday, 1975.

Bode, Janet. *View From Another Closet*. New York: Hawthorn Books, 1976.

Boston Women's Health Collective. *Our Bodies, Ourselves: A Book by and for Women*. New York: Simon and Schuster, 1971.

Boston Women's Health Collective. *Ourselves and Our Children*. New York: Random House, 1978.

Brown, Rita Mae. *Rubyfruit Jungle*. Daughters, Inc., 1973.

Clark, Don. *Loving Someone Gay*. Millbrae, California: Celestial Arts, 1977.

Dodson, Betty. *Liberating Masturbation*. New York: Bodysex Designs, 1974.

Fairchild, Betty, and Hayward, Nancy. *Now That You Know, What Every Parent Should Know about Homosexuality*. New York: Harcourt Brace Jovanovich, 1979.

Falk, Ruth. *Women Loving: A Journey Toward Becoming an Independent Woman*. New York: Random House/Berkeley, The Bookworks, 1975.

Fleming, Jennifer Baker, and Washburne, Carolyn Kott. *For Better, for Worse: A Feminist Handbook on Marriage and Other Options*. New York: Charles Scribner's Sons, 1977.

Friday, Nancy. *My Mother, My Self*. New York: Delacorte, 1977.

Friday, Nancy. *My Secret Garden: Women's Sexual Fantasies*. New York: Trident, 1973.

Galper, Miriam. *Co-Parenting: A Source Book for the Separated and Divorced Family*. Philadelphia: Running Press, 1978.

Gay Activists Alliance. *Twenty Questions About Homosexuality*. New York, 1972.

211

Greer, Germaine. *The Female Eunuch*. New York: McGraw-Hill Book Company, 1970.

Jong, Erica. *Fear of Flying*. New York: Holt, Rinehart and Winston, 1973.

Key, Ellen, *Love and Marriage*. Translated by Arthur G. Chater. New York: G.P. Putnam's Sons, 1911.

Kinsey, Alfred C.; Pomeroy, Wardell B.; Martin, Clyde E.; *Sexual Behavior in the Human Female*. Philadelphia; W.B. Saunders Co., 1953.

Kinsey, Alfred C.; Pomeroy, Wardell B.; and Martin, Clyde E. *Sexual Behavior in the Human Male*. Philadelphia: W. B. Saunders Co., 1953.

Klein, Fred, M.D. *The Bisexual Option*. New York: Arbor House, 1978.

Mead, Margaret. *Male and Female: A Study of the Sexes in a Changing World*. New York: W. Morrow, 1949.

Money, John, and Tucker, Patricia. *Sexual Signatures: On Being a Man or a Woman*. Boston-Toronto: Little, Brown and Company, 1975.

Nicolson, Nigel. *Portrait of a Marriage*. New York: Atheneum, 1973.

O'Neill, Nena, and O'Neill, George. *Open Marriage*. New York: M. Evans and Co., 1972.

Otto, Herbert A. *The New Sexuality*. Palo Alto, California: Science and Behavior Books, Inc., 1971.

Phillips, Debora, and Tudd, Robert. *How to Fall Out of Love*. Boston: Houghton Mifflin Company, 1978.

Rogers, Carl R. *On Becoming a Person*. Boston: Houghton Mifflin Company, 1961.

Rosenbaum, Salo, and Alger, Ian. *The Marriage Relationship—Psychoanalytic Perspectives*. New York: Basic Books, Inc. 1968.

Seaman, Barbara. *Free and Female*. Greenwich, Conn.: Fawcett Crest, 1972.

Seaman, Dr. Florence, and Lorimer, Anne. *Winning at Work: A Book for Women*. Philadelphia: Running Press, 1979.

Seligson, Marcia. *Options*. New York: Random House, 1977.

Slater, Phillip. *The Pursuit of Loneliness*. Boston: Beacon Press, 1970.

Smith, James R., and Smith, Lynn G. *Beyond Monogamy*. Baltimore: Johns Hopkins University Press, 1974.

Vida, Ginny. *Our Right to Love: A Lesbian Resource Book*. Englewood Cliffs, New Jersey: Prentice-Hall, 1978.

Weinberg, George. *Society and the Healthy Homosexual*. New York: St. Martin's Press, 1972.

ADDITIONAL RESOURCE

A Gay Bibliography, prepared by Task Force on Gay Liberation, American Library Association. (Available from Barbara Gittings, Box 2383, Philadelphia, Pa. 19103.)

Index